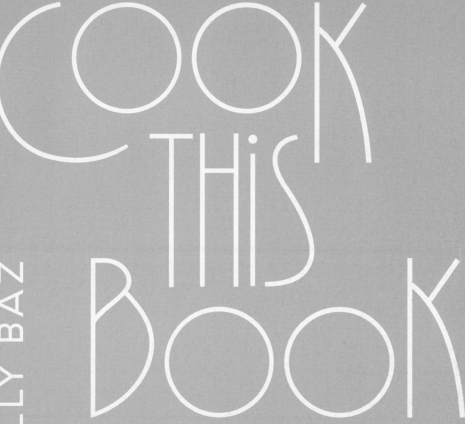

COOK THIS BOOK

MOLLY BAZ

**Techniques That Teach
& Recipes to Repeat**

Clarkson Potter/Publishers *New York*

To my epic husband, Ben,
whose endless support, brilliant eye,
and discerning palate single-handedly
enabled me to write this book

Library of Congress Cataloging-in-
Publication Data is available on request.

ISBN 978-0-593-13827-4
Ebook ISBN 978-0-593-13828-1

Printed in China

Principal Photographers:
  Taylor Peden and Jen Munk
Supplementary Photographer:
  Alex Kweskin
Creative Director: Ben Willett
Food Stylists: Christopher St. Onge and
  Alison Attenborough
Prop Stylist: Eli Jaime
Photography Assistant: Niko Feldman
Studio Kitchen Assistant: Shelley Ellis
Production Assistant:
  Asmite Gherezgiher
Designers: Violaine et Jérémy
Editor: Jennifer Sit
Production Editor: Terry Deal
Production Manager:
  Jessica Heim
Composition:
  Merri Ann Morrell,
  Hannah Hunt
Copy Editor: Kathy Brock
Indexer: Elise Hess

10 9 8 7 6 5 4 3 2 1

First Edition

Contents

Intro

I used to think that cooking from recipes was extremely un-cool. The way I saw it, recipes were for amateurs— those who needed hand-holding and couldn't think for themselves in the kitchen. I spent the formative years of my food- and cooking-obsessed life (my early twenties) determined to become the opposite of that. I yearned to be a "profesh." Recipes were for home cooks, and I was well on my way to becoming a chef (a label that now makes me cringe with regard to my own title). To rely on a recipe was to acknowledge how much I *didn't* know, and honestly when you've still got years and years of expertise to gain and the finish line is barely visible, there's nothing more un-fun than that. Fast-forward ten years—I now work as a recipe developer, and my primary responsibility is to teach regular people (read: decidedly UN-profesh chefs) to become great home cooks. Of course, recipes are absolutely core to that education. Recipes now course through my veins. I go to sleep thinking about them, dream about them, occasionally have night terrors about them, and almost always wake up still thinking about them. If that sounds really intense, it is. But mostly in a good way.

And, guess what?! Thirty-three-year-old Molly freakin' loves recipes. Not only do I love to develop and write recipes, I love to cook from recipes—especially those that aren't my own—**because recipes are actually the coolest.**

The sheer existence of a recipe suggests that the dish you're about to cook has been highly and repeatedly considered, tested, and tasted before it was even a twinkle in your pantry, which guarantees you're that much closer to securing yourself a delicious meal. Recipes are the culmination of exactly that free-balling journey I once prided myself on: a fridge full of seemingly random ingredients, which, after much consideration and many rounds of testing, come together to create something even greater than they once were.

Like most cookbooks, this one is full of recipes. But these are recipes that actually teach. They are packed with useful information that will answer your burning, never-stupid, always-valid questions (this is a safe space) and will help to shed some light on the mystery of the kitchen. I've tried to anticipate what those questions will be and provide answers to them within the recipes. I've spent a lot of time observing the way my non-food-industry friends and fam navigate their kitchens, and through my observations I have noticed that time management, ingredient prep, and order of operations can really trip up the home cook. That's a lot of GD stuff to manage at one time! Take my husband, for example, whom I would not call a novice at this point—he's been far too exposed to the kitchen by now. Even after everything I've taught him and all of the recipe development and testing he's witnessed in our home kitchen, he will

still, on occasion, start assembling a salad, dress it completely, and only then realize that his chicken still needs thirty minutes in the oven and his salad has no chance of surviving. (To his credit, he makes a mean salad, despite its occasional sog factor.)

Following a recipe takes an enormous amount of concentration and foresight, and frankly I think most recipes ask too much of the home cook. The recipes in this book were created with YOU, the home cook, in mind. I've done the heavy lifting for you and planned out all of the prep work in advance, meaning you can jump right into a recipe and rest assured that the time management aspect of things has already been considered. I'll be right there with you to tell you when to start chopping your onions and at what point you should get the rice going in order to make the most efficient use of your very valuable time. You'll also notice that ingredient quantities are listed in the ingredient lists and reiterated in the procedure text. This way, you can use the ingredient lists as a shopping guide, without having to go back and reference them every time an ingredient is called upon. To that end, I've organized the ingredients by where they're most likely to be found in a grocery store or in your home kitchen, to help streamline both your shopping trips and your movement around your kitchen as you gather ingredients and prepare to cook. **A great cook is an efficient cook, and these recipes will teach you to be just that.**

As you cook your way through this book, you'll encounter all of the techniques, both big and small, that I consider fundamental to modern home cooking. Each recipe chapter will cover an essential cooking category and teach you the core techniques you'll need to know. In the chicken chapter, for example, you'll find recipes for a foolproof roast chicken, a braise-y chicken stew, some shatteringly crisp chicken thighs, perfectly poached chicken breasts, and so on. If you cook your way through that entire chapter, you'll have learned the quintessential techniques for cooking chicken at home.

Once you've got the basic techniques down, another thing every cook must learn is how to build flavor and make food that tastes not just good but GREAT. So, we're going to cover that, too. The way I see it, **Technique × Flavor = Cooking.** You'll find all the tools you need to start thinking about flavor in How to Make Food Taste Great (page 32), because, after all, that's why you're here in the first place.

And one more thing . . .

COOKING IS REALLY FUN. I SWEAR. I'm in the business of having lots of fun and eating only the most delicious foods, and I would never have committed to a lifetime of cooking if it didn't deliver on those two promises. You simply need to set yourself up for success in the kitchen in order to truly enjoy it. What I really hope is that you'll commit to cooking through all of the recipes in this book, front to back, and by the end of it realize you just took a culinary-school crash course but didn't notice you were in school because you were having such a ridiculously great time while enrolled. I guarantee you'll come out the other end a confident, capable, creative, calm, collected, cool-as-fuck cook. So throw on that cross-back apron (or go get one immediately), bust out the kosher salt, and let's

COOK THIS BOOK!

QR Codes

I had a realization while trying to write out the step-by-step instructions for how to chop an onion: some techniques are best expressed visually. So instead of making you suffer through my long, clumsily written explanations, I shot a bunch of super-quick video tutorials for each of these hard-to-explain techniques. As you make your way through the recipes, you'll occasionally encounter a QR code floating inside a cute little egg-head, hanging out next to the text that relates to a specific technique. Simply open your camera app on your smartphone and hover it over the QR code, centering the code on your screen, and you'll be automatically directed to the corresponding video. Watch the on-the-go teaching moment and jump right back into the recipe you're cooking.

If you pull up this QR code, you'll find all of the techniques collected in one place. All of the QR codes can also be found on page 298, so you can easily access them anytime should you need a visual refresher on one of these foundational techniques.

The Anatomy of a COOK THIS BOOK Recipe:

(Title)

Here's the recipe title,
not that you really needed me
to point that out!

(Ingredient Lists)

All of the ingredients are categorized
by their department in the grocery store,
which generally translates to where they're most likely
to live in your kitchen. This way, you can shop efficiently
and then gather ingredients without running circles in
your kitchen looking for everything. To that end, you'll
always find the ingredients listed in their whole,
shop-able form, and not in their prepped state
(i.e., 1 lemon, not 2 tablespoons lemon juice).
I encourage you to pull out all of your ingredients before
jumping into a recipe for the smoothest sailing.

(Servings/Yield)

Most of the recipes in this book
serve four people, which means they just as
easily serve two with leftovers.
Feel free to halve or double any recipe
to suit your specific needs!

(Hednote)

This paragraph (a.k.a. the hednote or headnote)
usually contains a tidbit or two of useful
information that will serve you as you cook
through the recipe, and sometimes a silly
anecdotal story, thought, or reflection to keep
you entertained as you cook.

(Process)

Here's where I'll walk you through
every step of the recipe, starting with any prep
you'll need to do before diving in. I've written the recipe
procedures in chronological order, which means that you
can cook through them from start to finish without ever
having to worry about what comes next, or how to time
things out on your own. The recipes themselves are likely
lengthier than you are used to. That's only a factor
of the way they are written and all of the information
packed into each of them to support you as you cook—it
doesn't mean they're complicated. Don't let the procedure
length scare you away, it's all there to help you.

(QR code)

The QR codes can be accessed through the camera
app on your phone and link to short, sweet, technique-
driven videos. They help to demonstrate some of the
knifework and other fundamental skills that the recipes
require, which is oftentimes a lot easier to grasp by
watching a video than by reading text.

(Footnote)

A footnote in a recipe denotes an extra
tidbit of information that explains why
I've asked you to do something, as a means of
providing you with more education and more
context for each step along the way.

Toona Fish Salad

Serves 4

PRODUCE
1 medium shallot
2 celery stalks
½ cup dill leaves
2 small lemons

PANTRY
2 dill pickles
⅓ cup mayonnaise
4 teaspoons Dijon mustard
2 tablespoons dill pickle brine
1 tablespoon hot sauce
2 (5-ounce) cans oil-packed tuna
Kosher salt and freshly ground black pepper

I have a deep and unwavering love of tuna salad, and it's not just because my extremely long and perfect wiener dog is named Tuna. On the contrary: Tuna got her name due to my obsession with and utmost respect for canned tuna (oil-packed only in this house!) and all of its glorious applications. When purchasing canned tuna, be sure to steer clear of anything labeled either "water-packed" or "salt-free," both of which basically guarantee you a watery, bland, unseasoned product. You deserve better than that! We all do.

① **Do some knife work:**

+ Finely chop 1 medium shallot.
+ Cut 2 celery stalks lengthwise into ¼-inch-thick strips. Finely chop the celery.
+ Cut 2 dill pickles lengthwise into ¼-inch-thick planks. Cut the planks lengthwise again into ¼-inch strips. Finely chop the pickles.
+ Chop ½ cup dill leaves.

② **Assemble the tuna salad:**

+ In a medium bowl, combine the shallots, celery, pickles, and dill. Stir in ⅓ cup mayonnaise, 4 teaspoons Dijon mustard, the juice of 2 small lemons, 2 tablespoons dill pickle brine, and 1 tablespoon hot sauce.[1]
+ Crack open 2 (5-ounce) cans of oil-packed tuna. Drain any excess oil. **Not super familiar with tuna? Pull this up to get acquainted with her.**

+ Add the tuna. Use a fork to flake it apart, then vigorously stir the tuna salad to encourage the tuna to break down into smaller pieces and become one with the remaining ingredients. Season the salad well with salt and black pepper.

[1] The secret ingredient to a really great tuna salad is a little bit of hot sauce—not so much that the salad registers as spicy, but just enough to brighten things up, and give it that "je ne sais quoi."

Equipment

In my opinion, there is nothing worse than walking into a kitchen, excited to eat and ready to cook dinner, and realizing that the only available skillets are nonstick, the largest knife is a paring knife, and the cutting boards are the size of greeting cards. Being properly equipped is integral to successful cooking and will make your life in the kitchen SO. MUCH. EASIER. You will never achieve that deeply charred, crispy exterior on a steak by searing it in the wrong kind of pan. And your salads will never be properly dressed if you're working with a bowl that's half the size that it should be. Investing in the right equipment will make your life in the kitchen a million bajillion times more pleasant. These are the tools that I constantly reach for and the ones that I encourage you to invest in, regardless of your level of expertise. Ironically, the longer I cook, the fewer tools I find myself reaching for on a regular basis. Staying lean and purposeful in the kitchen–gadget department makes for a more efficient, less disjointed cooking experience. The recipes in this book will never call for anything not listed here, so once you've built out this tool kit, you're golden.

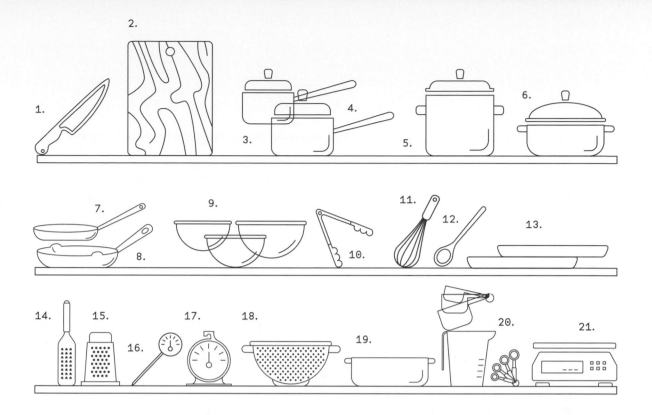

1. 7- to 9-inch Chef's Knife

2. Large Wooden Cutting Board (at least 18 inches wide)

3. Small (1- to 1.5-quart) Saucepan with Lid

4. Medium (3-quart) Saucepan with Lid

5. Large Pasta Pot

6. 6- to 8-quart Dutch Oven

7. 10- to 11-inch Nonstick Skillet

8. 12-inch Cast-Iron Skillet

9. Small, Medium & Large Mixing Bowls

10. Large Metal Tongs

11. Medium Whisk

12. Wooden Spoon

13. 2 Large Rimmed Baking Sheets (Half Sheet Pans)

14. Microplane Rasp Grater

15. Box Grater or Handheld Cheese Grater

16. Instant-Read Meat Thermometer

17. Oven Thermometer

18. Large Fine-Mesh Strainer

19. 9 × 5-inch Loaf Pan

20. Dry & Wet Measuring Cups & Measuring Spoons

21. Digital Scale

1. 7- to 9-Inch Chef's Knife

If you invest in one good-quality knife, let it be this one. Depending on the size of your hands, you may want one with a blade that is slightly shorter or slightly longer. If you can, shop for this in person so you can really feel the knife in your palm. Every knife is weighted differently, so take the time to find one that's juuuuuust right. Goldilocks that shit! And keep it sharpened! Dull knives are far more dangerous than sharp ones.

2. Large Wooden Cutting Board

If you hate the idea of washing your cutting board eight times throughout the course of a recipe, and I'm guessing you do, invest in a large and in-charge, heavy wooden cutting board that is spacious enough to chop more than just a single onion. Extra space on your cutting board means more efficient prep work, which, in turn, means dinner on the table that much faster. Anything 18 inches wide or larger will give you the room you need.

3. Small (1- to 1.5-Quart) Saucepan with Lid

A small saucepan with a lid is essential for some of the smaller, simpler tasks in life. Think toasting nuts in butter or warming up some olives. You'll use this saucepan in moments when a larger one would be too spacious, therefore making it difficult to cook something gently and evenly. Cooking is all about control, so choose this saucepan when working with smaller quantities of ingredients to maximize yours.

4. Medium (3-Quart) Saucepan with Lid

A few poached eggs, some leftover soup that needs to be reheated—these are the moments in which you will reach for a medium saucepan. Not too big, not too small. No need to invest in something fancy here, just a stainless-steel pot with a tight-fitting lid, the latter of which is absolutely crucial for making a perfect pot of rice.

5. Large Pasta Pot

This is an obvious one, but an important one nonetheless. It should be at least 12 inches in diameter, so as to contain enough water that even a long pasta shape like spaghetti or bucatini can be fully submerged as it cooks. Breaking your spaghetti in half to make it fit in a smaller pot is *not* the solution. Looking at you, Mom!!

6. 6- to 8-Quart Dutch Oven

I could write an entire book about the merits of a great Dutch oven. Mine holds permanent residence on my stovetop and is the pot I reach for most frequently in my day-to-day cooking. It's the go-to cooking vessel when the 3-inch-high sides of a cast-iron skillet won't cut it, and I find that to be the case more often than you'd think. Choose a round Dutch oven if you're purchasing only one—it's the shape that best suits the round nature of a stovetop burner.

7. 10- to 11-Inch Nonstick Skillet

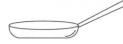

There are a few techniques that simply cannot be achieved in anything other than a nonstick skillet. Almost all skillet-cooked egg preparations are more easily executed in a nonstick pan than a cast-iron one. Get one measuring between 10 and 12 inches that you can use to fry eggs for four, make an omelet for two, or scramble eggs for up to six. It's also the perfect tool for crisping up leftover rice, which is one of life's greatest pleasures.

8. 12-Inch Cast-Iron Skillet

If you buy only one cast-iron skillet, I recommend a 12-inch, which is large enough to comfortably hold five or six chicken thighs, or two good-size strip steaks. It's a perfectly sized skillet for recipes intended for a family of four, or for a family of two that likes to get down on leftovers (that's me!). If you are rocking a single-person household, some of the recipes in this book (which all generally feed four people) may yield too much food, in which case, go for a 10-inch cast-iron skillet and halve the recipes as you see fit. This skillet has short-sided walls that don't trap steam inside the pan, which is great when you are looking for crispy-skinned chicken, well-seared mushrooms, and deeply charred steaks.

9. Small, Medium & Large Mixing Bowls

I keep a big stack of relatively inexpensive aluminum nesting bowls of all sizes in my kitchen—they don't take up a ton of space if stacked properly and will make your life a lot easier and less prone to mess. As a general rule of thumb, if you're unsure what size bowl to use, err on the side of slightly *too* large to avoid sloshing and spillage.

10. Large Metal Tongs

A good pair of metal tongs (not plastic ones—they can melt!) will act as an extension of your hands when things get a little too hot to touch. They are essential for tossing pasta, flipping steaks, turning Brussels sprouts, lifting a whole roast chicken, and just the general arranging and manipulation of ingredients while you cook. Grab a pair that is at least 12 inches long so that when you're cooking over high heat, your grip is far enough away from the fire that splattering oil won't burn your fingers.

11. Medium Whisk

If you invest in only one whisk, I recommend a medium-size one. A medium whisk is small enough to get into the curve of a medium mixing bowl in which you might emulsify a salad dressing or aioli, and large enough to whip cold cream into soft peaks without straining your forearm.

12. Wooden Spoon

This is another obvious one, but it's essential nonetheless. There are some tasks that tongs and whisks simply cannot achieve, and in those moments you'll reach for a wooden spoon. It will never melt, and the wood is gentle enough to use with nonstick cookware and when stirring in your precious cast-iron or Dutch oven without fear of scratching.

13. 2 Large Rimmed Baking Sheets (a.k.a. Half Sheet Pans)

Large rimmed baking sheets are essential for all sorts of roasting and baking so it's wise to invest in more than one. Besides being perfectly sized for your home oven, they also make for great mise en place organizers. If I'm prepping more than one dish simultaneously, I often organize my prepped ingredients for each on a rimmed baking sheet so as to keep things orderly in my kitchen. Look for baking sheets with a lip or a rim so that things don't slide off as they go in and out of the oven.

14. Microplane Rasp Grater

If you've ever cooked through one of my recipes, you've undoubtedly encountered the almighty Microplane. There are a bajillion different versions of a Microplane out there, but I stand by the "classic series," which has a very fine rasp. It's the kind of thing that you never knew you always needed, and once you've got one, you'll wonder how you ever lived a DAMN. DAY. IN. YOUR. LIFE. without one.

15. Box Grater or Handheld Cheese Grater

For grating any cheese that's not as hard as Parmesan, you'll have much more success using a box grater or handheld cheese grater than a Microplane. The larger holes make grating softer cheeses such as mozzarella and cheddar a breeze, especially when working with large quantities. Nothing fancy needed here, though I prefer the stability of a box grater.

16. Instant-Read Meat Thermometer

If you're a meat eater, ya gotta have one. I'm partial to the digital kind—it's the most instantaneous and accurate right down to the degree, while the analog kind is less precise when it comes to getting a very specific reading. A good meat thermometer is crucial because the difference between a perfectly cooked, juicy steak and a dry, tough, overcooked one is a matter of as little as 5 or 10 degrees.

17. Oven Thermometer

Wow. I truly cannot stress enough the importance of this tool. Every oven is calibrated slightly differently. I've cooked in ovens that run as much as 50 degrees higher than their dial would suggest. Fifty degrees! That's insane!!! The difference between an oven set to 375°F and an oven set to 425°F is far too significant to operate without an oven thermometer. Buy one, throw it in there right on the middle rack, halfway back, and start to get to know your oven.

18. Large Fine-Mesh Strainer

The best way to rinse a can of beans, strain oil, and drain cooked pasta or grains is to use a large strainer with mesh fine enough to catch little bits like lentils and quinoa; it should be able to hold a pound of cooked pasta, though a big colander can handle that job. Fine-mesh strainers are often sold in nesting sets of three sizes, which is the best-case scenario—you'll always have the appropriately sized tool and such a set is great if you're low on storage space.

19. 9 × 5-Inch Loaf Pan

All recipes in the Baking chapter utilize nothing more than the equipment listed here and a 9 × 5-inch loaf pan. This is my favorite cake pan. It's cheap, small, easy to store, and for some reason puts wary bakers at ease. It's the perfect entry-level, low-commitment, extremely casual baker's cake pan. Loaf pans should be measured from inside edge to inside edge, right up at the top opening of the pan. Avoid measuring from outside edge to outside edge, as that can throw off the measurement by as much as an inch. For most cake recipes that call for a 9 × 5-inch loaf pan, an 8½ × 4½-inch loaf pan will work just as well if that is what you have on hand, but I stock my kitchen with the larger one just to be on the safe side.

20. Dry & Liquid Measuring Cups & Measuring Spoons

The most important thing to note here is that liquid measuring cups (those glass or plastic pitcher-shaped ones with a spout) are not interchangeable with dry measuring cups (the plastic or metal scoop-shaped ones with a handle). While technically they both measure ingredients by volume, they're designed specifically with certain types of ingredients in mind and don't function as well when used improperly. Dry measuring cups are meant to be filled to the brim and leveled off with the back of a knife or a straightedge for the most accurate measurement. If you were to fill a dry cup measure to the brim with a liquid ingredient—such as oil, milk, or water—you'd likely lose some to a counter spill along the way. Liquid measuring cups generally come in larger sizes than dry ones. They have built-in spouts (whereas dry measuring cups do not) that make it easy to decant liquids. As for measuring spoons, one full set should suffice. I keep a few sets on hand so that I don't have to continually wash them as I cook.

21. Digital Scale

Most people consider owning a digital scale to be a little 2.0 when it comes to home cooking. I disagree. Throughout the recipes that follow, you'll notice that I've given weight measurements for all baking recipes and for any ingredients that are difficult to measure in volume. Grated Parmesan cheese is a perfect example of the utility of a digital scale in your home kitchen. For example, ½ cup Parmesan cheese that's been grated on a Microplane weighs ½ ounce, while ½ cup Parmesan cheese that's been grated in a food processor (like the pre-grated grocery-store kind) weighs 2 ounces. That's eight times as much cheese, for the same exact volume measurement. Measuring ingredients by weight is far more accurate than by volume, and for this reason, I highly recommend you invest in a digital scale.

Stock That

In many ways, what you choose to stock your pantry with is entirely personal. There is a whole helluva lot of stuff in my pantry at any given moment, including many weird and wacky things I've become attached to over time, but that doesn't mean you need to go out and buy the same things yourself. What you should do, however, is invest in some of the very basic building blocks of flavor that will support you in the kitchen. The items on the following list are almost always present in my pantry. They represent a wide range of flavor profiles and uses, and appear frequently in the recipes in this book. Start here and then continue to build your personal pantry according to your specific taste.

Pantry!

1. Salt

It would be entirely impossible to condense everything I want you to know about salt and how it is used in this book into a short paragraph. So instead, I wrote 3 pages about it! Flip to page 36 for all of my very strong opinions regarding salt. **And if you don't do that, please remember this: All of the recipes in this book were tested with Diamond Crystal kosher salt. If you're using a different brand, make sure you get to know its seasoning power or you will end up with sorely over- or underseasoned food.** But also, I reallllllly would prefer that you only use Diamond Crystal kosher salt. Okay? THANKS!

2. Extra-Virgin Olive Oil

Certainly there is no point in purchasing anything less than a decent-tasting olive oil. If it doesn't taste good straight out of the bottle, it's not going to taste good in your food either. But that doesn't necessarily mean spending an arm and a leg. When purchasing olive oil you should always look for bottles that are labeled "extra-virgin," which means the oil is made purely of cold-pressed olives, and not "virgin" or "light" olive oil, which denotes a blend that contains refined olive oil, which has been filtered and stripped of its flavor.

3. Freshly Ground Black Pepper

Though most people consider black pepper to be salt's counterpart, I believe that it should be appreciated as an ingredient on its own and not automatically deployed every time a recipe calls for salt. Freshly ground black pepper is floral and fragrant and can bring a lot of very specific flavor to a dish. Salt is for seasoning, pepper is for flavor. The difference between pre-ground black pepper (the pepper shaker kind) and black peppercorns that are freshly ground (the pepper mill kind) is an order of magnitude, so invest in a mill and some whole black peppercorns and get cracking, folks.

4. Red Pepper Flakes

There are a lot of ways to bring heat to a dish, and the red pepper flake is but one of them. It's a great spice to keep in your spice drawer because it delivers a pretty neutral flavor with substantial heat and therefore won't interfere with other flavors present in your dish. Gochugaru, Aleppo pepper, and cayenne are all great substitutes, though each chile varies in spiciness, so start slow and taste as you add them to get to know their strength.

5. Lemons

A truly magical fruit. If I open my fridge to find an inventory of less than two lemons on any given day, I feel naked, lost, and ill at ease. All hell breaks loose. You just never know when you might need a squeeze of lemon to brighten up and bring some balance and clarity to a dish. And as if the magical sour power of lemon juice wasn't enough, this fruit also provides us with lemon zest, which, when finely grated with a Microplane, can bring the citrusy, floral essence of a lemon to a dish without introducing any liquid. Lemons are a desert-island ingredient for me, and I'd bet that after cooking through the many lemony recipes in this book, they'll be one for you as well.

6. Vinegar

Though most people associate vinegars with vinaigrette, they're just as essential as additions to braises and roasts, caramelized vegetables, and pasta salads, bringing much-needed acidity and lift to deeper roasty-toasty flavors. Start experimenting by adding a splash of vinegar here and there just before serving a roast chicken, or right after you rest a fatty marbled steak. Toss some crispy roasted potatoes with splash of distilled white vinegar,

continues →

or stir a tablespoon of red wine vinegar into a slow-cooked tomato sauce and you'll begin to know their true power. I try to keep a wide variety of different types and tastes of vinegar on hand—one or two wine-based vinegars, a rice vinegar, an apple cider vinegar, and distilled white vinegar—to keep things interesting and ensure that my food doesn't meld into one-notedness.

7. Fresh Herbs

Herbs, glorious herbs! Herbs are a major player in the freshness factor of your food, which is an important element to consider when crafting crave-worthy meals. If ever you don't care for one of the herbs I've called for in this book, feel free to swap it out for one you like. I tend to keep four or five different fresh tender herbs (e.g., cilantro, parsley, mint, dill, chives, basil) in my fridge at once, 'cause frankly, I never want to have to choose, but set yourself up with a rotating selection of one or two, and use them freely and with reckless abandon.

8. Parmigiano-Reggiano (Parmesan) Cheese

In my opinion, the king of cheeses. It's the perfect grating cheese for finishing any and all pasta dishes and can lend a ton of depth in the form of that mysterious flavor profile known as umami. Because of the rate at which I blow through Parmesan cheese, I like to purchase the freshly pre-grated kind. Most high(ish)-end grocery stores grate their own Parm by throwing it in a food processor, which yields perfect little itty-bitty Parm pellets that are just delightful. Of course, the best-case scenario would be to purchase a wedge of Parmigiano-Reggiano, cut it into smallish pieces, and throw them into a food processor, blitzing them up yourself. Otherwise, buy fresh and buy frequently.

9. Eggs

Do I really need to convince you of the importance of a fridge stocked with eggs? Okay, fine. They are breakfast, they are lunch, and they are dinner. They are packed full of protein. They are quick cooking. They are versatile. They are delicious. They are healthy. They are pretty. All the recipes in this book featuring eggs were tested with large eggs, so keep that in mind when shopping.

10. Dried Spices

Dried spices are powerful workhorses in cooking, as they lend tons of flavor—fast—to whatever they're added to. Toasting whole spices and grinding them in a mortar and pestle or spice grinder will yield the absolute freshest and most fragrant flavor. That said, putting in that extra legwork is not always necessary and shouldn't be a deterrent from cooking with any spices at all. There are two measures you can take to optimize the potential of pre-ground spices:

① **Buy your spices in small quantities from a busy supermarket (or better yet, a bulk bin!)** to guarantee that they're moving through their inventory quickly, and retire any spices that have been sitting in your spice drawer for more than a year. Spices are, in many cases, the dried version of a fresh, living, breathing plant or herb. Just as you would not use super old, lifeless fresh herbs, you should not use stale, expired spices.

② **Always toast spices (both pre-ground and freshly ground) in some form of fat to bloom them and activate all their flavor.** That could mean stirring them into a pot of onions sizzling in olive oil until the spices are fragrant before adding any liquid. Or in the case of Pastrami Roast Chicken with Schmaltzy Onions & Dill (page 61), mixing them into some olive oil and using that paste to coat the chicken before it goes into the oven, knowing that the heat of the oven will toast them and bring out their flavor.

What you absolutely do not want to do is to wait until the very last minute to stir a pinch of untoasted spices into a soup, giving them nothing to work their flavor into and no time to spend doing so.

11. Cultured Dairy

This broad category of cultured and/ or soured dairy products includes but is not limited to sour cream, Greek yogurt, regular (unstrained) yogurt, labneh, crème fraîche, cottage cheese, and buttermilk. What makes this category of dairy products unique is its ability to simultaneously introduce both richness and acidity to a dish, which not many ingredients can do. This makes cultured dairy perfectly suited to stirring into salad dressings and sauces, when the goal is to a strike a balance of fat and acidity. Furthermore, a dollop of sour cream or Greek yogurt swirled into a spicy, savory soup or stew can move mountains of flavor. See K–bas & Cabbage Soup (page 234).

12. Nuts

I love nuts. They appear often in this book for the simple fact that they simultaneously bring tons of flavor, texture, and fat to whatever they're added to, making them a super-versatile pantry staple. If possible, purchase raw nuts and toast them yourself. Raw nuts last longer, and toasting them unlocks their freshest flavor. Due to their high fat content and tendency to burn easily, nuts and large seeds should always be toasted in a 325°F oven for the most even browning. Store them in your fridge or freezer, since they tend to spoil pretty quickly, unless you blow through at rate like I do, in which case, no need.

13. Alliums

Allium refers to a group of aromatics that includes onions, garlic, chives, leeks, scallions, shallots, and ramps. They are pungent and piquant when raw, and turn very mellow and sweet when cooked, which makes them a must–have pantry staple. Alliums provide big flavor fast and are essential building blocks of flavor. It's a good idea to keep a stash of garlic and some, if not several, of the aforementioned onion family members on hand at all times. Store them at room temperature in a dry area, and always buy them whole and fresh for best flavor (resist the temptation to buy the preminced jarred or dried stuff). You'll find that most recipes in this book (desserts aside) feature at least one of them.

Before you dive into cooking, you are legally obligated to read the following section.

ABS: Always! Be! Seasoning!

A lifetime of cooking and eating, and thinking about cooking and eating, has led me to conclude that inadequate seasoning is the number one culprit of lackluster food. And just to clarify, when I say "season," I'm referring to the addition of salt (we'll get to other flavors later on). There are, of course, many variables that factor into tasty food, which we'll also discuss, but I truly can't stress enough how important it is to learn to properly salt your food. If ever you've wondered why the food you cook at home never seems to taste as vibrant, full-flavored, and downright delish as the food you eat in restaurants, well, now ya know. It's not butter, it's not sugar, it's salt.

Salt makes food taste more like itself. I'm going to repeat that because it's a bit of a head-scratcher: *Salt makes food taste more like itself.* That is to say, a tomato tastes more intensely of tomato when sprinkled generously with salt. An egg will taste like an egg when properly salted; without salt, it will taste sulfurous and bland. Salt makes our taste receptors fire, sending signals to our brain that tell us food tastes good. Without it, those signals aren't transmitted, and food just doesn't taste like much of anything at all. And what a fucking bummer that is.

The Unnecessarily Vast World of Salts

If the bad news is that you may have been underseasoning your food your whole life, the good news is it's a very easy problem to fix. So let's get fixing. I firmly believe that despite the innumerable varieties of salt available out there (lookin' at you, Himalayan pink salt, table salt, and fleur de sel), you need only invest in two kinds: kosher salt and flaky sea salt. I've sustained a fruitful career in food filled with lots of perfectly seasoned meals using those two kinds of salt exclusively, and I have never felt the need to expand my collection, so as far as I'm concerned, neither do you. So what's the diff between the two and when should you reach for each?

Kosher salt is your go-to, all-purpose, use-with-abandon, season-everything salt. Its evenly sized, medium-coarse crystals are just large enough to pinch between your fingers without falling through them. This makes them ideal for distributing a very even shower of salt over your food as you season it. Kosher salt is best deployed as you are cooking, starting right at the beginning and continuing throughout the process. You'll reach for this stuff 95 percent of the time and plow through it much more quickly than flaky sea salt. Diamond Crystal and Morton are the two most popular and widely available kosher salt brands on the market, but, unfortunately, they are by no means interchangeable. Morton kosher salt flakes are much denser than Diamond Crystal kosher salt flakes, making them much saltier when used in equal measure. I am a die-hard Diamond Crystal girl—because, if it's not already apparent, I like the ability to salt liberally without worrying about overseasoning. I strongly encourage you to seek out this brand when stocking your pantry. All of the recipes in this book were developed with Diamond Crystal kosher salt, so if you choose to cook with a different brand, keep in mind that it will affect the saltiness of your food.

Flaky sea salt, on the other hand, is your "finishing" salt. Its large, irregularly shaped crystals contribute an addictive crackly-crunch factor and should really only be used to that effect—a finishing touch just before diving in. The different sizes of the flakes create little salty pockets of flavor that light up your taste receptors whenever they hit your palate. I like to keep a few pinch bowls of flaky salt around in both my kitchen and on my dining room table so that I'm never more than an arm's reach away from a little flaky-flake. You never know when your food might need a hit. Both Jacobsen Salt Co. and Maldon Salt Company make great flaky sea salts that are pretty widely available.

The Three-Finger Pinch

Knowing what types of salt to use is only half the battle—the rest is on you, the cook. If you consistently season with the same brand of salt using the same method every time you cook, eventually your fingertips will become your own very convenient, highly attuned measuring spoons. I like to grab a large pinch of salt between my thumb, forefinger, and middle finger, and then, raising it high above whatever I am seasoning, scatter the salt in a back-and-forth zigzag motion, while rubbing my fingers together to allow the salt to evenly drop from my grip. This is known as the "three-finger pinch" and while it sounds like a lot of fancy finger work, it's actually a super-duper simple, important skill to learn. In most of the recipes in this book, I've included salt measurements (based on Diamond Crystal kosher salt), but once you're comfortable with your own three-finger pinch, you should feel empowered to ignore those measurements and season according to how it feels in your fingers and tastes on your tongue. **If you want to learn how to season like a pro, pull up this vid and get acquainted with the ol' three-finger pinch.**

If there's one thing I hope you will take away from this book, it is the confidence to properly season your food. Every palate is different, so it's important to get to know your personal capacity and tolerance for salt. Part of figuring that out may mean oversalting your food to the point of inedible in the name of determining where your personal threshold maxes out. But one overly salty meal in the service of many, many perfectly seasoned, bang-up future meals seems like a worthwhile investment to make, dontcha think? And if you find this section useful or interesting, I recommend picking up a copy of Samin Nosrat's *Salt, Fat, Acid, Heat*. It's a genius cookbook by many accounts, and it takes an even deeper dive into the chemical properties of salt, its effect on food, and all of the nuanced ways to use it—it's an essential read (not to mention a fun one!) for all burgeoning home cooks.

The Challenge

The easiest way to truly understand the power of salt? This very simple test. While you're purchasing both kosher salt and flaky sea salt, also purchase a couple of large cucumbers, ripe avocados, or ripe tomatoes (if in season!).

Step 1: Dice up whatever you've got and divide it into two bowls—you should have two decently sized bowls of chopped veg to work with. Assign one of those decently sized bowls as your control set—the bowl that will never be seasoned and will serve as a comparison to the other.

Step 2: Pour a good amount of kosher salt (let's say at least ¾ cup) into a small bowl or ramekin. It's helpful to always maintain enough salt in your bowl that you can grab a very consistent three-finger pinch every time, so refill it as funds get low.

Step 3: Raise that hand up high and using the aforementioned method at left, *lightly* season the other bowl of diced veg with whatever amount of salt means "lightly" to you—everyone will differ. Give the veg a toss or a stir. Take a taste of the unseasoned veg. Register its deliciousness. Next, take a taste of your seasoned veg. Register that.

Step 4: Now, re-season those lightly seasoned cukes, avos, or tomatoes with what you would consider a moderate amount of salt (bearing in mind that they are already lightly seasoned). Taste both bowls again. Are the seasoned ones starting to taste more like . . . cukes, avos, and tomatoes? Are they suddenly very delicious?

Step 5: Repeat this exercise until things start tasting really great and then continue seasoning until they start to register as salty. Take note of how many three-finger pinches it took you before things started getting really tasty, and at what point they started tasting salty. The more you practice, the sooner perfect seasoning will become as passive as breathing, so keep at it.

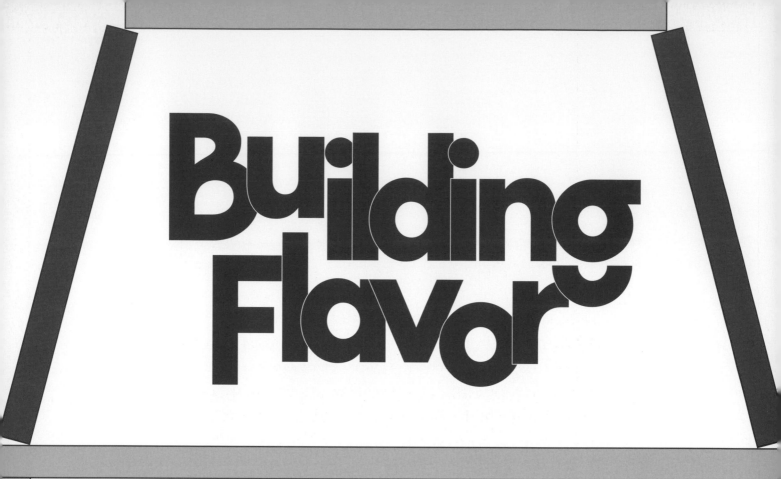

Building Flavor

Technique × Flavor = Cooking

Once you become comfortable and familiar with some of the basic, foundational cooking techniques, you can begin to start thinking about the other hugely important component of great cooking: **FLAVOR.** This is a tricky one. Flavor is, of course, subjective. No two palates are exactly alike, which means there's no single combination of flavors in a given recipe that is indisputably the most delicious combination. What's absolutely *take-me-to-church* delicious to me might taste only pretty good to you. Your personal experience, upbringing, and culture greatly influence the types of foods you are most drawn to, and each of us has a unique history of eating that informs the way we relate to food and flavor and register taste. Every time you eat, your brain files away information about ingredients and flavor that you can later reference. You can use that memory log to your advantage as you cook, by pulling inspiration and insight from the tens of thousands of meals you've eaten in your lifetime to help guide you as you go. I encourage you to make alterations to the recipes in this book according to your likes, dislikes, and personal preferences. That's the ticket to a life filled with deliciousness.

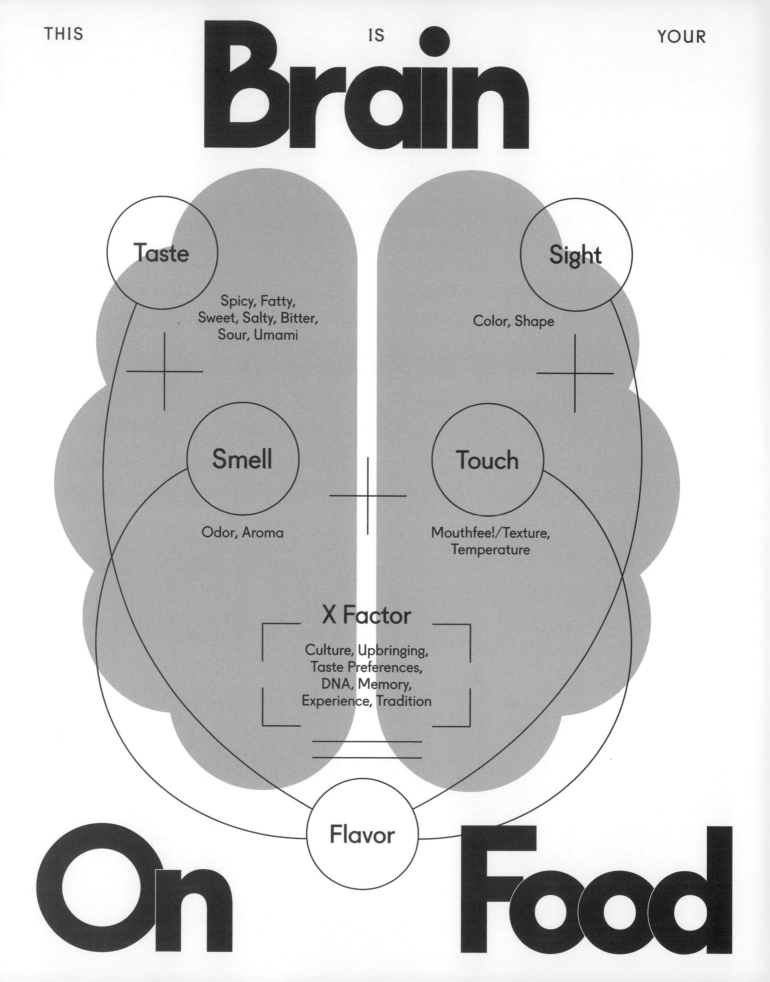

THIS   IS   YOUR

Brain

Taste

Spicy, Fatty,
Sweet, Salty, Bitter,
Sour, Umami

Sight

Color, Shape

Smell

Odor, Aroma

Touch

Mouthfee!/Texture,
Temperature

X Factor

Culture, Upbringing,
Taste Preferences,
DNA, Memory,
Experience, Tradition

Flavor

On   Food

Your perception of flavor is a direct result of the information that your senses send to your brain as you eat. Your ability to taste, touch, smell, and see collectively determines what tastes good to you. While all of your senses are at work as you cook and eat, your sense of taste, and your sense of touch have the strongest, most meaningful impact on your perception of flavor, and you possess the power to manipulate your food in favor of those senses. So let's talk about taste and touch and how to make your food taste really great . . .

Taste & Balance
The Spectacular Seven

Scientifically speaking, it is commonly held that our taste buds perceive five different flavor profiles: salty, sweet, bitter, sour, and umami. Each of your taste buds house receptors for one or several of these flavor profiles. Now, I'm no scientist, but for the sake of explaining how all of these flavor profiles end up affecting one another and the way our food tastes, I've also included "spicy" and "fatty" in the group. Exactly how the brain registers the sensation of spicy or fatty is less important here than acknowledging that those two flavor profiles interact with the other five flavor profiles (salty, sweet, bitter, sour, umami) to create flavors that are greater than the sum of their parts. The magic happens when any number of these seven "tastes" come into harmony and balance in a dish, inspiring that WOW factor you experience when you taste something supremely delish.

Part of being a great cook is learning how to manipulate the seven tastes and combine them in various ways to create tasty—for lack of a better word—flavors. Each of the tastes (a.k.a. flavor profiles) possess an enhancing or suppressing effect on each other when combined. There's no hard-and-fast rule that states a dish must include *all* seven of the tastes in order to taste delicious (if there were, mastering flavor would be a whole helluva lot simpler!). What you should know, however, is that delicious food results from striking a balance between any number of those tastes simultaneously. Once you are aware of these relationships, you'll be able to control the outcome of your food and start to create new flavors.

If you've ever eaten a super-spicy Thai papaya salad, for example, you may know how powerful a creamy, sweet Thai iced tea consumed alongside can be in tempering that heat. Or maybe you've been told to drink a glass of whole milk to quell the burn of unbearably spicy buffalo wings. These are examples of the suppressing effect that "fatty" and "sweet" ingredients have on "spicy" ones. Likewise, the next time you accidentally oversalt a soup or stew, try adding a splash of lemon juice or vinegar—it will help mask the saltiness. Sour ingredients temper salty ingredients when used in small quantities. When it comes to offsetting bitterness, a radicchio salad dressed with a sweet or fatty dressing will register less bitter than a leaf of radicchio eaten on its own. That's simply because sweet and fatty ingredients both suppress bitter ones when used in moderation. Similarly, sourness, in moderate quantities, can suppress fattiness and bring harmony to a dish. Consider a simple salad dressing or vinaigrette. If you were to dress a salad of leafy greens in olive oil alone, your mouth would be coated in fat and greatly miss that balance and vibrancy that a sour (acidic) note brings.

As you begin to combine ingredients together that introduce multiple flavor profiles, you create complements and contrasts within dishes that yield an infinite possibility of flavor. Take, for example, a classic no-frills macaroni and cheese. At its very core, this dish is composed of

pasta, cheese, butter, milk, and salt. Though it seems simple, mac and cheese elicits *salty* (in the form of cheese and salt), *umami* (from the cheese), and *fatty* and *sweet* (butter, cheese, milk). When executed properly, these four tastes work in unison to balance and contrast each other.

Now consider what happens when you add lots of black pepper to that same macaroni and cheese. The black pepper is spicy, which contrasts and complements the already present umami, fatty, salty, and sweet, creating a new version of the dish. If you've ever wondered why *cacio e pepe,* the classic Roman pasta dish, is so freakin' delish, well, now ya know.

Furthermore, if you've ever had *pasta al limone,* with its sauce made of cheese, butter, black pepper, salt, and lemon juice, then you know what a little acidity (sour) can do for a dish. *Pasta al limone* is nothing more than mac and cheese turned *cacio e pepe,* with a good hit of lemon juice right at the end. It's a dish that fires up almost all of your taste buds simultaneously (salty, umami, fatty, sweet, spicy, sour). Head to page 144 for my variation, Orzo al Limone, if you want to get to know what I'm talking about.

All three of these dishes elicit different combinations of the seven *tastes,* culminating in three distinct but equally delicious flavors. Being able to categorize the ingredients in your dish by their flavor profile will allow you flexibility within recipes. Not a big black pepper fan but love the heat of fresh chiles? Sounds great. As long as you're checking off that "spicy" box, you should feel empowered to swap them out for a variation that you think will best suit your palate.

When it comes to making your food taste great, it's totally up to you to steer the ship. Once you possess the knowledge that all flavors are composed of some combination of those seven tastes, you'll be able to improvise more freely in the kitchen. Navigating the many different possibilities of flavor within each of the seven tastes is as easy as thinking about the set of ingredients you are cooking with and the myriad dishes you've eaten in the past and then drawing your own experience–based conclusions. Make a mental note of what something tastes like the next time you eat a really delicious meal at a restaurant, and bring those flavors home to your own kitchen. Sometimes you'll knock it out of the park, and other times you'll decide you wish you'd chosen a different flavor profile or ingredient substitution altogether. This is all part of becoming a flexible and inspired home cook, not just an expert at following recipes.

Need Some Inspo?

SWEET

Granulated Sugar
Brown Sugar
Molasses
Honey
Maple Syrup
Apples
Pears
Dried Fruits
Cooked Onions
Stone Fruit
Berries
Bananas
Sweet Potatoes
Tropical Fruits
Carrots
Oranges
Ketchup
Hoisin Sauce
Jam or Jelly
Cooked Tomatoes
Winter Squash

SALTY

Salt
Anchovies
Olives
Capers
Fish Sauce
Soy Sauce
Miso Paste
Bacon
Parmesan Cheese
Pecorino Cheese
Feta Cheese
Cured Meats
Smoked Salmon
Clam

BITTER

Citrus Zest
Chocolate
Coffee
Amaro
Beer
Mustard Greens
Radicchio
Broccoli Rabe
Dandelion Greens

UMAMI

Parmesan Cheese
Piave Cheese
Cheddar Cheese
Walnuts
Fish Sauce
Mushrooms
Anchovies
Monosodium
Glutamate (MSG)

Use these lists for reference when improvising or looking for a substitution on the fly. Whether you're just not a fan of an ingredient I've called for or can't find it at the grocery store, there's always a suitable substitute. These suggestions are by no means exhaustive, but they should certainly get your wheels turning.

Kimchi
Sardines
Oysters
Miso Paste
Cured Meats
Soy Sauce
Chicken Broth

FATTY

Heavy Cream
Crème Fraîche
Sour Cream
Cream Cheese
Butter
Nuts
Seeds
Avocado
Mortadella
Sausage
Cheese
Tahini
Olive Oil

Neutral Oil
(vegetable, canola, grapeseed, safflower)
Sesame Oil
Coconut Oil
Coconut Milk
Mayonnaise
Bacon
Lard
Yogurt
Schmaltz

SPICY

Fresh Chile Peppers
Ground Dried Chiles
Black Peppercorns
Szechuan Peppercorns
Fresh Ginger
Mustard
Mustard Seeds
Harissa Paste
Gochujang
Sambal Oelek

Chile Oil
Chile Crisp
Sriracha
Horseradish
Hot Sauce
Wasabi

SOUR

Vinegar
Lime
Lemon
Grapefruit
Buttermilk
Cottage Cheese
Yogurt
Wine
Pickles
Cornichons
Pickled Onions
Tomato
Sauerkraut
Kimchi

Touch

The way food feels in your mouth as you eat it also plays an important role in determining its tastiness, and as with all things related to our senses, texture in food is highly subjective. Your upbringing and unique food culture greatly influence what textures you deem desirable in certain dishes. Crispy, creamy, chewy, soft, moist, dry, crumbly, crunchy, bouncy, tough, firm, smooth, gritty, sticky, fudgy—the list goes on and on and on. Part of selecting ingredients when you cook involves considering what textures will be at play. Just as balancing flavor profiles within a dish is tantamount to its deliciousness, creating a balance of contrasting textures can also heighten your enjoyment of a dish. A side of tender roasted vegetables, for example, might benefit greatly from the addition of chopped toasted nuts or a crispy bread-crumb topping to contrast with the inherent softness of the vegetables. A slab of melty butter schmeared on toast introduces moistness to something otherwise dry. A tangy sour cream dip served alongside a platter of crudités offers a creamy contrast to the crispness and crunch of the raw veg.

Temperature (as perceived by your sense of touch) is also powerful in influencing the yum-factor of your food. If you've ever had a bite of cold scrambled eggs, you'll know what I'm talking about. There's a reason that a bowl of Really Great Chicken Soup (page 233) is at its optimal deliciousness when served piping hot and is pretty unpleasant when served cold. Conversely, a salad like the Minimalist Wedge (page 181) is truly a bummer to eat when not served cold and crisp—warm iceberg slathered in mayonnaise is certainly not my idea of a great time. Finding balance between two opposing temperatures can do wonders for a dish. A dish like Miso Apple Tart (page 275) is very tasty served warm out of the oven but is taken to an entirely different, superior level when accompanied by a cold, creamy scoop of vanilla ice cream that mingles with the warm caramel–y apples as it melts. Fiery chile-flecked dishes often crave cold or refreshing counterparts to provide both heat relief and temperature contrast. Helloooo, Hot 'n' Crispy Chicken Cutlets with Kimchi Ranch (page 66)! Let your innate knowledge of textures and temperatures help guide you as you decide which ingredients to add to a dish, or which to substitute in an existing recipe. Remember that your perception of flavor is heightened when you eat food that is hot and dulled when you eat food that is cold. For the best possible assessment of flavor, always taste your food at its intended serving temperature to ensure that it is properly seasoned.

&
Texture

Flavor Flex-ing

Let's talk about how to put all of what we just discussed into practice in a real and meaningful way in your own kitchen. As we've just learned, the way something tastes is a direct result of the convergence of many different variables, as perceived by our senses. Understanding the big flavor picture is vital to your ability to *flavor-flex* in the kitchen. Equipped with this knowledge, you should feel emboldened to take the reins of your own cooking pursuits and tackle whatever snafus and sitchus come your way. You're about to start to flex your shit in the kitchen, and it's going to feel REAL good. To make things easier, I've crafted a couple of checklists that distill all of the above into a clean, easy-to-follow flow chart to reference whenever you hit a road bump within a recipe. They live on the following pages and are there for you whenever you need 'em.

Checklists

"I just made a meal and it tastes pretty meh ...."

① CHECK FOR SEASONING

✓ Add a bit of salt to a spoonful or forkful of whatever you made and taste it again. Did the flavor improve? If so, go ahead and reseason the whole dish. Underseasoning was likely your problem.

② TASTE FOR BALANCE

✓ What is the prevailing flavor profile you are tasting? Is it overpowering? What ingredient do you wish you could taste more (or less)? What can you do to accentuate or diminish that flavor? Could you balance the flavors with a bit more of an ingredient already present in the dish?

✓ What other flavor profile could you introduce to modify the flavor and steer it in a more delicious direction? Refer to the ingredients lists and comb through for something you have on hand that seems like it will complement the other flavors present in your dish.

✓ If it's a slow-cooked dish or a deeply roasty-toasty one, could you introduce something fresh to balance those deeper cooked notes?

③ ASSESS FOR TEXTURE

✓ Is the dish feeling uni-textural? Could it use a little contrast? What quick-fix items do you have on hand that might add some dimension? Crack open your pantry and search for nuts, seeds, croutons, bread crumbs, crackers, chips, and other highly textural sprinkly things that often solve the prob.

④ MAKE ADJUSTMENTS AND CARRY ON!

"Aiii, I'm missing an ingredient!"

① DIG DEEP

✓ What will you lose by not including this ingredient in the recipe? If your gut tells you it won't change much, you can likely stop right there. If you think it's going to play a crucial role, carry on.

✓ Does the dish you are making remind you of something you've had in the past? Can you place it in a familiar cultural or culinary context?

② CONSULT THE LISTS

✓ Flip back to those lists on pages 46—47 and pick a few substitute ingredients that you think might be comparable in flavor and appropriate within the dish. If you're not already familiar with them, taste those ingredients first.

③ ASSESS THE NEW INGREDIENT

✓ What makes this substitute ingredient different from the original? How might this new ingredient affect the dish as a whole, if at all? What adjustments will you need to make to the dish to compensate for this change in ingredient?

✓ Is it more intense in strength of flavor? If yes, then use less of the chosen substitute.

✓ Does it also introduce another flavor profile? As needed, hold back a smidge of another like-minded ingredient in the recipe to account for the added flavor.

✓ Is the texture different? Consider how this new texture will change the outcome of the dish. Is it desirable?

✓ Does it change the overall look of the dish or eating experience? Is it a different color or shape than the original ingredient? How can you cut, tear, slice, dice, or prepare the new ingredient in a way that will accord with the rest of the dish?

✓ Does it smell good? If not, uhh . . . you should probs chuck it and pivot!

④ MAKE THAT SUBSTITUTION AND CARRY ON!

Molly's Golden Rules

1

Read the Recipe First

Recipes are a lot. They're packed with information, and they ask you to synthesize all of it while simultaneously cooking. If you take the time to read through a recipe from start to finish before you begin, you'll get a sense of the big picture and free up some of your attention for the finer things that require more focus. When it comes time to start cooking, you'll have a better idea of the endgame and what kind of time commitment you'll need to make, and the whole experience will be a lot less stressful. Plus, you will avoid accidentally overlooking critical ingredients and might save yourself an extra trip to the grocery store.

2

Cook Through Every Recipe More Than Once (Unless You Hated It the First Time)

You know how when you see a movie for a second time, you start to notice the little details you missed the first time and gain a deeper appreciation for the film as a whole? Recipes operate the same way. The first time you cook through a recipe, you will expend an incredible amount of brainpower just wrapping your head around the ingredients, the prep work, and the way it all comes together on the plate. Cook through that same recipe again, and suddenly you'll free up some brainpower to focus on the little things you couldn't before— the nuances of a dish that can elevate it from good to great to GD delish.

3

The Importance of MISE. EN. PLACE.

Three words. The single most important concept to internalize as a home cook. Mise en place (French for "put in place") refers to the act of prepping all the necessary ingredients for a dish in advance, to prepare you to cook in a streamlined, timely, and unchaotic manner. If you put in the time to read through and complete the necessary prep before you even turn on that burner, you will be rewarded with a lifetime of stress-free cooking and a kitchen that doesn't look like it got bombed at the end of the night.

4

Work Clean

Cooking can be very messy and almost always results in some quantity of dirty dishes. The thought of having to do a deep clean after spending an hour in the kitchen cooking is just a little too much to stomach for a lot of people. I get it. But if you clean as you go, hand wash or fill the dishwasher periodically while you cook, wipe down surfaces, and discard garbage as you create it, the dishes won't pile up, and after all is said and done, you'll sit down to a delicious meal with a clean kitchen. Sounds simple, but trust me—this practice has the potential to really change your relationship to cooking.

5
Your Food Is Only as Good as Your Ingredients

Be thoughtful about which ingredients you invest in—spending a little extra can go a very long way when you're cooking simple recipes like these. Some of the best meals I've ever made were built upon just four or five truly excellent, high-quality ingredients, and they made all the difference in the world. It's even more important to choose good-quality, seasonal, and local food when you're cooking simply—there's nowhere for subpar flavor to hide.

6
You Control the Heat, the Heat Doesn't Control You

I believe that much of the angst that plagues novice cooks involves a fear of navigating the mysterious and intimidating stovetop. But guess who controls that stovetop and those burners? YOU. If you think your onions are getting too dark, turn down the flame. If the chicken skin isn't getting crisp, turn it up! A recipe can only go so far in guiding you. It's your kitchen and you own that stove, so tell it who's boss.

7
Season as You Go

Adding salt to your food little by little as you cook allows you to season each individual element of a dish separately, which results in food that tastes seasoned but not salty. On the flip side, if you season only after something has finished cooking, the salt will only interact with your food superficially and will more likely register as salty.

8
Your Palate Is the Only Palate That Matters

Although everyone loves to have an opinion about food, and believe me, I am no exception, your palate is the only palate that matters in your world and, above all else, in your kitchen. So cook with conviction and make informed decisions according to your own taste preferences and no one else's. You'll never satisfy yourself if you're constantly trying to satisfy others.

9
Cook to the Visual Indicator

This is a crucial one. Despite what most people think, time ranges in recipes are meant to function only as guidelines and never as dogma. Since every burner on every stove and every oven differs in size and power, there is no possible way to prescribe perfect timing in a recipe. Instead, follow the visual indicator given in conjunction with the suggested time frames, and make your best judgment call based on those signals. If a recipe says, "Sear the steak until deeply golden brown, 4 to 5 minutes," and after 5 minutes has passed your steak is only lightly golden, continue to sear it until it reaches that visual indicator, and no less. Trust your instinct—if it doesn't look delicious, it probably isn't.

10
NEVER! STOP! TASTING!

I can't stress this enough. Whenever I see someone cook through a recipe, serve it, and sit down to eat it without ever having stopped to taste it along the way, a little (read: ENORMOUS) part of my soul dies. The only way to be sure your food tastes delicious is to taste, taste, and taste again. If you start tasting at the beginning, you'll give yourself the opportunity to avoid train wrecks before they happen, instead of leaving the end result up to fate.

Pastrami Roast Chicken with Schmaltzy Onions & Dill

Serves 4

PRODUCE

2 large red onions

2 whole garlic heads

½ cup dill leaves

MEAT

1 (3½- to 4-pound) whole chicken

PANTRY

5 tablespoons extra-virgin olive oil

Kosher salt

1 teaspoon freshly ground black pepper

1 tablespoon sweet paprika

1 tablespoon light brown sugar

Dijon mustard, for serving

Of all the ways to prepare a chicken, nothing quite compares to the glory and satisfaction of pulling a whole roasted bird out of the oven. The key to perfectly cooked, moist, tender meat is arranging the chicken with the legs pointing to the back of the oven (the hottest part), so that the breasts don't overcook by the time the legs have reached optimal temperature. The spice rub that gets slathered on this chicken is loosely inspired by my husband's extreme and undying love of pastrami. Believe it or not, he loves a roast chicken even more than I do, so I decided to fuse two of his favorite foods into one epic Sunday night roast. The onions get all schmaltzy and caramelized as they cook below the chicken, and I have to say it's really something.

---

① Position a rack in the middle of your oven. Preheat the oven to 450°F.

② **Get your mise on:**

✦ Cut 2 large onions in half through the root end and slice into ¾-inch-thick wedges. Scatter the onions in a 12-inch cast-iron pan (or on a large rimmed baking sheet).

✦ Cut 2 heads of garlic in half crosswise and nestle them into the onions, cut-sides down, skins and all.[1]

✦ Drizzle 3 tablespoons olive oil all over the onions and garlic and season with 1 teaspoon salt, tossing to coat.

③ **Season the chicken:**

✦ Pat the chicken dry with paper towels.[2]

✦ In a small bowl, combine 4 teaspoons salt, 1 teaspoon black pepper, 1 tablespoon paprika, 1 tablespoon brown sugar, and 2 tablespoons olive oil, mixing with your fingertips until a paste forms.[3]

✦ Place the chicken breast-side up on top of the onions in the skillet. Rub the paste evenly over the chicken, making sure to hit all the nooks, crannies, and undersides.[4]

④ **Roast the chicken:**

✦ Transfer the skillet to the oven, with the legs toward the back of the oven, and roast 50 to 65 minutes, giving the onions a stir once or twice after at least 30 minutes for more even cooking. The chicken is done when the skin is deeply golden brown and the thickest part of the leg registers 165°F on an instant-read thermometer. If the rub is getting too dark, lightly tent the darkest areas with aluminum foil for the remainder of the cook time.

✦ Remove the skillet from the oven and let it rest 15 to 20 minutes.[5] Using tongs, tilt the chicken to allow the juices from the cavity to drip into the skillet, then transfer the chicken to a large cutting board.

⑤ **Serve:**

✦ Stir ½ cup dill leaves into the onions and garlic in the pan.

✦ Carve the rested chicken, removing the legs from the carcass first, then the breast and wings. Slice the breasts crosswise into ½-inch-thick pieces and cut between the drumstick and thigh to separate them. No idea what I'm talking about? No problem. **Pull up this video for a quick carving tutorial. It will all make a lot more sense.** Return the chicken to the skillet, on top of the onion mixture, and serve with Dijon mustard for slathering.

---

[1] The papery skins help protect the garlic from burning, and it's a lot less tedious to squeeze them out once they're all roasted and soft than peeling them now. Your time is valuable! I'm not trying to waste it.

[2] Any water on the surface of the bird is going to prevent the skin from getting golden brown and crisp.

[3] If your chicken is smaller than 3 pounds or larger than 5, either hold back 1 teaspoon salt or add 1 teaspoon accordingly! Generally speaking, it's good to shoot for about 1 teaspoon of salt per pound of meat.

[4] If you have the time to season the chicken in advance, GO FOR IT! Even a few hours of advance seasoning will help the salt penetrate the meat and result in more evenly seasoned, tender meat. It can sit, uncovered, in the fridge with the seasoning for up to 24 hours.

[5] This allows the chicken to finish cooking through residual heat. It'll also make it easier to carve without burning your fingers!

Crispy McCrisperson Chicken Thighs with Herby Peas & Fennel

Serves 4

PRODUCE
1 large fennel bulb (about 1 pound)

6 scallions

3 garlic cloves

2 lemons

1 cup mint, dill, and/or basil leaves

DAIRY
3 tablespoons unsalted butter

MEAT
2½ pounds bone-in, skin-on chicken thighs (about 6)

PANTRY
Kosher salt and coarsely ground black pepper

½ teaspoon red pepper flakes

FROZEN
1 (10-ounce) bag frozen or fresh English peas

If you've ever wondered how to make juicy, tender chicken thighs with shatteringly crisp skin, well, this is your lucky day. This recipe deploys a technique called the "cold-pan method," which was first introduced to me by Chris Morocco. Things have not been the same for me since. When you start chicken thighs skin-side down in a cold pan (that's right—cold!) and allow the skin to very gradually cook, it releases all of their moisture and fat, landing you smack-dab in CrispyTown, USA.

---

① Position a rack in the bottom third of the oven. Preheat the oven to 425°F.

② **Prep the fennel:** Trim off the tough root end and any stalks or fronds of 1 large fennel bulb. Cut in half lengthwise and slice into ½-inch-thick wedges. **Never handled a fennel before? Watch this video, it's super simple.**

③ **Crisp up that chicken skin:**

✦ Pat 2½ pounds of bone-in, skin-on chicken thighs dry with paper towels to remove any surface moisture.[1] Season the chicken all over with 2½ teaspoons salt and a few good cranks of coarsely ground black pepper. Arrange the thighs skin-side down in a dry, unheated 12-inch cast-iron skillet. Set over medium heat and cook, undisturbed, until the skin releases easily from the pan and is light golden brown, 12 to 14 minutes.

✦ Once released, move the chicken thighs around a bit to ensure even browning. Parts of your skillet will get hotter than others. Continue to cook until the skin is very crisp and deep golden brown, 4 to 6 minutes longer. Use tongs to transfer the thighs to a plate, skin-side up.

④ **Add the fennel:** Using tongs, add the fennel wedges to the skillet, turning them to coat in some of the rendered chicken fat. Season with ½ teaspoon salt. Return the chicken to the skillet, skin-side up. Transfer the skillet to the oven and roast 10 to 15 minutes, flipping the fennel halfway through for even browning, until the chicken meat is no longer pink and the fennel is caramelized.

⑤ **Finish your mise:**

✦ Meanwhile, thinly slice 6 scallions and 3 garlic cloves.

⑥ **Finish the chicken:**

✦ Remove the skillet from the oven and transfer the thighs to a plate, skin-side up to stay nice and crisp.

✦ Add 3 tablespoons butter, the scallions, and the garlic to the fennel in the skillet. Cook over medium heat until the scallions and garlic have softened but not browned, 1 to 2 minutes.[2]

✦ Stir in 10 ounces peas, ½ teaspoon red pepper flakes, ½ cup water, and ½ teaspoon salt, scraping up any browned bits from the bottom of the skillet (that's flavor!), and cook until the peas are bright green and just cooked through, 3 to 4 minutes. Turn off the heat.

✦ Stir in the juice of ½ lemon. Taste the peas and add more salt or lemon juice as needed until it tastes super lemony and really tasty.

⑦ **Serve:** Cut whatever lemon remains into wedges for serving. Divide the peas and fennel among 4 shallow bowls and top each with a chicken thigh or two, a lemon wedge, and some torn mint.

---

[1] Surface-area moisture will inhibit browning, so whenever it's a nicely seared crispy crust you're after, make sure you're starting with the driest surface possible.

[2] Browning the garlic brings out bitter notes in the flavor, so most often it's best to avoid getting any color at all.

Milk-Braised Chicken with Bacon, Beans & Kale

Serves 4

PRODUCE
1 whole garlic head

1 lemon

3 sage sprigs

2 bunches lacinato kale, mustard greens, or Swiss chard

DAIRY
2½ cups whole milk

MEAT
3 thick-cut bacon slices

4 bone-in, skin-on chicken leg quarters or 6 thighs (about 2½ pounds)

PANTRY
Kosher salt and freshly ground black pepper

2 tablespoons extra-virgin olive oil, plus more for drizzling

½ teaspoon red pepper flakes (optional)

1 (14.5-ounce) can cannellini beans

Of all the ways to cook a chicken, I'll admit this one is certainly not the most beautiful. But what this dish lacks in beauty, it makes up for astronomically in taste. Cooking whole chicken legs in milk yields meat that is unfathomably tender and flavorful. As the milk cooks with strips of lemon peel, it naturally breaks, separating into curds and whey—you're essentially creating ricotta as the chicken braises. It becomes a rich sauce of bouncy little full-flavored cheese curds to spoon over your chicken. To know milk-braised chicken is to LOVE milk-braised chicken. So get to know it already, would ya??

---

① Preheat the oven to 375°F.

② **Start prepping:**

- Firmly smash and peel all of the cloves from 1 garlic head.

- Using a vegetable peeler, peel 6 (3-inch-long) strips of zest from a lemon. Halve the lemon and set it aside.

- Cut 3 thick-cut bacon slices in half crosswise.

③ **Brown the chicken:**

- Pat 4 chicken legs dry and season all over with 1 tablespoon salt and lots of black pepper.

- Heat 2 tablespoons olive oil in a large Dutch oven over medium-high heat. Add the chicken legs in a single layer, skin-side down, and cook until the skin is very crisp and deep golden brown, 9 to 11 minutes.[1]

④ **Build the sauce:**

- Use tongs to flip each chicken leg skin-side up.

- Add the lemon zest, all but one of the garlic cloves, the bacon, 3 sage sprigs, and ½ teaspoon red pepper flakes (if using), nestling everything around the chicken as best as possible. Cook 1 minute to bloom the lemon zest in the oil.

- Pour 2½ cups whole milk down the sides of the pan.

⑤ **Braise the chicken:** Cover the pot, leaving the lid just slightly askew, and transfer to the oven. Braise for 40 minutes, until the chicken is cooked through but not yet fall apart-y.

⑥ **Add the kale and beans:**

- Meanwhile, strip the leaves from 2 bunches of lacinato kale; discard the stems. Tear the leaves into 3-inch(ish) pieces. Drain and rinse 1 (14.5-ounce) can of cannellini beans. Once the chicken has been cooking for 40 minutes, use tongs to transfer the chicken legs to a large plate. Stir the beans and kale into the sauce. Nestle the chicken back into the pot, skin-side up.

- Return the pot to the oven, uncovered, and braise until the chicken is very tender when prodded with a fork and the joint between the leg and the thigh wiggles loosely, 10 to 15 minutes longer. The sauce will have separated and formed tiny delicious curds swimming in a garlicky bacon broth, so fear not if it looks unusual. This is what makes this dish so special.

- Transfer the chicken to a plate. Pluck out and discard the bacon, which has lent incredible depth of flavor to the dish but is now flabby and unappealing.

⑦ **Serve:**

- Divide the chicken legs among 4 serving bowls.

- Finely grate the reserved garlic clove into the broth. Squeeze the juice of the lemon halves into the sauce. Taste and add more salt if it needs it.

- Divide the kale, beans, and sauce among the serving bowls and drizzle with more olive oil.

---

[1] You may need to move them around after 7 or 8 minutes if certain areas are browning faster than others. There are hot spots on every burner, so pay attention to where yours are.

Hot 'n' Crispy Chicken Cutlets with Kimchi Ranch

Serves 4

PRODUCE
1 garlic clove
1 lemon
1 small bunch chives

DAIRY
¾ cup labneh or plain whole-milk Greek yogurt

MEAT
2 large boneless, skinless chicken breasts or 4 chicken cutlets (about 2 pounds)

PANTRY
2 cups kimchi, plus 3 tablespoons kimchi brine
1 tablespoon plus 2 teaspoons onion powder
1¼ teaspoons cayenne pepper
Kosher salt
½ cup mayonnaise
2 cups neutral oil, such as canola, vegetable, or grapeseed
2 cups panko bread crumbs

My husband is quite possibly the world's greatest buffalo wing fan. The man asks me to make him buffalo wings no less than twice a week. It's rare that I actually do (let's be honest, I never have), but I did promise him there'd be a nod to his favorite guilty pleasure in this book. Chicken cutlets get bathed in Korean kimchi brine, which imparts a ferment-y acidic punch, before they're breaded, shallow-fried, and served with a tangy, garlicky labneh-based condiment that is basically what ranch dressing wishes it could be. What results is a dish that really has nothing to do with buffalo chicken wings at all but is 100 percent Ben Willett–approved. You're welcome, ma babes.

① **Marinate the chicken:**

✦ In a medium bowl, whisk together ¼ cup labneh, 3 tablespoons kimchi brine, 1 tablespoon onion powder, and 1¼ teaspoons cayenne pepper.

✦ Pat 2 chicken breasts dry and slice each in half lengthwise to create 2 thin cutlets. Season the cutlets all over with 2 teaspoons salt and transfer to the marinade, turning to coat. Marinate the chicken at least 15 minutes at room temperature and up to 8 hours in the fridge.

② **Make the kimchi ranch:**

✦ In a small bowl, whisk together ½ cup mayonnaise, 2 teaspoons onion powder, and ½ cup labneh.

✦ Finely grate 1 garlic clove and zest half of a lemon into the labneh–mayo mixture. Cut the lemon into wedges and set them aside for serving.

✦ Thinly slice half of the chives and stir them into the ranch. Slice the remaining chives on the bias into 1½-inch(ish)-long matchsticks for garnishing later.

✦ Finely chop ¾ cup kimchi and stir it into the ranch. If it looks a little thick, add a splash or two of water until it is swooshable and spreadable. Season with salt.

③ **Heat the oil:** In a large Dutch oven, heat 2 cups neutral oil over medium heat; the oil should be about 1½ inches deep. It's ultimately going to need to reach about 400°F,

so use a deep-frying thermometer to check from time to time and adjust the heat as needed to maintain that temp. If you don't have a thermometer, throw a few pieces of panko in the oil, and if they sizzle like cray, you're in the right ballpark for frying.

④ **Bread the chicken:**

✦ Place 2 cups panko in a medium bowl.

✦ Working one at a time, use tongs to dip each chicken cutlet into the panko and use your fingers to press and pack the panko onto the chicken until very well coated. Transfer to a plate.

⑤ **Fry the chicken:**

✦ Line a rimmed baking sheet or a large plate with paper towels.

✦ Once the oil reaches 400°F, working in 2 batches, fry the chicken cutlets until deeply golden brown all over, flipping halfway through, 3 to 5 minutes per side.[1]

✦ Transfer the cutlets to the paper-towel-lined baking sheet and season well with salt.[2] Transfer the cutlets to a cutting board and slice across the grain (perpendicular to the point of the breast) into ½-inch-thick pieces.

⑥ **Plate 'em up:** Spread some kimchi ranch on each plate, add the cutlets and the remaining 1¼ cups kimchi, top with the reserved chives, and serve extra ranch alongside.

[1] Adding them all at once will drastically reduce the oil temperature, and they won't get all golden brown and crisp, which would truly be a bummer.

[2] As a general rule, anything that gets fried in oil should be seasoned as soon as it comes out of the oil, for best salt stickage.

Poached Chicken over Brothy Rice with Cilantro Scallion Sauce

(a.k.a. I LOVE YOU, NONG'S)

PRODUCE
2 whole garlic heads
1 (4-inch) piece
fresh ginger
4 scallions
1 large bunch cilantro
2 jalapeños
1 lime

MEAT
2 bone-in, skin-on
chicken breasts
(about 2 pounds)

PANTRY
1 cup long-grain white
rice, such as basmati
or jasmine
Kosher salt
¼ cup extra-virgin olive
oil or neutral oil

Serves 4 (with lots of yummy leftover broth!)

If you've never been to Nong's Khao Man Gai, a Portland, Oregon–based street cart gone brick-and-mortar that specializes in Thai chicken and rice (the dish that is its namesake), you truly have not lived. The stuff is absolutely legendary. This dish is an ode to Nong Poonsukwattana's but takes quite a few different turns along the way to bring you something that is at once very delicious and achievable on a weeknight. Some people eat cheeseburgers when they're hungover; I eat this. Instead of cooking an entire bird like tradition dictates, you'll take a time-saving shortcut by poaching chicken breasts in a flavorful gingery broth until just shy of cooked through (to account for carryover cooking) and then ladle the fortifying chicken broth that is created in its wake over the chicken and rice just before serving. When I don't have a bottle of Nong's fermented soybean sauce on hand, I turn to a super-quick spicy, cilantro-scallion sauce to tie the whole thing together.

① **Cook the rice:**

✦ Rinse 1 cup long-grain rice in a fine-mesh strainer, swirling the rice with your hands until the water runs clear, 1 to 2 minutes.

✦ Combine the rinsed rice, 1¼ cups cold water, and ¼ teaspoon salt in a small saucepan and bring to a simmer over medium-high heat. Cover the pot immediately with a tight-fitting lid and reduce the heat to very low. Cook 16 minutes (set a timer). Turn off the heat, leave the lid on, and let the rice steam for another 10 minutes; uncover and fluff with a fork.

② **Meanwhile, prep the broth:**

✦ Cut 2 heads of garlic in half crosswise. No worries if they fall apart a bit.

✦ Thinly slice 1 (4-inch) piece of ginger lengthwise into planks.[1]

✦ Cut 4 scallions in half crosswise, separating the dark green parts from the light green and white parts.

✦ Cut 1 large bunch of cilantro in half, separating and reserving the thick stems from the tender leaves and stems.

③ **Poach the chicken:**

✦ Place 2 bone-in, skin-on chicken breasts skin-side up in a medium saucepan. Add the halved garlic heads, sliced ginger, dark scallion greens, thick cilantro stems, 4 cups water, and 2 tablespoons salt. The chicken should be just submerged in the water; if it's not, add more water.

✦ Bring the water to a simmer over medium-high heat. Using tongs, flip the chicken breasts so they're skin-side down.[2] Cook until an instant-read thermometer inserted into the thickest part of the breasts (insert the probe near top part, i.e., the rounded part of the breast) reaches 150°F. This will take 10 to 20 minutes.[3]

recipe continues →

[1] You don't need to peel the ginger since it's just going to simmer in the broth and impart its flavor, unless the skin looks super dirty, in which case peel it using a vegetable peeler.

[2] The bottom of the pot is quite a bit hotter than the top. This ensures the chicken will cook evenly.

[3] The residual heat within the chicken breasts will continue to cook them once they're out of the broth, and you'll ultimately hit the perfect 160°F to 165°F doneness range.

④ **Make the scallion sauce:**

✦ Thinly slice the light green and white parts of the remaining scallions crosswise. Finely chop the cilantro leaves and tender stems.

✦ Trim the stems of 2 jalapeños. Cut the jalapeños in half lengthwise and pull out the seeds and inner ribs. Finely chop the jalapeños. Combine the scallions, cilantro, and jalapeños in a small bowl.

✦ Stir in ¼ cup olive oil and the juice of 1 lime; season with salt.

⑤ **Back to that chicken:**

✦ Once the chicken reaches 150°F, use tongs to transfer the breasts to a cutting board and let cool for about 10 minutes. Once cool enough to handle, remove and discard the skin. Carve the meat of each breast off the bone and cut each against the grain into ½-inch-thick slices. **Here's a video to help guide you through that process.**

✦ While the chicken cools, add 3 cups water to the broth and return to a simmer. Remove from the heat.

⑥ **Serve:**

✦ Place a big mound of cooked rice in each of 4 serving bowls and top with the chicken breast slices. Ladle some broth over top (no need to strain it; just avoid the big pieces of garlic and scallion floating around).

✦ Spoon the scallion sauce generously over the chicken. Serve more broth alongside for sipping.[4]

---

[4] You'll have a lot of broth left over. That's a good thing! You can strain it and use it in any other recipes that call for stock or water. Just remember that it is highly seasoned already, so you may want to hold back on salt in whatever you use it for.

Spiced, Grilled & Swaddled Chicken Thighs with the Works

Serves 4

PRODUCE
2 medium red onions

5 garlic cloves

2 lemons

1 bunch mint or cilantro

DAIRY
1¾ cups plain whole-milk yogurt

MEAT
2 pounds boneless, skinless chicken thighs (about 6 small thighs)

PANTRY
1 cup distilled white vinegar

½ cup sugar

Kosher salt

1 tablespoon vegetable oil, plus more for the grill

1 tablespoon sweet smoked paprika

1 tablespoon ground cumin

¾ teaspoon ground cinnamon

½ teaspoon cayenne pepper

4 pitas

I've always dreamt of somehow jerry-rigging a shawarma spit setup in my home kitchen. I mean, how amazing would it be to bring the intoxicating scent of spit-roasted meat (if you're a New Yorker you know—nothing is more delicious than the smells that waft off a shawarma cart) into your home kitchen and to shave off in real time for your guests when you entertain?! Sadly, in a Brooklyn apartment kitchen, that is far from realistic. So when the craving hits, I take things outdoors and make a version of these spiced and grilled chicken thighs, swaddle them in warmed pitas with piles of herbs and pickled onions, and forget for a second just how far I am from realizing that dream.

---

① **Pickle the red onions:**

✦ Slice 2 red onions crosswise into ⅛-inch-thick rings.

✦ In a small saucepan, heat 1 cup white vinegar, 1½ cups water, ½ cup sugar, and 1 tablespoon salt over medium heat, stirring often to dissolve. Once the vinegar mixture comes to a simmer, remove from the heat and immediately add the onions. Let cool to room temperature. The onions can be made up to several days in advance; they only get better with time.

② **Make the garlic yogurt:**

✦ Finely grate 1 garlic clove into a small bowl and stir in 1 cup plain yogurt. Season with salt and set aside for serving.

③ **Marinate the chicken:**

✦ Finely grate 4 garlic cloves into a large bowl.

✦ Stir in ¾ cup plain yogurt, the juice of 1 lemon, 1 tablespoon vegetable oil, 2½ teaspoons salt, 1 tablespoon smoked paprika, 1 tablespoon cumin, ¾ teaspoon cinnamon, and ½ teaspoon cayenne pepper and whisk well to combine.

✦ Add 2 pounds boneless, skinless chicken thighs to the marinade and turn to coat. Let sit at room temperature for at least 30 minutes while you prepare a grill for medium heat (or heat a cast-iron grill pan over medium heat). If you're going to marinate them longer (which you totes should; they only improve with time), cover and keep chilled in the refrigerator for up to 6 hours and pull them out 30 minutes before cooking.

④ **Back to grilling that chicken:**

✦ Once the grill is preheated to medium (you should be able to hold your hand over the grate for about 5 seconds before it gets too hot), lightly oil the grill grates.

✦ Remove the chicken from the marinade with tongs, letting any excess drip back into the bowl, and transfer it to the grill. Cook, undisturbed, until it's nicely charred underneath and naturally releases from the grates, 5 to 6 minutes. Pay attention to the hot spots of your grill or grill pan, and move the thighs around accordingly to ensure even browning. Flip the thighs and cook until just cooked through, 4 to 7 minutes longer. (An instant-read thermometer should register 165°F in the thickest part of the thigh.) This will vary depending on how large your chicken thighs are, so keep an eye on temperature more than timing in this case! Let the chicken thighs rest on a plate while you grill the pitas.

⑤ **Warm the pitas and serve:**

✦ Warm the pitas on the grill while the chicken rests, about 1 minute per side.

✦ Cut a lemon into 4 wedges and pick the leaves from 1 bunch of mint.

✦ Slice the chicken against the grain into ½-inch-thick strips and serve on a big platter alongside the pitas, pickled onions, garlic yogurt, lemon wedges, and mint for a build-your-own kinda sitch.

Golden Brown & Delicious Chicken Breasts with Crispy Bread Salad

Serves 4

PRODUCE
1 medium head radicchio (about 8 ounces)

3 garlic cloves, unpeeled

DAIRY
2 ounces Piave, Parmesan, or pecorino cheese

3 tablespoons unsalted butter

MEAT
2 large bone-in, skin-on chicken breasts (about 2 pounds)

PANTRY
Kosher salt and freshly ground black pepper

5 tablespoons extra-virgin olive oil

1 cup Castelvetrano olives

¼ baguette (about 3 ounces)

3 oil-packed anchovy fillets

3 tablespoons sherry vinegar

Honey, for drizzling

Chicken breasts get a bad rap in the food world. Truth be told, it's a lot easier to overcook chicken breasts than it is legs or thighs, which contributes to their reputation for being dry and tough. To combat that, it's important to roast chicken breasts with both their skin and bone intact. The skin provides a protective barrier for the meat, keeping it moist, while the bone lends a lot of flavor to the breast as it cooks. If you've never repeatedly basted a piece of meat with frothy, foaming garlic butter, you are about to experience one of the greatest pleasures of cooking.

---

① Preheat the oven to 425°F.

② **Season the chicken:** Pat the chicken dry and season it evenly all over with 2½ teaspoons salt and lots of black pepper.

③ **Cook the chicken:**

✦ Heat 2 tablespoons olive oil in a 12-inch cast-iron skillet over medium-high heat until just beginning to smoke. Place the chicken breasts skin-side down in the skillet and reduce the heat to medium. Cook, undisturbed, until the skin is golden brown, 6 to 8 minutes. Move the breasts around the pan if the chicken seems to be browning more quickly in some parts than others.

✦ Transfer to the oven (skin-side down). Roast until an instant-read thermometer registers 145°F when inserted into the thickest part of the breast, 25 to 30 minutes.

④ **Prep the salad:**

✦ Meanwhile, tear 1 medium radicchio head into large pieces and transfer to a large bowl.

✦ Using a vegetable peeler, shave 2 ounces Piave cheese right into the radicchio.

✦ Smash 1 cup Castelvetrano olives with the bottom of a mug or glass measuring cup. Discard the pits and add the olives to the salad.

✦ Tear ¼ of a baguette into irregular 1-inch pieces. Set aside.

⑤ **Baste the chicken:**

✦ Smash 3 garlic cloves but don't peel them.[1]

✦ When the chicken is done, remove the skillet from the oven and transfer it to the stovetop. Keep the oven on.

✦ Flip the chicken breasts skin-side up. Add 3 tablespoons butter, the garlic, and 3 anchovy fillets to the skillet and set over medium heat. Tilt the pan slightly toward you, let the melted butter collect at the side of the pan, and, using a large spoon, continuously baste the chicken breasts with the butter for 2 minutes. **Need a quick butter-basting tutorial? See here.** Transfer the chicken to a cutting board to rest, leaving the anchovy-garlic butter behind.

✦ Add the torn bread to the butter and stir the pieces around to coat. Return the skillet to the oven and bake until the croutons are crisp and golden brown, 8 to 10 minutes.

⑥ **Dress the salad:**

✦ Add the croutons and garlic to the bowl of salad.

✦ Drizzle 3 tablespoons sherry vinegar and 3 tablespoons olive oil over the radicchio; toss well. Season with salt and black pepper. Lightly drizzle the salad with honey, tossing once to create pockets of sweetness.

⑦ **Serve:** Carve the chicken breasts off the bone, slice them crosswise, and serve with the salad. **Not sure how to carve a chicken breast? Watch this.**

---

[1] The skins protect the garlic from burning.

Slow-Roasted Piri-Piri(ish) Chicken with Crushed Potatoes & Aioli

Serves 4

PRODUCE

1 whole garlic head

2 red Fresno or serrano chiles or 1 Thai bird's-eye chile

2 pounds baby Yukon Gold potatoes

2 lemons

DAIRY

2 large egg yolks

MEAT

1 (3½– to 4–pound) whole chicken

PANTRY

Kosher salt

4 tablespoons extra–virgin olive oil

2 tablespoons double–concentrated tomato paste

1 tablespoon smoked paprika

2 tablespoons red wine vinegar or sherry vinegar

1 cup vegetable oil

Enter the slow-roasted chicken, one of the all-time most reliable techniques when it comes to cooking chicken. Compared to classic roast chicken that's cooked at a higher temperature, a slow-roasted chicken isn't inherently more complicated. Yes, this recipe takes 2½ to 3 hours in the oven, but the low-and-slow method makes this technique nearly foolproof against dry and overcooked meat. And those are entirely inactive hours, meaning you could be doing literally anything else at all while this bird transforms from something great into something sublime. The result is meat so tender that you can pull it apart with your hands, meaning no mastery of carving necessary either. The chicken gets rubbed in a smoky-hot chile paste, reminiscent of piri piri sauce, a Portuguese condiment made of super-hot piri piri chiles (native to West Africa) that made its way into Portuguese cuisine in the fifteenth century. Piri piri chiles can be hard to come by in the United States, so I've offered some more common alternatives.

---

① Preheat the oven to 400°F.

② **Season the chicken:** Place the chicken on a rimmed baking sheet. Season the chicken all over with 4 teaspoons salt, being sure to season the cavity as well.

③ **Make the chile paste:**

+ Lightly smash and peel 6 garlic cloves. Using a Microplane, finely grate 4 of the cloves into a small bowl. Set the remaining 2 cloves aside for making the aioli later on. Cut what's left of the head of garlic in half crosswise for roasting alongside the chicken. Lots of garlic in this dish—no wonder it's so good!

+ Finely grate 2 Fresno chiles into the bowl, discarding the stem. You can also finely chop the chiles and mash them to a paste with the side of your chef's knife.

+ Whisk in 2 tablespoons olive oil, 2 tablespoons tomato paste, 1 tablespoon smoked paprika, and 2 tablespoons red wine vinegar until combined.

+ Using a pastry brush or the back of a small spoon, rub the entire chicken with all of the chile paste, getting in all the nooks and crannies—no need to coat the inside of the cavity.

④ **Season the potatoes:** On the baking sheet with the chicken, toss 2 pounds baby Yukon Gold potatoes and the halved garlic with 2 tablespoons olive oil and season with salt. Arrange them around the chicken (the chicken sits directly on the baking sheet, not on top of any of the vegetables; this will ensure that all of the potatoes cook at the same rate).

⑤ **Roast the chicken and potatoes:** Transfer the chicken and potatoes to the oven to roast for 10 minutes, then reduce the heat to 325°F.[1] Continue to roast until the legs are so tender that when wiggled with a pair of tongs you could almost pull them off the carcass, 2½ to 3 hours, and the potatoes are tender and easily pierced with the tines of a fork. While roasting, baste the chicken two or three times: shake the pan, then tilt the pan toward you slightly to collect some of the accumulated juices in a spoon and pour it back over the chicken.

---

[1] The reason we start the oven at 400°F and then drop it to 325°F is that it takes quite some time for a cold chicken and a lot of potatoes to heat up in a low oven. This allows them a blast of heat at the beginning to get everything hot before reducing the temperature to ensure a gentle, slow cook for the next couple of hours.

recipe continues →

⑥ **Make the aioli:**

✦ Finely grate the reserved 2 garlic cloves into a medium bowl. Add 2 egg yolks and whisk well to combine. Place a damp kitchen towel under the bowl to stabilize it.

✦ Slowly whisk in 1 cup vegetable oil in a very thin stream at first, then more generously once the aioli starts to thicken and lighten in color. Fear not: this is a pretty foolproof aioli, since it has 2 eggs to help bind the oil. **Still need a little assistance with that aioli? Pull up this video to see how it's done.**

✦ Once all of the oil has been incorporated, add the juice of 1 lemon and season well with salt.[2] Cover the aioli until you're ready to serve.

⑦ **Serve:** Let the chicken rest for at least 15 minutes. Cut 1 lemon into wedges for serving. Carve the chicken. **You can pull the legs right off the carcass without a knife, but if you want a refresher on how to carve a chicken, pull up this video.** Serve it with the potatoes, halved garlic, lemon wedges, aioli, and any juices left in the skillet.

---

[2] It's going to take a lot more salt than you might think to season a full cup of oil and 2 egg yolks, so really go for it until things start to taste good. This recipe yields a full cup of aioli, which might be unnecessary for the number of people the dish serves (depending who you ask), but this way you'll have ample leftovers for slathering on . . . everything.

Beef, & Pork Lamb

Skirt Steak with Red Chimichurri

Serves 4

PRODUCE
2 garlic cloves

1 small shallot, or ¼ small red onion

1 red Fresno chile or jalapeño

MEAT
1 pound skirt steak, trimmed

PANTRY
Kosher salt

⅓ cup red wine vinegar or sherry vinegar

2 teaspoons sugar

2 teaspoons sweet smoked paprika

⅓ cup plus 2 tablespoons extra-virgin olive oil

½ cup drained roasted red peppers

Flaky sea salt

One of the thinnest cuts of beef out there, skirt steak was basically made for weeknight meals because of its quick-cooking nature. If you can't find skirt, flank steak will work just as well, although I prefer the marbling typical of skirt steak. Fat is flavor, after all. Regardless, the trick here is to preheat your pan until it is unfathomably hot, so the steak can achieve a good dark sear on the outside before overcooking on the inside. A small amount of sugar in the marinade helps expedite that process to ensure a deeply caramelized crust. The whole thing is topped with a bright, spicy, Argentinean-style red chimichurri sauce. Unlike the green version that's jam-packed with herbs, this one is made with both sweet and spicy peppers.

---

① **Marinate the steak:**

+ Pat 1 pound of skirt steak dry with paper towels. Cut it crosswise into 3 equal pieces.[1] Season all over with 1½ teaspoons kosher salt. Transfer to a shallow bowl or baking dish.

+ Finely grate 2 garlic cloves into a glass measuring cup. Add ⅓ cup red wine vinegar, 2 teaspoons sugar, 2 teaspoons smoked paprika, and ⅓ cup olive oil and whisk to combine. Pour half of that marinade over the steak, turning to coat. Let sit at least 15 minutes at room temperature or up to 4 hours in the refrigerator.

② **Make the chimichurri sauce:**

+ Finely chop 1 shallot. **Not totally sure how? Right this way for a quick demo.**

+ Thinly slice 1 Fresno chile crosswise, discarding the stem and seeds, and finely chop it.

+ Finely chop ½ cup roasted red peppers. Add the shallot, chile, and roasted red peppers to the remaining marinade. Season with kosher salt.

③ **Cook the steak:**

+ Preheat a dry 12-inch cast-iron skillet over medium-high heat for at least 4 minutes to be sure it's nice and hot right off the bat. You should be able to see some very light wisps of smoke coming off the pan.

+ Remove the steak from the marinade, allowing any excess liquid to drip back into the bowl. Pat dry with paper towels.[2]

+ Working in 2 batches, add 1 tablespoon olive oil to the pan, allow it to heat up for about 30 seconds, then add half the steak and cook, undisturbed, until charred on the underside, 2 to 3 minutes. Flip and cook 1 minute on the second side. Transfer to a cutting board to rest for 5 minutes.[3]

④ **Serve:** Look at the steak and figure out which way the grain is running (i.e., which way the muscle fibers run). Thinly slice crosswise against the grain, perpendicular to the fibers. **Not sure what the grain is or how to find it? Right this way.** Transfer to a platter along with any juices on the cutting board (that's FLAVOR—don't leave it behind). Spoon some of the chimichurri over the steak and serve the remainder alongside. Season with flaky sea salt.

---

[1] This makes it easier to fit them into the pan and will yield shorter, more manageable slices in the end.

[2] Moisture is the enemy of browning (it creates steam!), so the drier the steak, the better the sear.

[3] You really don't need to worry about taking the internal temperature of a steak this thin because it cooks so quickly—your biggest concern is not overcooking it, so as long as the pan is hot, you should be golden.

Beef & Celery Stir-Fry with Wilted Basil

Serves 4

PRODUCE

4 celery stalks

1 red Fresno or serrano chile

4 garlic cloves

1 (2-inch) piece fresh ginger

1½ cups packed basil leaves

MEAT

1 pound boneless beef short ribs

PANTRY

3 tablespoons unseasoned rice vinegar

3 teaspoons toasted sesame oil

4 teaspoons light brown sugar

Kosher salt

3 tablespoons vegetable oil

White rice (page 169), for serving (optional)

Most people associate short ribs with slow roasts and braises, and assume they require a significant time commitment in order to coax them into tenderness. This recipe exists to convince you otherwise. Short ribs are very fatty and marbled, which actually makes them great for a high-heat stir-fry, as the meat stays juicy and moist. Freeze the short ribs (be sure to get them boneless so you don't have to deal with cutting out the bone) for a short period of time to firm up the meat, so you'll have a much easier time slicing them into thin, even slices. The short ribs are the star of this dish, but the crunchy celery is a close second—and the perfect juicy complement to the flavorful strips of meat.

① If you're serving rice with this dish, get that rice cooking! (There's a recipe for Really Reliable Rice on page 169.) It's also totally acceptable to run down the street and buy a pint of rice from your local take-out joint; nobody's judging.

② **Chill the short ribs:** Place the short ribs on a small plate and freeze for 15 to 20 minutes.[1]

③ **Do some prep:**

✦ Slice 4 celery stalks on the bias about ¼ inch thick.

✦ Thinly slice 1 red Fresno chile crosswise into rings, seeds and all; discard the stem.

④ **Make the marinade:**

✦ Using a Microplane, finely grate 4 garlic cloves and a 2-inch piece of ginger into a medium bowl. (You don't need to peel the ginger unless the skin seems super tough and gnarly.)

✦ Add 1 tablespoon rice vinegar, 2 teaspoons sesame oil, 4 teaspoons light brown sugar, 2 teaspoons salt, and 2 tablespoons vegetable oil and stir together with a fork.

⑤ **Slice the beef:** Once the beef is firm, trim off any gristly hard fat attached. Thinly slice against the grain into 2-inch-long strips.[2] **Not sure how to find the grain? Pull up this video.** Transfer the beef to the marinade and use your hands to toss and coat everything. Set aside at room temperature for at least 15 minutes and up to 1 hour.

⑥ **Start stir-fryin':**

✦ Heat a large nonstick skillet over medium-high heat for 3 minutes, or until very hot. Add the remaining 1 tablespoon vegetable oil to the skillet. Using tongs, add half the beef to the skillet in a single layer and cook, undisturbed, until deeply brown and caramelized, 3 to 4 minutes. Flip and cook the second side until no longer pink, just 30 seconds longer. Transfer the beef to a plate. Repeat with the remaining beef; there should be enough fat left in the skillet.

✦ Turn off the heat and quickly add the sliced celery, Fresno chile, 2 tablespoons rice vinegar, 1 teaspoon sesame oil, and 1½ cups basil leaves. Season with salt and toss to combine until the celery is just barely heated through and the basil is wilted and bright green. Serve on top of steamed rice (if desired).

---

[1] This makes it easier to thinly slice the meat. It doesn't need to freeze all the way through, just enough to firm up the meat. A sharp knife will help, too!

[2] The thinner, the better, but don't beat yourself up about it—as always, the most important thing is that the slices are equal in thickness to encourage even cooking.

Strip Steaks au Poivre

Serves 4

PRODUCE
1 large shallot

4 garlic cloves

3 thyme sprigs

DAIRY
3 tablespoons unsalted butter

½ cup heavy cream

MEAT
2 (1½-inch-thick) New York strip steaks (about 1½ pounds total)

PANTRY
Kosher salt and freshly ground black pepper

1 tablespoon whole black peppercorns

2 tablespoons vegetable oil

⅓ cup cognac, dry sherry, or brandy

Flaky sea salt

I recently got a text from my husband, who was having dinner at beloved all-day café/market/dream restaurant Gjusta in Venice, California. He was eating steak au poivre (a French dish of steak drenched in creamy pepper sauce) and just absolutely LOVING every minute of it. "I think you should bring back the steak au poivre" was what it said. A week later, this recipe was born and that was that.

---

① **Prep your mise:**

✦ Pat 2 New York strip steaks dry with paper towels. Season all over with 2½ teaspoons kosher salt and a generous amount of ground black pepper. Set aside for at least 15 minutes.[1]

✦ Finely chop 1 large shallot.

✦ Thinly slice 2 garlic cloves. Firmly smash 2 additional garlic cloves to really break them open so that they are able to release a lot of flavor when they hit the skillet.

✦ Place 1 tablespoon whole peppercorns in a sealable plastic bag, seal the bag, place it on your countertop, and crush with the bottom of a small saucepan to coarsely crack them. If you have a mortar and pestle, use that! They should be coarser than ground black pepper.

② **Cook the steaks:**

✦ Heat a 12-inch cast-iron skillet over medium-high heat for 4 minutes.

✦ Add 2 tablespoons vegetable oil to the skillet. Add the steaks and cook, undisturbed, until a deep golden brown crust forms underneath, about 3 minutes. Flip and cook on the second side until equally golden brown, 3 minutes longer. (If the steaks have a fat cap, upend them on their sides, stabilizing them with tongs, and sear the edges, until browned, 2 to 3 minutes per edge.)

③ **Baste:** Reduce the heat to medium-low. Add 1 tablespoon butter, 3 thyme sprigs, and the 2 smashed garlic cloves to the pan. Use a spoon to continuously baste the steak, about 2 minutes. **If you've never basted a steak and want to learn how, right this way!** Insert your instant-read thermometer into the thickest part of the steak. Once it registers 120°F, transfer it to a cutting board to rest.

④ **Make the pan sauce:**

✦ Add 2 tablespoons butter to the skillet along with the sliced garlic, shallot, and crushed peppercorns. Cook, stirring often, until the shallot and garlic are softened but not browned, 4 to 5 minutes.[2]

✦ Turn off the heat (cognac is flammable!) and add ⅓ cup cognac. Return the skillet to medium heat and cook until the cognac has mostly evaporated and your spoon leaves streaks in the skillet when you stir, 1 to 2 minutes.

✦ Add ½ cup heavy cream, bring to a simmer, and cook until it coats the back of a spoon, about 1 minute. Season with kosher salt.

⑤ **Serve:**

✦ Slice the steak against the grain. **Not sure what the grain is or how to find it? Right this way.** Transfer to a serving platter.

✦ Pour any resting juices back into the skillet and stir them into the sauce. Spoon the sauce generously over the steak, season with flaky sea salt, and serve immediately.[3]

---

[1] This will give the salt a chance to penetrate the meat, so it won't fall off the steaks when you sear them.

[2] Cooking the peppercorns helps bloom their flavor and infuses the butter with peppery heat in a way that simply stirring them in at the end does not.

[3] The sauce will thicken and congeal as it cools down, and it won't feel as luxurious on your palate.

Sunday Brisket

Serves 6 to 8

PRODUCE
2 medium red onions

1 whole garlic head

1 large rosemary sprig

1 cup packed parsley leaves

½ lemon

MEAT
5 to 6 pounds flat or point brisket, untrimmed

PANTRY
Kosher salt and freshly ground black pepper

1 tablespoon extra-virgin olive oil

2 tablespoons white miso paste

1 cup dry red wine

1 (28-ounce) can crushed tomatoes

1 teaspoon red pepper flakes

2 (14.5-ounce) cans chickpeas

Growing up, we were more of a chicken-cutlet-and-frozen-peas-for-Sunday-dinner kinda family than an all-day-affair-Sunday-sauce kinda household. And I'm not mad about it. I still really love chicken cutlets. But I do regret the fact that I don't have a decades-old family tradition of sitting down to a long-cooked piece of meat on a lazy Sunday evening. So, this is a Sunday sauce, *my way*. Only time will tell if this recipe lives on to grace the tables of my grandchildren, but a girl can certainly dream.

You'll likely encounter two different cuts of brisket at the store—the flat and the point—and both of them work great in this gentle, slow-cooked tomato-based braise, but I'm partial to the point, because it's quite a bit fattier and therefore more flavorful. This recipe makes a lot of food, but that's the spirit of a Sunday sauce—the leftovers are even more delicious.

---

① **Season the brisket:** Set a 5- to 6-pound brisket on a rimmed baking sheet and season it all over with 3 tablespoons salt and lots of freshly ground black pepper. Transfer the brisket to the fridge to chill, uncovered, for at least 8 hours and up to 24.[1]

② **Do some prep:**

✦ Position a rack in the lower third of your oven. Preheat the oven to 300°F. Remove the brisket from the refrigerator.

✦ Cut 2 medium red onions in half through the root end. Peel and discard the skins and then cut each half into 3 wedges through the root end.

✦ Firmly smash and peel a head's worth of garlic cloves. Set 1 clove aside for the gremolata.

③ **Build the braise:**

✦ Heat a large Dutch oven over medium-high heat for 4 to 5 minutes until it's really hot. Pat the brisket dry. Add 1 tablespoon olive oil to the pot, swirling the pot to coat the surface. Add the brisket, fattier-side down, and cook, undisturbed, until you establish some good golden brown color, 8 to 10 minutes. Using tongs and a spatula, flip the brisket and sear the other side until golden brown, 8 minutes longer. Transfer the brisket to a rimmed baking sheet.

✦ Spoon out and discard all but enough fat to lightly coat the bottom of the pot. Add the onions in a single layer and cook until brown on one side, 3 to 4 minutes. Flip and brown the other side, 3 to 4 minutes longer.

✦ Stir in the smashed garlic and season with 1 teaspoon salt. Cook until the garlic just begins to take on a little bit of color and is fragrant, 1 to 2 minutes.

✦ Add 2 tablespoons miso paste and stir to incorporate.[2]

✦ Add 1 cup dry red wine and cook, stirring and scraping the bottom of the pot, until it has reduced slightly, is a bit thicker and more viscous, and no longer smells as harshly alcoholic, about 4 minutes.

✦ Stir in 1 (28-ounce) can of crushed tomatoes, 1 large rosemary sprig, 1 teaspoon red pepper flakes, and 1 teaspoon salt. Nestle the brisket back into the pot. Add enough water so that the brisket is only peeking out of the liquid by about 1 inch (about 1½ cups water). Bring the liquid to a simmer over medium-high heat.

---

[1] Unfortunately, this is a step you shouldn't skip. The brisket is so dense that it really needs the time to sit so the salt can gradually penetrate and season the meat throughout.

[2] Miso paste might sound crazy in the context of tomato-based braise, but it actually brings a ton of depth of flavor without being noticeably miso-y.

④ **Braise the brisket:** Cover the pot with a tight-fitting lid and transfer it to the oven to braise until the brisket is very tender when prodded in the thickest part with a fork, 3 to 4 hours total, depending on how thick your brisket is. While it cooks, once every hour, spoon the sauce up and over the brisket.

⑤ **Finish the sauce:**

✦ Let the brisket cool, uncovered, in the pot for 10 minutes. Using a pair of tongs and a large spatula, transfer the brisket to a large cutting board.

✦ Ladle or spoon off as much of the rendered fat that has risen to the top of the pot as you can and discard it.[3]

✦ Drain 2 (14.5-ounce) cans of chickpeas into a fine-mesh strainer and rinse. Stir into the sauce. Set over medium heat and cook the sauce, stirring occasionally, until slightly reduced, 5 to 10 minutes longer.

⑥ **Make the gremolata:** Finely chop 1 cup packed parsley leaves and transfer to a small bowl. Finely grate the zest of ½ lemon and the reserved garlic clove into the bowl. Stir with a fork to combine.

⑦ **Serve:**

✦ Once the brisket has rested for at least 10 minutes, slice into ½-inch-thick slices against the grain with a serrated knife. **Not sure how to find the grain? Right this way.**

✦ Spoon some of the chickpeas and sauce into shallow serving bowls and top each with a few slices of brisket and a sprinkle of gremolata.

---

[3] There is plenty of fat in the brisket for flavor, so it doesn't hurt to get rid of a little off the top to avoid greasiness.

Miso-Marinated Pork Steaks & a Big Pile of Spicy Cukes

Serves 4

PRODUCE

1 English (hothouse) cucumber

MEAT

2 (1-inch-thick) bone-in pork shoulder steaks (about 2½ pounds total)

PANTRY

½ cup white miso paste

½ cup sake

3 tablespoons plus 2 teaspoons sugar

Kosher salt

2 tablespoons vegetable oil

2 tablespoons unseasoned rice vinegar

¾ teaspoon red pepper flakes

Most people eat pork chops; I eat pork shoulder steaks. I don't really believe in cooking pork chops at home because they require advance planning to brine them so that they actually taste like something and aren't tough and bland. Instead, when I'm looking for a quick-cooking cut of pork I reach for shoulder steaks, a fattier, more marbled (i.e., more forgiving and flavorful) cut. It's not terribly common to see pork shoulder steaks that have been preportioned into 1-inch-thick chops, but almost any butcher will be able to cut them that way for you. The marinade that coats these pork steaks is a combination of miso, sake, and sugar—a marination technique that has long-standing roots in Japanese cuisine. It's both intensely sweet and savory and a perfect match for the fatty pork.

---

① **Marinate the pork:**

✦ In a medium bowl, whisk together ½ cup white miso, ½ cup sake, and 3 tablespoons sugar untll well combined. Add 2 bone-in pork shoulder steaks and turn them to coat. Cover the bowl and refrigerate for at least 2 hours and up to overnight.

✦ Pull the pork out of the fridge and let sit at room temperature for about 30 minutes.

② **Make the cucumber salad:** Cut 1 English (hothouse) cucumber in half lengthwise. Slice crosswise as thinly as possible into half-moons. Transfer the cucumber to a medium bowl and season with 1½ teaspoons salt. Chill in the fridge for at least 15 minutes and up to 2 hours.[1]

③ **Cook the pork:**

✦ Using a spatula, scrape off most of the marinade from the pork steaks, letting the marinade drip back into the bowl, and transfer them to a large plate or rimmed baking sheet. Stir ½ cup water into the leftover marinade.

✦ Heat a 12-inch cast-Iron skillet over medium-high heat for 5 minutes to get it super-duper hot.

✦ Pat the pork dry with paper towels. Season with 1 teaspoon salt and coat all over with 2 tablespoons vegetable oil. Adding oil to the meat itself versus directly to the skillet helps minimize the spattering and smoke when it hits the pan.

✦ Add the pork to the skillet, decrease the heat to medium, and cook until it begins to brown on one side, about 2 minutes. Using tongs, flip the pork and cook on the other side until beginning to brown, 2 minutes longer. Continue cooking, flipping every minute or two, until the steaks are deeply caramelized and an instant-read thermometer reaches 145°F, 4 to 5 minutes longer.[2] Transfer the steaks to a cutting board to rest for 10 minutes. Reserve the skillet.

✦ While the pork rests, tip off and discard any liquid that has collected in the bowl of cucumbers. Add 2 tablespoons rice vinegar, ¾ teaspoon red pepper flakes, and 2 teaspoons sugar and toss to coat.

✦ Cut the pork steaks off the bone—there may be a few bones that run through each steak, so navigate your way around them. Slice the meat across the grain into ½-inch-thick pieces. **Not sure how to find the grain? Right this way.** Transfer the sliced pork and any juices that have accumulated on the cutting board to a serving platter.

④ **Make the pan sauce and serve:**

✦ Carefully tip out and discard any fat left behind in the skillet. Return the skillet to medium heat and stir in the reserved marinade. Cook, stirring and swirling the skillet constantly, until the sauce comes to a simmer and turns glossy and deep golden brown. Remove from the heat. Add a splash of water if it looks too thick. Season with salt.

✦ Spoon the pan sauce over the sliced pork. Top with a big pile of the spicy cucumbers.

---

[1] Salting the cucumbers will help draw out some of the water in them. This will leave them extra flavorful and supremely crunchy.

[2] There is sugar in the marinade that will caramelize in the hot skillet and help give it deep color and depth of flavor.

Pork Sausages with Mustardy Lentils & Celery

Serves 4

PRODUCE
4 celery stalks

1 lemon

1 cup parsley leaves

4 garlic cloves

1 medium yellow or white onion

MEAT
1 pound fresh pork sausages (any kind)

PANTRY
Kosher salt

1½ cups French green lentils (a.k.a. lentilles du Puy) or black beluga lentils

4 tablespoons extra-virgin olive oil

2 tablespoons Dijon mustard

Freshly ground black pepper

This dish takes inspiration from two classic French flavor combinations—pork + lentils and sausage + Dijon mustard—combines them into one savory, hearty meal, and tops it all off with a bracing celery leaf salad. The lentils cook in boiling water, just like pasta, and are drained so you don't need to worry about the precise amount of water they will absorb. It's a foolproof method for perfectly cooked lentils every time.

---

① **Cook the lentils:** Fill a medium saucepan about three-quarters full with water. Season with 1 tablespoon salt and bring to a boil. Add the lentils, adjust the heat to medium-low to maintain a simmer, and cook, stirring once or twice, until just tender but not mushy, 20 to 30 minutes. Drain the cooked lentils in a fine-mesh strainer.

② **Meanwhile, make the celery salad and prep your vegetables:**

+ Pick off any leaves attached to 4 celery stalks and place them in a medium bowl.[1] Trim any nasty brown ends off the stalks, thinly slice on a bias, and add to the bowl with the leaves.

+ Zest about half a lemon into the celery. Cut the lemon in half and squeeze the zested half into the bowl, tossing to combine. Reserve the remaining lemon half for the lentils.

+ Add 1 cup parsley leaves to the bowl, but don't toss the salad yet; we'll get to that later, closer to serving time so it stays crisp. Keep chilled.

+ Thinly slice 4 garlic cloves.

+ Finely chop 1 medium yellow onion. **Not sure how? Right this way for a quick onion dicing lesson!**

③ **Cook the sausages:** Once the lentils have been cooking for about 15 minutes, heat a 12-inch cast-iron skillet over medium heat. Add 3 tablespoons olive oil and 1 pound pork sausages and cook, turning occasionally, until well browned and cooked through, 10 to 13 minutes.[2] Transfer them to a plate.

④ **Finish the lentils:**

+ Add the onion and garlic to the skillet and return it to medium heat. Cook, stirring often, until the onion is softened, 4 to 5 minutes.

+ Add the lentils, 2 tablespoons Dijon mustard, and 1 cup water. Stir, scraping up any browned bits from the pan, until saucy, 3 to 5 minutes. Remove from the heat, squeeze the juice from the reserved lemon half into the pan, and stir again to combine. Taste and add salt if needed.

⑤ **Serve:**

+ Toss the parsley leaves with the celery, drizzle with 1 tablespoon olive oil, and season with salt and black pepper.

+ Slice the sausages on the bias. Divide the lentils among 4 bowls and top each with several slices of sausage and some of the celery salad.

---

[1] Celery leaves are packed with celery flavor—they're like free herbs!

[2] Check the internal temperature with a thermometer—they should register about 150°F and will continue to climb between 155 and 160°F after they're out of the skillet. If you don't want to bother with a thermometer, you can press on the sausages lightly with your fingers—they should not feel mushy as they did when they were raw; they'll be more taut and bouncy, but not totally firm (which means they're overcooked).

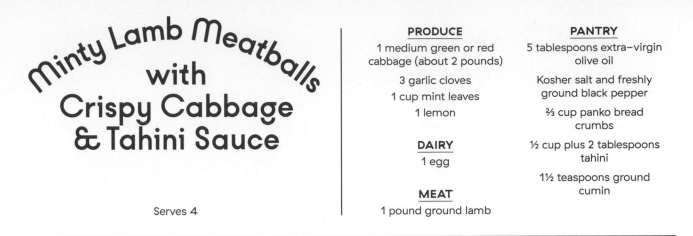

Minty Lamb Meatballs with Crispy Cabbage & Tahini Sauce

Serves 4

PRODUCE

1 medium green or red cabbage (about 2 pounds)

3 garlic cloves

1 cup mint leaves

1 lemon

DAIRY

1 egg

MEAT

1 pound ground lamb

PANTRY

5 tablespoons extra-virgin olive oil

Kosher salt and freshly ground black pepper

⅔ cup panko bread crumbs

½ cup plus 2 tablespoons tahini

1½ teaspoons ground cumin

While some might say the meatballs are the stars of this dish, I say it's the cabbage. If you've never roasted cabbage until all of its moisture has been driven off and it's been rendered charred and crisp, then you are in for a treat. This recipe employs not one but two baking sheets, allowing you the control to achieve a range of different textures (juicy, perfectly cooked meatballs and crispy charred cabbage) within the finished dish. The Middle Eastern–style minty lamb meatballs are extra juicy thanks to the tahini and olive oil mixed into them, so you don't have to worry about drying them out as they cook.

---

① Position one rack in the upper third of your oven and a second one in the middle. Preheat the oven to 450°F.

② **Prep the cabbage:**

✦ Quarter 1 medium cabbage through the root end. Trim out the core of each quarter. Cut each quarter in half crosswise to create 8 pieces total. Separate all of the leaves and scatter them across 2 rimmed baking sheets—it's okay if they overlap.

✦ Drizzle each baking sheet with 2 tablespoons olive oil and season each with ¾ teaspoon salt and lots of black pepper. Use your hands to massage the oil into the cabbage so that it's evenly distributed. Roast the cabbage until it is charred in some places and has lost some of its volume, 13 to 15 minutes. Remove from the oven and combine all of the cabbage on one baking sheet, reserving the other pan for the meatballs.

✦ Increase the oven temperature to 500°F.

③ **Meanwhile, make the meatballs:**

✦ In a large bowl, lightly beat 1 egg. Add ⅔ cup panko, 2 tablespoons tahini, 1½ teaspoons ground cumin, 1¼ teaspoons salt, and 1 tablespoon olive oil and whisk to combine.

✦ Finely grate 2 garlic cloves into the panko mixture.

✦ Chop ½ cup mint leaves and add them to the mixture along with about ⅓ pound ground lamb. Use your hands to gently mix the panko mixture into the lamb until it is evenly distributed and no pockets of panko remain—beware of overworking the mixture or the meatballs may get tough. Mix in the remaining ⅔ pound ground lamb.[1]

✦ Roll the meatball mixture into 12 equal-size balls about 1½ inches wide. Arrange the meatballs on the empty baking sheet.

④ **Cook the meatballs and cabbage:** Return both baking sheets to the oven, placing the meatballs on the top rack to encourage better browning.[2] Roast until the meatballs are browned and bounce back when you press on them gently and the cabbage is mostly charred and crisp, 7 to 9 minutes. If the cabbage looks like it could use a few more minutes, leave it in the oven and pull out only the meatballs to avoid overcooking them.

⑤ **Meanwhile make the tahini sauce:** While the meatballs roast, stir together ½ cup tahini, ⅓ cup water, the juice of 1 lemon, and ¾ teaspoon salt in a small bowl. Finely grate 1 garlic clove into the tahini. Whisk the sauce to combine. It should have a pourable consistency; if it looks too thick, whisk in another splash of water.

⑥ **Assemble and serve:** Spread some of the tahini sauce on each plate, and top with the cabbage, meatballs, and ½ cup mint leaves.

---

[1] It's best to begin by adding a small amount of lamb to encourage even distribution of the panko mixture, introducing more only once it's been evenly dispersed.

[2] There won't be a pan hovering above them, which would trap the steam and inhibit browning.

Yogurt-Crusted Lamb Chops with Charred Lemons & Sesame

Serves 4

PRODUCE
2 garlic cloves

2 lemons

1 small red onion or large shallot

1½ cups mint leaves

DAIRY
1½ cups plain whole-milk Greek yogurt

MEAT
8 lamb rib chops (about 3 pounds)

PANTRY
Kosher salt

1 tablespoon fennel seeds or cumin seeds

1 teaspoon red pepper flakes

½ teaspoon sugar

3 tablespoons extra-virgin olive oil

1 tablespoon toasted sesame seeds

For the majority of my life I was not a fan of lamb. These lamb chops changed that for me. Anything that is slathered in yogurt and garlic is already well on its way to having my heart. In the case of this recipe, which takes a marinating cue from Indian tandoori-style marinades, a spiced yogurt tenderizes the lamb chops, while also seasoning them and aiding in caramelization as they cook. This is an ideal weeknight entertaining dish—the chops can be marinated up to 24 hours in advance, and the execution takes just minutes once you've done that. They look impressive and taste even better. Serve them alongside a big pile of crispy oven-roasted potatoes (see page 226 for my take) and drop the mic.

---

① **Season and marinate the lamb:**

+ Arrange the lamb chops on a rimmed baking sheet. Season the chops all over with 1 tablespoon salt.

+ Finely grate 2 garlic cloves into a small bowl. Add ¾ cup whole-milk Greek yogurt and stir to combine.

+ Finely chop 1 tablespoon fennel seeds (or crush them with a mortar and pestle if you have one); stir into the yogurt along with 1 teaspoon red pepper flakes.

+ Smear the yogurt mixture all over the lamb chops. Let them sit for at least 30 minutes at room temperature and up to overnight, covered, in the refrigerator.

② **Pickle the onions:**

+ Cut 2 lemons in half crosswise.

+ Cut 1 small onion in half through the root end, then thinly slice.

+ Toss the onion in a medium bowl with the juice of half a lemon, a big pinch of salt, and ½ teaspoon sugar.

③ **Sear the chops:**

+ Heat 2 tablespoons olive oil in a large cast-iron skillet over medium-high heat.

+ When the oil is very hot, arrange 4 lamb chops (marinade and all!) in the skillet and cook, undisturbed, until deeply caramelized, 3 to 4 minutes. Flip the lamb chops and cook on the second side for 3 minutes. Using tongs, upend the chops and sear them on the fat cap until golden brown, about 1 minute. Transfer to a plate to rest while you repeat with the remaining 4 chops and 1 tablespoon olive oil.

+ Once all the chops are cooked, add the remaining 3 lemon halves to the pan, cut-sides down. Sear them in the residual fat until deeply charred, 3 to 4 minutes.

④ **Serve:**

+ Spread ¾ cup Greek yogurt on a serving platter and arrange the lamb chops on top.

+ Add 1½ cups mint leaves and 1 tablespoon toasted sesame seeds to the bowl of pickled onions, tossing to combine. Season with salt and serve piled on top of the lamb chops with the charred lemons alongside.

Seafood

Shrimp Cocktail with Dilly Horseradish Cream

Serves 2 to 4

PRODUCE
1 small shallot
½ cup dill leaves
2 lemons

DAIRY
½ cup crème fraîche or sour cream

SEAFOOD
1 pound (size U10 or U15) shell-on shrimp

PANTRY
Kosher salt
¼ cup sugar
2 tablespoons prepared horseradish
Freshly ground black pepper

Shrimp cocktail and a martini so cold it hurts your fingers: it simply does not get much better than that. Shrimp are sorted and sold by size and marked according to about how many pieces of shrimp compose 1 pound. I like the larger size of U10 or U15 (meaning, 10 to 15 shrimp per pound) for shrimp cocktail, but if you can't find them, go for slightly smaller ones (16/20). Most important, make sure they are shell-on—this is crucial when poaching shrimp, as the shell acts like a protective barrier for the flesh. Smaller shrimp will cooker faster, so if you're using size 16/20, knock off 30 seconds from the cooking time. Sounds fussy, but it makes all the difference in the world, I swear.

---

① **Build the poaching liquid:** Combine ¼ cup salt, ¼ cup sugar, and 6 cups water in a medium pot and bring to a boil over medium-high heat.

② **Prep the shrimp:** Using a pair of scissors, snip through the shrimp shells down the backs of each shrimp, stopping right where the tail begins.[1] If you see any dark veins running down the line that you snipped, use a paper towel to pull them out. **Here's a quick tutorial on deveining shrimp if you've never done it before.**

③ **Cook the shrimp:** Have a timer at the ready—shrimp can overcook VERY easily, so you need to be prepared. Once the water comes to a boil, turn off the heat, add the shrimp, and cover. Set the timer for 4 minutes; the shrimp should be pink and have turned opaque.[2]

④ **Shock the shrimp:** Meanwhile, fill a large bowl with ice and water. Drain the shrimp and plunge them into the ice bath. Let sit until very chilled, 10 to 15 minutes.

⑤ **Make the dilly horseradish cream:**

✦ In a medium bowl, stir together ½ cup crème fraîche and 2 tablespoons prepared horseradish.

✦ Finely chop 1 shallot.

✦ Finely chop ½ cup dill leaves. Add the dill to the crème fraîche along with the chopped shallot.

✦ Finely grate the zest of ½ lemon into the crème fraîche mixture and squeeze in the juice. Cut 1½ lemons into wedges for serving.

✦ Season with salt and lots of black pepper.

⑥ **Peel and serve:** When the shrimp are completely chilled, peel them, leaving just the tails attached. Transfer to a shallow serving bowl full of ice cubes (or over crushed ice if you're fancy). Cold shrimp is key! Serve with the lemon wedges and horseradish cream.

---

[1] You're not going to remove these shells until after they're cooked, but this will make it a hell of a lot easier to peel them.

[2] We turn off the heat because shrimp are very easy to overcook.

Slow-Roasted Cod Tostadas with Juicy Cucumber Salad

Serves 4

PRODUCE

1 large garlic clove

3 limes

¼ small red onion

2 serrano chiles or jalapeño

1 English (hothouse) cucumber

1 ruby red grapefruit

1 ripe avocado

2 cups mint and/or cilantro leaves

SEAFOOD

1½ pounds cod or other flaky white fish, such as halibut or pollack

PANTRY

Kosher salt

2 tablespoons extra-virgin olive oil, plus more for drizzling

Store-bought corn tostadas or tortilla chips, for serving

When, after hitting a bit of a writer's block, I asked Ben what in the world I should write about in the headnote for this dish, he responded, "Oh, cod, I love you." Not gonna lie, he didn't exactly nail it, but the sentiment is there. Slow-roasted cod is in fact something that I love. Cooking lean white fish at a low oven temperature greatly reduces your risk of overcooking it and yields tender, silky flesh. The cucumbers that accompany it get tossed in an acidic, spicy bath reminiscent of Mexican aguachile, made of lime juice, chiles, mint, and red onion, then spooned over the still-warm fish and scooped up with big broken shards of tostada.

---

① Place a rack in the center of the oven. Preheat the oven to 300°F.

② **Prep and cook the fish:**

✦ Place 1½ pounds of cod in a 12-inch cast-iron skillet. (You may need to cut the fish into a few pieces so that it all fits.) Season the fish all over with 1½ teaspoons salt. Finely grate 1 large garlic clove over top and drizzle with 2 tablespoons olive oil, rubbing it gently with your hands to coat.

✦ Roast until the flesh just begins to flake away easily when prodded with the tines of a fork, 18 to 25 minutes.[1]

③ **Meanwhile, make the salad:**

✦ Cut 2 limes in half and squeeze the juice into a medium bowl.

✦ Thinly slice ¼ small red onion through the root end. Add to the lime juice and season with 2 big pinches of salt. (There's a lot of acid in this salad, so we need to season it highly to balance some of that.)

✦ Thinly slice 2 serrano peppers and 1 large English cucumber crosswise into rounds; add to the onions.

✦ Remove the pith of the grapefruit by cutting ½ inch off both the top and bottom of the grapefruit, then slicing away the peel and pith along the contour of the fruit. Use your knife to release the segments of flesh from between the membranes, adding them to the salad as you go. The segments are called "suprêmes." **Never done this before? This video should help.** Let this marinate for a bit in the fridge until you're ready to eat it so the onion lightly pickles and the salad stays cool, crisp, and refreshing.

④ **When ready to eat, assemble:**

✦ Cut 1 avocado in half lengthwise and discard the pit. Using a metal spoon, scoop out small curls of the flesh (sort of like how you'd use a melon baller) and add them to the salad.

✦ Add 2 cups mint leaves. Very gently stir to combine, taking care to avoid mashing the avo up too much. Taste and add more salt if it needs it.

⑤ **Serve:** Cut 1 lime into wedges. Divide the fish among serving dishes, flaking it apart with a fork into large pieces as you do so. Pile the salad on top of the fish. Drizzle each dish with more olive oil and serve with tostadas and the lime wedges.

---

[1] The time will vary based on what type of fish you are cooking, so if you've got thin fillets, start checking on the early end of things.

Coconut Shrimp with Crushed Chickpeas & Basil

Serves 4

PRODUCE
1 (2-inch) piece fresh ginger

5 garlic cloves

1 cup packed basil leaves

2 limes

SEAFOOD
1½ pounds (size U10 or U15) shrimp, peeled, tails left on, and deveined

PANTRY
¼ cup sambal oelek

1 tablespoon honey

Kosher salt

1 (14-ounce) can full-fat coconut milk

¼ cup unsweetened shredded coconut

2 (14.5-ounce) cans chickpeas

2 tablespoons vegetable oil

I know I'm not alone when I say that breaded coconut shrimp, the kind that's covered in sweet, candylike shredded coconut, deep-fried and served with chile sauce, will forever make me weak in the knees. It may have something to do with the fact that this particular dish is usually accompanied by a fat piña colada and an abundance of sunshine, but who's to say? With sambal oelek (an Indonesian chile sauce) and coconut milk in the marinade, this recipe is a far cry from the original, though I think it captures a similar spirit. Shrimp are notorious for turning from just barely cooked to sorely overcooked and bouncy within minutes, so timing is key here. They really only need to get a sear on one side and a quick kiss in the pan on the other.

---

① **Marinate the shrimp:**

+ Finely grate 1 (2-inch) piece of ginger (no need to peel it!) and 5 garlic cloves into a medium bowl.

+ Whisk in ¼ cup sambal oelek, 1 tablespoon honey, 2 teaspoons salt, and 1 (14-ounce) can coconut milk.

+ Add 1½ pounds shrimp to the marinade, turning to coat. Let sit at room temp for at least 15 minutes or, covered, in the fridge for up to 1 hour.[1]

② **Toast the coconut:** Heat a large nonstick skillet over medium. Add ¼ cup unsweetened shredded coconut and toast, stirring often, until golden brown all over, 3 to 4 minutes. Transfer to a small bowl to cool. Wipe out and reserve the skillet.

③ **Cook the shrimp:**

+ Drain and rinse 2 (14.5-ounce) cans of chickpeas in a fine-mesh strainer.

+ Line a plate or rimmed baking sheet with a few layers of paper towels. Using tongs, remove the shrimp from the marinade, shaking off any excess, and transfer to the paper-towel-lined plate. Reserve the bowl of marinade.[2]

+ Heat 1 tablespoon vegetable oil in the reserved skillet over medium-high heat until just beginning to show wisps of smoke.[3]

+ Add half of the shrimp in a single layer and cook, undisturbed, until browned on one side, 3 minutes. Flip and cook 30 seconds longer. Transfer to a serving bowl and repeat with the remaining shrimp and 1 tablespoon vegetable oil.

④ **Finish the sauce:**

+ Add the drained chickpeas and reserved marinade to the skillet and cook, smashing some of the chickpeas into the sauce with a wooden spoon to release their starch, until the sauce has thickened slightly and is a few shades darker in color, 4 to 5 minutes.

+ Turn off the heat and stir in 1 cup basil leaves.

+ Cut 1 lime in half, squeeze the juice into the chickpeas, and stir to combine. Taste the sauce and add more salt if needed.

⑤ **Serve:** Cut 1 lime into wedges. Top the shrimp with the chickpea sauce and toasted shredded coconut, and serve with the lime wedges.

---

[1] If you leave them in there any longer, the salt will begin to actually cook the shrimp (ceviche-style), and the texture will start to change.

[2] Yes, we are wiping off some of the marinade (dry shrimp = good browning), but the leftover marinade is ultimately going to end up back in the skillet to reduce into a sauce, so we won't lose out on any flavor, I promise.

[3] Shrimp cook EXTREMELY quickly, so we need that oil to be piping hot in order to get color on the shrimp before they overcook.

Crispy-Skinned Salmon with Harissa & Citrusy Fennel Salad

PRODUCE
1 grapefruit
1 orange
1 lemon
2 medium fennel bulbs

SEAFOOD
4 (6-ounce) salmon fillets

PANTRY
2 tablespoons harissa paste, plus more
1½ teaspoons toasted sesame oil
2 tablespoons extra-virgin olive oil
Kosher salt

Serves 4

When I realized that the secret to shatteringly crisp salmon skin was to start it in a cold, dry nonstick pan, my relationship with cooking fish at home changed forever. I don't know about you, but the thought of dropping a piece of fish into a ripping-hot pan of oil at home and watching it spit and sputter its fishiness all over my apartment is really not my idea of a fun time. Thankfully, we'll never have to endure that stress again. The cold-pan method gently and slowly renders out any fat and moisture in the skin, leaving behind the crispiest damn fillet of salmon you ever did eat. Hot tip: Harissa (a Tunisian hot chile pepper paste) can vary a ton in terms of spiciness jar to jar, so always taste it before you add it to a dish to get a sense of its heat factor.

① Prep and assemble the salad:

✦ In a large bowl, whisk together 2 tablespoons harissa, 1½ teaspoons sesame oil, 2 tablespoons olive oil, and ½ teaspoon salt until incorporated.

✦ Use your knife to cut away the peel and any white pith from 1 grapefruit and 1 orange; discard. Remove the grapefruit and orange segments from between the membranes and tear them in half, creating irregular 1-inch pieces of flesh. **Not sure how to tackle that task? Right this way for a citrus prep tutorial.** Add them to the harissa vinaigrette.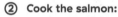

✦ Cut 1 lemon in half, and squeeze the juice from 1 of the halves into the bowl, stirring to combine. Cut the remaining half into wedges for serving. Wipe your cutting board clean.

✦ Trim and discard the stalks and fronds of 2 medium fennel bulbs and cut the bulb in quarters through the root end. Then slice lengthwise as thinly as possible. **Pull up this video if you need some help in the fennel slicing department.**

✦ Add the sliced fennel to the bowl but don't combine just yet.[1] Chill the salad until ready to serve.

② Cook the salmon:

✦ Pat the salmon fillets dry with paper towels.[2] Season the fillets all over with 2 teaspoons salt. Place each skin-side down in a large, dry nonstick skillet.[3]

✦ Set the skillet over medium heat and cook, undisturbed, pressing firmly on each fillet to make sure all the skin is making contact with the pan, until the skin is very crispy and releases easily from the pan, 10 to 12 minutes.

✦ Flip the salmon and cook until not quite cooked through but close to it, just 1 minute longer. You will be able to tell by looking at the sides of the fillet, which turn from translucent to opaque as the salmon cooks. The sides should appear mostly opaque with a small area of translucency in the middle.

✦ Transfer each fillet to a plate, skin-side up to keep it nice and crisp.

③ Serve:
Toss the fennel and citrus a few times to evenly coat in the dressing. Taste the salad; if you think it could use a little more heat, add another tablespoon or two of harissa. Pile the salad alongside the salmon, drizzling any extra vinaigrette over top, and serve with the lemon wedges alongside.

---

[1] Fennel can wilt quickly in the presence of acid and salt, so wait till the last few minutes to toss it with the vinaigrette.

[2] Moisture is the enemy of crispy skin since it creates steam in the pan, making salmon skin soggy.

[3] The oily nature of salmon skin allows us to add it to the nonstick skillet without any additional oil.

Seared Scallops with Curry Butter, Sweet Corn & Sungolds

Serves 4

PRODUCE
12 ounces Sungold or cherry tomatoes

1 medium shallot

2 limes

2 ears corn

2 garlic cloves

½ cup cilantro leaves

DAIRY
3 tablespoons unsalted butter

SEAFOOD
16 (size U10 or U20) dry-packed sea scallops

PANTRY
Kosher salt

3 tablespoons vegetable oil

1 tablespoon curry powder, such as Madras

For some reason, most people shy away from scallop cookery at home. I get it—there's a lot at stake when you're working with a protein at such a high price point. But proper scallop-searing technique is actually no different than, say, searing a steak or a pork chop, so forget your fears and let's go! The key to that highly coveted crispy golden crust is a really fucking hot pan. Scallops cook incredibly quickly, which means the oil they cook in has to be ripping hot in order to maintain a high enough temperature to develop good browning before they overcook. The other defense you can take is to pat your scallops dry right before you cook them. Dry scallops equal golden brown scallops, and that's what we're here for.

---

① **Do some prep:**

+ Cut 12 ounces of Sungold tomatoes in half; place in a medium bowl.

+ Thinly slice 1 medium shallot crosswise into rings. Add the shallot rings and the juice of 1 lime to the tomatoes and gently stir to combine. Season with ½ teaspoon salt.

+ Shuck 2 ears of corn and cut off the kernels; discard the cobs. **Want to learn the easiest way to do that? Take a look at this video.**

+ Thinly slice 2 garlic cloves.

+ Cut a second lime into 4 wedges for serving.

② **Cook the scallops:**

+ In a 12-inch cast-iron skillet, heat 3 tablespoons vegetable oil over medium-high heat just until it begins to give off wisps of smoke. This will take 3 to 4 minutes, so don't rush it because super-hot oil is the key to restaurant-worthy scallops with a golden brown crust.

+ Pat 16 scallops dry with paper towels and season all over with 1½ teaspoons salt.

+ Using tongs, arrange the scallops in a single layer in the pan (be careful, they may sputter a bit).

Cook, undisturbed, to establish a good crust, rotating the skillet 90 degrees on the burner every minute or so to encourage even browning, 3 to 4 minutes total.

+ Take a peek at the bottom of the scallops and flip them when they're looking nice and golden brown. Quickly add 3 tablespoons unsalted butter and 1 tablespoon curry powder to the skillet. Using a large spoon, baste the scallops with the melted butter for 1 minute longer, so they get coated in nutty, curried, buttery deliciousness. **Never butter basted before? Here's how to do it.** Turn off the heat and transfer the scallops to a plate, leaving the butter in the skillet.

③ **Cook the veg:** Add the corn and garlic to the skillet and return the pan to medium heat. Cook, stirring often, until the corn is bright yellow and just cooked through and the garlic is softened but not browned, 1 to 2 minutes. Remove the skillet from the heat, stir in the marinated tomatoes and shallots, and season with salt.

④ **Serve:** Arrange 4 scallops on each plate. Spoon the corn, tomatoes, and all the tomato juices over top, leaving no butter or juices behind! Top with ½ cup cilantro leaves and serve with the lime wedges alongside.

Would you rather work one hundred hours a week and eat like an absolute king, or work ten hours a week and eat only pureed baby food?

Clams on Toast with Bacon & Old Bay Mayo

Serves 4

PRODUCE

2 ears corn

6 garlic cloves

2 large leeks

1 small bunch chives

SEAFOOD & MEAT

32 littleneck or manila clams

6 ounces cold thick-cut bacon

PANTRY

¾ cup mayonnaise

2½ teaspoons Old Bay seasoning

Kosher salt

½ teaspoon red pepper flakes

¾ cup dry white wine

2 large (1-inch-thick) slices country bread

3 tablespoons extra-virgin olive oil

This recipe takes everything you love about classic New England–style clam chowder and gives it the ultimate upgrade: a fat slice of fried bread sitting right underneath to soak up all that sweet, bacon-y, briny broth. You'll know the clams are cooked once their shells open up. They can be finicky when steamed and won't all open at once, so take the time to pluck out those that open first to allow the more stubborn ones the time they need.

---

① **Mise it out:**

✦ Submerge the clams in a large bowl of cold water set in the sink, swooshing them around to release any grit. Use a clean sponge to scrub any that seem particularly dirty. Let them sit for at least 1⊙ minutes while you start the broth so they expel any sand inside them.

✦ Remove the husks from 2 ears of corn. Working one at a time, stand an ear upright inside a medium bowl. Working from the top down, shave the kernels off the cob into the bowl. Discard the cobs

✦ Thinly slice 5 garlic cloves and add them to the bowl of corn.

✦ Trim off and discard the dark green tops and hairy root end of 2 leeks. Peel off and discard the first two layers; dice the leeks. If the leeks look dirty, rinse them under cold water in a fine-mesh strainer to release any grit, then pat dry. Add the leeks to the corn.

✦ Thinly slice 1 small bunch chives and set aside.

② **Make the Old Bay mayo:** Stir together ¾ cup mayonnaise and 2½ teaspoons Old Bay seasoning in a small bowl. Finely grate 1 garlic clove into the mixture. Stir and season with salt.

③ **Build the broth:**

✦ Dice 6 ounces cold bacon into ½-inch pieces.[1] Place in a large Dutch oven and set over medium heat. Cook, stirring often, until crisp and golden brown, 8 to 1⊙ minutes.

✦ Add the corn mixture, ½ teaspoon red pepper flakes, and 1 teaspoon salt to the Dutch oven. Cook, stirring occasionally, until the vegetables are very soft but not browned, 8 to 1⊙ minutes.

✦ Meanwhile, drain the clams in a colander.

✦ Once the vegetables are soft, add ¾ cup white wine and simmer until the pot is almost dry again to cook off some of the winey alcohol flavor, 2 to 3 minutes.[2]

④ **Cook the clams:** Add the clams to the pot and stir to coat. Cover the pot and cook until all the clams open, 8 to 15 minutes. Start checking at around 8 minutes; this timing will vary greatly depending on their size. Transfer the cooked clams to a bowl, letting the remaining clams cook longer (discard the clams that don't open; that's an indicator that they were dead to begin with).

⑤ **Fry the bread:**

✦ While the clams cook, cut 2 slices of bread in half crosswise so that you have 4 pieces total.

✦ In a large cast-iron skillet, heat 3 tablespoons olive oil over medium-low heat. Add the bread slices and cook on one side only, until deeply golden brown and crisp, 5 to 6 minutes.[3] Slather some Old Bay mayo on the fried side of each of the toasts and place one toast in each of 4 shallow bowls, fried-side up.

⑥ **Serve:** Spoon the clams into the bowls over the toast and top with the broth, vegetables, and lots of sliced chives.

---

[1] Bacon is easiest to cut when it's cold, since as it warms and softens, the fat starts to melt and things get messy.

[2] This way, the final dish will have the essence of wine and benefit from its acidity without tasting like . . . a glass of Sauvignon Blanc.

[3] The bread gets fried on one side only so that the untoasted side can soak up all the brothy deliciousness in the bowl, while the fried side stays crisp.

Roasted Salmon with Marinated Olives & Potato Chips

Serves 4

PRODUCE
2 garlic cloves
1 lemon

SEAFOOD
1 large (1½–pound) salmon fillet

PANTRY
Kosher salt
⅓ cup plus 1 tablespoon extra–virgin olive oil
1 cup Castelvetrano olives
2 tablespoons capers, drained
Freshly ground black pepper
½ cup kettle–cooked potato chips

Technically, this is a slow-roasted salmon recipe, as it utilizes the low-and-slow method of cooking a piece of fish at a low temperature, ever so gently, until it just flakes apart. But I really hate to call it that because the words *slow* and *roasted* imply a long cook time, and that would be an entirely inaccurate description of this recipe. This dish spends a total of about 20 minutes in the oven, which is, by all accounts, very quick when it comes to getting dinner on the table. Whereas high-heat stovetop methods of fish cookery can lead to overcooked fish in a matter of seconds, this gentler method allows you, the cook, to calmly assess when the salmon is done.

① Position a rack in the center of your oven. Preheat the oven to 275°F.

② **Season the fish:** Season a 1½–pound fillet of salmon all over with 2 teaspoons salt. Place it in a 12–inch cast–iron skillet (if it won't fit whole, cut it into 2 pieces) and drizzle the flesh with 1 tablespoon olive oil, gently rubbing to coat.

③ **Cook the fish:** Roast until the flesh turns from translucent to mostly opaque and easily flakes when prodded with a fork, 20 to 30 minutes.[1]

④ **Meanwhile, marinate the olives:**
  ✦ Firmly smash 1 cup Castelvetrano olives with the side of a chef's knife or your palm to release the flesh from the pits. Discard the pits and tear the olives in half; add them to a saucepan.
  ✦ Thinly slice 2 garlic cloves.
  ✦ Using a vegetable peeler, remove 4 (2–inch–long) strips of zest from 1 lemon. Thinly slice the strips lengthwise. Add the lemon zest, garlic, 2 tablespoons capers, and remaining ⅓ cup olive oil to the saucepan.
  ✦ Set the saucepan over medium heat and cook, stirring occasionally, until the oil is bubbling furiously and the garlic has softened but not browned, 5 to 6 minutes. Remove the pan from the heat.
  ✦ Thinly slice about half of the peeled lemon crosswise into rounds (discarding the knobby, pithy end). Cut the slices into half–moons, pick out and discard any seeds, then add the lemon slices to the marinated olives. Squeeze the juice of what's left of the lemon into the olives. Season with salt and lots of black pepper and stir everything well to combine.[2]

⑤ **Finish the dish:** When the salmon is cooked, spoon the warm marinated olives and all of the oil over the fish. Just before serving, crush ½ cup kettle–cooked potato chips with your hands and scatter them over the fish. Serve with a large spoon for breaking the salmon flesh into smaller pieces.

[1] That's a pretty big window of time; salmon fillets can vary greatly in thickness, which is what determines how quickly they cook. Unlike some other fish, salmon is both safe and delicious when served medium, i.e., not totally cooked through.

[2] The marinated olives can be prepared to this point up to 6 hours in advance. Gently rewarm them in their saucepan over medium heat until hot just before serving.

Crispy Buttered Shrimp with 20 Cloves of Garlic

Serves 4

PRODUCE
2 heads garlic
1 lemon

DAIRY
8 tablespoons (1 stick)
unsalted butter

SEAFOOD
1 pound (size U1⊙ or U15)
shell-on shrimp

PANTRY
1 (14.5-ounce) can white
beans (such as cannellini
or navy)

Kosher salt and freshly
ground black pepper

Warm crusty bread, for
serving

Lemme guess: you are thinking to yourself, *That is WAY too much garlic*. I assure you it is not. I still vividly recall the intoxicating scent that permeated my entire house when I first cooked Ina Garten's iconic Chicken with Forty Cloves of Garlic fifteen or so years ago. It was in that precise moment that I realized that no amount of garlic is an unreasonable amount of garlic. That's a pretty powerful realization when you love garlic as much as I do.

So, I bring you shrimp with twenty cloves of garlic. Perhaps the scent of tons of garlic, sizzling in copious amounts of butter and mingling with the aroma of sweet sautéed shrimp will forever stick with you in a similar way. If you've never eaten shell-on shrimp, this is your moment. Spring for the highest-quality shrimp you can find and have yourself a real nice time.

① **Do some prep:**

+ Thinly slice 2⊙ garlic cloves.

+ Cut 1 lemon in half. Thinly slice half of the lemon crosswise into rounds, discarding any seeds that cling to the rounds. Reserve the other half for squeezing.

+ Drain and rinse 1 (14.5-ounce) can of white beans in a fine-mesh strainer.

+ Pat 1 pound of shrimp dry with paper towels. Season all over with 1 teaspoon salt.

② **Cook the shrimp:**

+ Heat a large cast-iron skillet over high heat for 2 minutes. Add 2 tablespoons butter and swirl to melt. Add the shrimp in a single layer and cook, undisturbed, until lightly golden brown and crisp underneath, 2 to 3 minutes. Flip the shrimp and cook just until pink, 1 minute longer. Season with lots and lots of black pepper. (We're talking many cranks.) Transfer the shrimp to a serving dish.

+ Reduce the heat to very low and add 6 tablespoons butter, the sliced garlic, and the lemon slices. Cook, stirring constantly, until the garlic is very fragrant and softened, just barely beginning to turn brown at the edges, 2 to 3 minutes.

+ Stir in the drained beans. Season with salt and more black pepper and cook, stirring, until the beans are warmed through, about 2 minutes.

+ Pour the garlicky beans over the shrimp. Squeeze the remaining ½ lemon over everything and serve with bread for soaking up all that garlic butter.

Poached Fish with Creamed Leeks & Toasty Hazelnuts

Serves 4

PRODUCE
4 medium leeks
12 garlic cloves
1 lemon

DAIRY
2 cups heavy cream

SEAFOOD
1½ pounds cod, halibut, or pollack fillets

PANTRY
½ cup blanched hazelnuts or blanched whole almonds

Kosher salt
3 tablespoons extra-virgin olive oil

This recipe owes its genius to my former work brother Andy, who once made the world's simplest, and most delicious, dish of cod poached in heavy cream. I mean, obviously fish poached in cream (plus lots of garlic) is delicious. I knew that. I just never had the balls to pour 2 whole cups of heavy cream over a fillet of fish and call it dinner. The irony is that Andy has approximately zero percent body fat and is by far the healthiest and cleanest eater I know. But enough about Andy and his sweet bod. The moral of this story is, now that I have the courage to poach my fish in heavy cream, I bring to you the indulgent deliciousness that is this dish.

---

① **Do some prep:**

+ Trim the roots and dark green tops of 4 medium leeks. Peel off and discard the first two layers of the leeks, which often contain lots of dirt. Cut the leeks crosswise into 1-inch rounds. If the leeks look especially gritty or dirty, give them a rinse under cold water.

+ Firmly smash and peel 12 garlic cloves.

+ Using a vegetable peeler, peel 4 (3-inch-long) strips of lemon zest from 1 lemon. Cut the lemon in half.

+ Coarsely chop ½ cup blanched hazelnuts.

② **Poach the leeks:** Combine 2 cups heavy cream, 1 cup water, the leeks, garlic, 2 teaspoons salt, and the lemon zest in a medium saucepan (choose one that fits the fish with a little wiggle room around it, about 3 quarts) and bring to a simmer over medium heat. Reduce the heat as needed to maintain a bare simmer with very gentle bubbles and cook until the leeks are very soft, 10 to 15 minutes. The cream may boil up vigorously, so stay nearby and stir the pot occasionally to avoid overflow.

③ **Toast the hazelnuts:** Meanwhile, in a small saucepan, combine the chopped hazelnuts and 3 tablespoons olive oil. Cook over medium-low heat, swirling the pan often, until the hazelnuts are golden brown, 5 to 6 minutes. Remove from the heat, and season with ½ teaspoon salt.

④ **Poach the fish:**

+ Season the fish all over with 1 teaspoon salt.

+ Using a spatula or large spoon, add the fish to the cream, submerging it. If the cream doesn't cover the fish all the way, add enough water to barely cover.

+ Return the liquid to a simmer over medium heat and simmer very gently until the flesh of the fish has just turned opaque and flakes with slight pressure from the tines of a fork, 6 to 8 minutes. Remove from the heat.

⑤ **Serve:** Divide the fish among 4 shallow serving bowls, using a serving spoon to flake it into large irregular pieces. Spoon over some of the melted leeks and cream, the hazelnuts and oil, and the juice of the zested lemon.

Mushroom Toast with a Molly Egg

PRODUCE

1 pound mushrooms, preferably oyster, maitake, and/or shiitake

1 large shallot

3 garlic cloves

6 thyme sprigs, or 1 large rosemary sprig

¼ cup parsley leaves

DAIRY

½ cup crème fraîche or sour cream

½ ounce grated Parmesan cheese (2 tablespoons), plus more for sprinkling

2 large eggs

PANTRY

⅓ cup plus 1 tablespoon extra-virgin olive oil

Kosher salt and freshly ground black pepper

2 tablespoons red or white wine vinegar

2 (1-inch-thick) slices country bread

Serves 2

During my days as a line cook, working the brunch shift at a restaurant called Allswell in Brooklyn, I gave birth to what I like to call the "Molly Egg." It's essentially a sunny-side-up egg that gets cooked so gently and slowly that the whites set into a soft blanket before any crispy fried edges form, which might otherwise be undesirable but, when served on top of a thick slice of toasted crusty bread, is exactly what the doctor ordered. As for the mushrooms, instead of cooking them in several batches (who has the patience??), I like to add them to the skillet all at once, and let time take care of the rest. Of course, at first overcrowded, they will steam, but eventually the water they release will cook off and they will achieve that crispy, caramelized exterior you are here for.

① **Do your mise:**

+ Tear 1 pound mushrooms into roughly 2-inch pieces, discarding any tough stemmy bits. If you're using shiitakes, tear off and discard the stems; they're too tough to eat.

+ Cut 1 large shallot in half through the root end. Peel, then finely chop.

+ Lightly smash and peel 3 garlic cloves. Thinly slice.

+ Pick the leaves from 6 thyme sprigs.

+ Chop ¼ cup parsley leaves.

② **Cook the mushrooms:**

+ Heat ⅓ cup olive oil in a 12-inch cast-iron skillet over medium-high heat until you just begin to see wisps of smoke coming from the pan.[1] Add the mushrooms and toss to coat in the oil using tongs, until all the oil has been absorbed by the shrooms.

+ Season with ½ teaspoon salt.[2]

+ Cook the mushrooms, undisturbed, until the mushrooms have developed good color on the underside, 4 to 5 minutes. Toss them around with your tongs to redistribute and cook, stirring once or twice,

until mostly golden brown all over and no longer tough, 4 to 5 minutes longer (taste one!).

③ **Finish the mushrooms:**

+ Reduce the heat to low, add the shallot, garlic, and thyme leaves to the skillet, and cook, stirring often, until the garlic and shallot are aromatic and softened but not browned, 1 to 2 minutes.

+ Stir in 2 tablespoons of red wine vinegar. Remove the skillet from the heat, stir in ½ cup crème fraîche and ½ ounce grated Parmesan cheese (2 tablespoons). Season with salt and black pepper. Cover to keep warm.

+ Toast 2 slices of bread (however is easiest for you).

④ **Cook the eggs:** Heat 1 tablespoon olive oil in a large nonstick skillet over medium-low heat. Crack 2 eggs into the skillet, season them with salt and black pepper, and cook until the whites have just set but are not crispy and the yolk is runny, 3 to 4 minutes.

⑤ **Serve:** Divide the toasts between 2 plates. Spoon the mushrooms over each piece of toast. Top each toast with more Parmesan, parsley, and an egg.

---

[1] The oil needs to be super-duper hot because adding all those mushrooms is going to greatly lower its temperature, and a lower temp means less browning.

[2] About that: I am a believer in adding salt to mushrooms right at the beginning of cooking, since the whole point of cooking them at high heat is to cook off all the water within them and then get them nice and

caramelized. Salt draws out moisture, so it aids in speeding up that process by drawing out water right from the get-go.

Jammy Eggs with Yogurt & Brown-Buttered Nuts

Serves 4

PRODUCE
1 small garlic clove

DAIRY
8 large eggs
1 cup plain whole-milk Greek yogurt or labneh
5 tablespoons unsalted butter

PANTRY
Kosher salt
⅔ cup walnuts, blanched hazelnuts, or shelled pistachios
2 teaspoons Aleppo pepper or other mild chile flakes
¼ teaspoon ground turmeric
Flatbreads or pitas, for dragging

This recipe is an ode to one of my favorite breakfasts: çilbir, a Turkish dish of poached eggs served over Greek yogurt and drowned in chile-flecked butter. Something glorious happens when garlicky yogurt mixes with roasty-toasty browned butter and jammy egg yolks. In this case we'll boil the eggs instead of poaching them. The key to jammy eggs is precise timing, so you'll cook them for exactly 7 minutes in boiling water before shocking them in an ice bath to stop the cooking. Seek out Aleppo pepper if you can—it's a deliciously fruity and very mild chile flake, which means you can use it liberally. If you can't find it, red pepper flakes will work, too, just hold back a bit since they tend to be much spicier.

---

① **Cook the eggs:**

+ Bring a medium pot of water to a boil. Using a slotted spoon, gently lower 8 eggs into the water; set a timer for 7 minutes.

+ Meanwhile, fill a medium bowl with ice water. Once the eggs have finished cooking, use a slotted spoon to transfer them to the ice bath to stop cooking. Let the eggs cool for at least 5 minutes, then peel them and set aside.

② **Make the garlic yogurt:** Finely grate 1 garlic clove into a small bowl, then stir in 1 cup plain whole-milk Greek yogurt. Season with salt.

③ **Make the brown-buttered nuts:**

+ Chop ⅔ cup walnuts so that all pieces are about the size of a lentil.

+ Wipe out the saucepan used for the eggs so that it is completely dry, then add 5 tablespoons butter and cook over medium-low heat until just melted and foamy. Add the walnuts and cook, stirring occasionally, until very lightly toasted, 2 to 3 minutes.

+ Add 2 teaspoons Aleppo pepper and ¼ teaspoon turmeric and continue to cook until the walnuts are toasted and golden brown and the butter is very nutty and fragrant, about 1 minute longer. Remove from the heat and stir in ½ teaspoon salt.

④ **Serve:** Divide the garlic yogurt among 4 shallow bowls. Nestle 2 peeled eggs in each bowl and drizzle the brown-buttered nuts over top. Season with more salt and serve with flatbread.

B-fast Tacos with Charred Scallion Salsa & Fried Pepitas

Serves 4

PRODUCE
10 scallions
2 limes
1 bunch cilantro

DAIRY
8 large eggs
3 tablespoons butter

PANTRY
Kosher salt
⅓ cup plus 2 tablespoons extra-virgin olive oil
½ cup raw pepitas
Hot sauce (your fave brand)
8 small corn or flour tortillas

I'd like to set the record straight and remind you that there is no right way to scramble eggs. There are many, many ways to do so, all of which yield different results—from fluffy large curds to custardy small ones. This is my preferred method—moist large curds that result from a short cook time in a medium-hot skillet. If you prefer very creamy small curds, turn down the heat to low and switch from a spatula to a whisk, which will break up the curds as you stir them. However you like to scramble, enjoy these tacos with this quick, earthy salsa, crunchy pepitas, and whatever kind of tortillas suits you best. These are nobody's b-fast tacos but your own.

---

① **Do some prep:**
+ Slice 10 scallions crosswise into ½-inch(ish)-long pieces.
+ Cut 1 lime in half (for the salsa) and another one into quarters for serving.
+ Finely chop the leaves and tender stems from 1 bunch cilantro. Transfer to a medium bowl.
+ Crack 8 eggs into a medium bowl. Season with 1 teaspoon salt and vigorously whisk until no white streaks remain.

② **Fry the pepitas:** Combine 2 tablespoons olive oil and ½ cup raw pepitas in a large nonstick skillet and cook over medium heat, swirling and stirring occasionally, until golden brown and you hear crackling and popping, 5 to 6 minutes. Remove from the heat. Using a slotted spoon, transfer the pepitas to a small bowl, leaving whatever oil remains in the pan. Season the pepitas with salt.

③ **Make the charred scallion salsa:**
+ Add the scallions to the skillet and return it to medium heat. Cook, turning the scallions occasionally, until they are charred all over and softened, 6 to 8 minutes. Transfer to the bowl of chopped cilantro. Reserve that skillet once more.
+ Stir ⅓ cup olive oil, the juice of 1 lime, and a few dashes of hot sauce into the scallion mixture. Season with salt—it should be very flavorful.

④ **Warm the tortillas:**
+ Place a tortilla directly over a gas burner set to medium heat. Cook, flipping halfway through, until charred around the edges, about 1 minute total. If using an electric burner, heat a large cast-iron skillet over medium and cook the tortilla in the skillet until warmed through, about 30 seconds per side. Wrap the tortilla in a towel and repeat with the remaining tortillas. Keep cozy until ready to serve.

⑤ **Scramble the eggs:** Wipe out the skillet. Add 3 tablespoons butter and melt it over medium-high heat. Add the eggs and cook, undisturbed, until a thin layer of cooked egg appears around the edge of the skillet, about 30 seconds. Using a rubber spatula in a figure-eight motion, stir the eggs gently, making sure all areas of the skillet get equal spatula play, and cook until fluffy and just barely set, about 2 minutes.[1]

⑥ **Serve:** Top each tortilla with some scrambled eggs, scallion salsa, and pepitas. Serve with the remaining salsa, the lime wedges, and hot sauce.

---

[1] The eggs should still look ever so slightly wet on top—they'll continue to cook a bit from the residual heat of the pan. If they're cooking too fast, take them off the heat for 15 seconds, continuing to stir, then return them to medium-low heat to finish cooking.

Niçoise Sando with Smashed Egg & Black Olive Mayo

Makes 2

PRODUCE
1 garlic clove
1 ripe medium tomato
½ cup basil leaves

DAIRY
4 large eggs

PANTRY
⅓ cup oil–cured black olives

6 tablespoons mayonnaise
2 (10–inch) soft hoagie rolls
1 (6.7–ounce) jar high–quality oil–packed tuna
Kosher salt and freshly ground black pepper
2 tablespoons red or white wine vinegar
2 handfuls potato chips

This was originally destined to be a niçoise salad, my attempt at taking a fresh look at the beloved French classic of tuna, olive, potato, and egg. I quickly realized that as a salad, the niçoise is perfect and iconic as is, and that I have no business trying to reinvent it. However, if you take all of those same flavors and rearrange them in the form of a sandwich (sorta à la pan bagnat), then I do have reason to get involved. Whatever you do, invest in the highest quality canned tuna you can find, and be sure it's oil-packed for best flavor. The boiled eggs here are cooked for exactly 9 minutes, which means they're just shy of hard-boiled (read: NOT chalky), perfect for a sandwich that is already quite juicy.

① **Cook the eggs:**
+ Bring a medium pot of water to a boil.
+ Using a slotted spoon, carefully lower 4 eggs into the water. Set a timer for 9 minutes.
+ Meanwhile, fill a medium bowl with ice and water. Once the eggs are cooked, transfer them to the ice bath to chill for at least 5 minutes to stop the cooking.

② **Make the olive mayo:**
+ Smash ⅓ cup oil–cured black olives with the bottom of a measuring cup and discard the pits.
+ Finely chop the olives and combine them with 6 tablespoons mayo in a small bowl.
+ Finely grate 1 garlic clove into the olive mayo and mix well to combine. No need to season this mayo, since oil–cured black olives are inherently very salty.

③ **Prep your other elements:**
+ Cut the hoagie rolls in half lengthwise and pull out some of the bread to hollow them slightly so that the ingredients have somewhere to sit.
+ Drain the oil from 1 (6.7–ounce) jar of oil–packed tuna.
+ Slice 1 medium tomato about ¼ inch thick. Season the slices with salt and black pepper and set on paper towels to drain (no soggy sandwich!). Wipe down that cutting board.

④ **Assemble:**
+ Slather the olive mayo on all 4 hoagie halves, dividing it evenly.
+ Peel the eggs. Tear each egg into a few pieces, then place them on the bread. Using the back of a fork, smash each egg down so that it sits more evenly on the sandwich. Season the eggs with salt and black pepper.
+ Layer the sliced tomatoes on the bottom halves of the sandwiches.
+ Flake apart the tuna and arrange it in an even layer on top of the eggs. Drizzle 1 tablespoon red wine vinegar over the tuna on each sandwich.
+ Top with some basil leaves, a handful of potato chips, and the top of the hoagie roll. Press down firmly to compress everything.

⑤ **Wrap and serve:** Wrap the sandwiches in parchment paper or foil to keep them tidy, then slice each sandwich in half before serving.

Turkey Club, Tuna Melt, BLT

F*ck, Marry, Kill?

Extremely Fried Eggs with Frizzled Shallots & Rice

Serves 4

PRODUCE
4 large shallots

DAIRY
4 large eggs

PANTRY
2 cups sushi rice or other short-grain rice
Kosher salt
1 tablespoon unseasoned rice vinegar
5 tablespoons extra-virgin olive oil
Shichimi togarashi and/or chile oil, hot sauce, or red pepper flakes, for serving (optional)

There are fried eggs. And then there are extremely fried eggs. I don't know about you, but I'm here for the latter. The glory of extremely fried eggs is the textural contrast between the runny yolk, the tender just-set whites, and the lacy fried edges. A little flick of the wrist is all you have to master here—crispy edges are born of continually basting the egg whites with some of the hot oil they're cooked in, such that the top edges fry as much as the bottom does.

---

① **Start the rice:**

+ Rinse 2 cups sushi rice in a fine-mesh strainer, swirling the rice vigorously as you rinse it, until the water runs clear, 1 to 2 minutes.[1]

+ Combine the rinsed rice with 2½ cups cold water and ½ teaspoon salt in a medium saucepan. Bring to a simmer over medium-high heat. As soon as it does, cover the pot with a tight-fitting lid and reduce the heat to very low. Cook for 16 minutes (set a timer), then turn off the heat and let the rice steam, covered, for 10 more minutes. Stir in 1 tablespoon rice vinegar and fluff with a fork. Cover to keep warm.

② **Meanwhile, frizzle the shallots:**

+ Thinly slice 4 large shallots crosswise to create lots of thin rings.

+ In a large nonstick skillet, combine 3 tablespoons olive oil and the shallots and cook over medium heat, stirring often, until they turn deep golden brown, even charred and crispy around the edges, 10 to 14 minutes.[2] Transfer the frizzled shallots to a small plate and season with a pinch of salt. Wipe out the skillet.

③ **Fry the eggs:** Add 2 tablespoons olive oil to the nonstick skillet and set over medium heat for 2 minutes, to allow the oil to get hot. Crack 4 eggs into the skillet (be careful, they may spatter a bit!) and cook, spooning some of the oil up over the whites, until the edges are brown and lacy and the whites are set, 3 to 5 minutes. **This is called basting, and it's a technique you can apply to many ingredients. Pull up this video to see it in action.** Season with salt.

④ **Assemble and serve:** Put a scoop of rice into each bowl. Top each with a fried egg, some frizzled shallots, and shichimi togarashi and/or chile oil (or any other fun spicy condiment you have on hand).

---

[1] This will take longer than you think, but it's a crucial step in evenly cooked, un-gummy rice. Don't skip it!

[2] Unlike slowly caramelizing onions over low heat, cooking the shallots at a higher heat for a shorter period of time, as we're doing here, yields jammy but crispy frizzled shallots. It's a different vibe and takes a lot less time than a carefully caramelized onion.

Fancy French Egg Salad

Serves 4

PRODUCE

¾ cup packed mixed tender herbs, such as dill, parsley, chives, tarragon, basil, mint, etc.

DAIRY

12 large eggs

PANTRY

1 tablespoon whole-grain mustard

1½ teaspoons Dijon mustard

3 tablespoons white wine vinegar

½ cup extra-virgin olive oil

8 cornichons

1 tablespoon capers, drained

Kosher salt and freshly ground black pepper

This slightly turnt-up version of the humble, traditional egg salad takes its inspiration from *gribiche*, a classic French sauce made of finely chopped hard-boiled eggs mixed with cornichons, mustard, and white wine vinegar. My version features 10-minute eggs, with yolks that are perfectly hard-boiled and a far cry from the dreaded overcooked yolks that egg salads often feature. They get torn and mixed into a bright, mustardy dressing and brought to life with a mix of tender herbs, which makes for an egg salad that is just as delicious served on toast or in a sandwich as it is spooned over roasted vegetables.

---

① **Cook the eggs:**

✦ Bring a large pot of water to a boil.

✦ Using a slotted spoon, gently lower 12 eggs into the pot and set a timer for 10 minutes.

✦ Meanwhile, fill a large bowl with ice water. Once the eggs are cooked, transfer them to the ice bath to chill for at least 5 minutes to stop the cooking.

② **Make the dressing:**

✦ In a medium bowl, whisk together 1 tablespoon whole-grain mustard, 1½ teaspoons Dijon mustard, and 3 tablespoons white wine vinegar. Whisking constantly, slowly stream in ½ cup olive oil until thick and emulsified.[1]

✦ Chop 8 cornichons and 1 tablespoon capers. Stir them into the dressing.

③ **Assemble and serve:**

✦ Peel the cooled eggs, then chop or tear them into bite-size pieces. Gently fold them into the dressing. Season with lots of salt and black pepper.

✦ Coarsely chop or tear ¾ cup packed mixed tender herbs and gently fold them into the egg salad.

✦ Choose your own adventure when it comes to serving this. It's good on pretty much everything.

---

[1] When the oil and the vinegar have come together into one homogeneous liquid and are not split or visibly distinct, they're emulsified.

Perfect Poached Eggs with Spiced Chickpeas & Smothered Pita Chips

Serves 4

PRODUCE
6 garlic cloves
1 jalapeño
1 medium yellow onion
1 cup cilantro leaves and tender stems, plus more leaves for serving

DAIRY
4 large eggs
Plain whole-milk yogurt, for serving

PANTRY
2 (14.5-ounce) cans chickpeas
¼ cup extra-virgin olive oil, plus more for drizzling
2 teaspoons ras el hanout (see headnote)
Kosher salt
1 (28-ounce) can crushed tomatoes
4 cups pita chips (6 ounces)

Poaching gets a bad rap because most people make it more complicated than it needs to be. The method you'll use in this recipe requires no vinegar and no frantically swirling vortex. As long as you have a fine-mesh strainer on hand, you've got everything you need. Once you've mastered the poach, you'll nestle the eggs into this spicy chickpea stew, which is jam-packed with crispy-gone-soggy (!!!) pita chips. The result offers impressions of North African shakshuka and Mexican chilaquiles, two dishes that I just so happen to love. Note: If you don't have ras el hanout, a Moroccan spice blend, you can use another warm spice blend such as Indian garam masala—just know that the flavors are not interchangeable and will take things in a different (though no less delicious!) direction.

① **Do some prep:**

+ Lightly smash and peel 6 garlic cloves; thinly slice them.

+ Trim and discard the stem of 1 jalapeño. (Discard the seeds if you are spice averse.) Finely chop the jalapeño.

+ Finely chop 1 medium yellow onion. **Not sure how to properly chop an onion? I got you.**

+ Chop 1 cup cilantro leaves and tender stems.

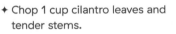

+ Drain and rinse 2 (14.5-ounce) cans of chickpeas. Set aside in a large bowl.

② **Build the stew:**

+ Heat ¼ cup olive oil in a 12-inch cast-iron skillet over medium heat. Add the garlic, onions, jalapeño, 2 teaspoons ras el hanout, and 1½ teaspoons salt and cook, stirring often, until the onion is very soft and just beginning to brown at the edges, 8 to 10 minutes.

+ Add the drained chickpeas (reserve that bowl) and cook, stirring often, to allow the chickpeas to absorb some of the flavor of the spices, 4 to 5 minutes.

+ Add 1 (28-ounce) can crushed tomatoes to the skillet. Bring the stew to a simmer and cook until slightly thickened, 15 to 20 minutes. Remove from the heat and stir in the cilantro. Taste and adjust the seasoning.

③ **Poach the eggs:**

+ Fill a large pot with 3 inches of water and bring to a boil.

+ Place the reserved large bowl right next to the sink so we can do some swift maneuvering here. Rest a fine-mesh strainer over the sink or a bowl. Crack an egg into the strainer, lift it up, and gently shake it to release some of the excess egg whites, discarding them. You'll be left with a yolk that is surrounded by a very contained, tight egg white orb. Carefully tip the egg out of the strainer into the large bowl. Repeat with 3 additional eggs, adding all of them to the same bowl. **If you've never strained eggs in this manner before, pull up this video.**

+ Once the water boils, turn off the heat. Immediately lower the lip of the bowl of eggs down into the water and gently let each egg slip out of the bowl and into the water, one by one. Set a timer for 3 minutes and let the eggs poach undisturbed.

④ **Serve:**

+ While the eggs poach, stir 4 cups pita chips into the stew.

+ Divide the stew among 4 serving bowls. Using a slotted spoon, transfer 1 poached egg to each bowl. Season the eggs with salt. Top each bowl with cilantro leaves, plain whole-milk yogurt, and more olive oil.

Saucy Eggs all'Amatriciana

Serves 4

PRODUCE
1 large yellow or white onion

5 garlic cloves

2 pounds cherry or Sungold tomatoes

2 oregano or marjoram sprigs

DAIRY
2 ounces grated Parmesan or pecorino cheese (½ cup), plus more for serving

4 large eggs

MEAT
8 ounces bacon or pancetta

PANTRY
¼ loaf of crusty bread (about 4 ounces)

4 tablespoons extra-virgin olive oil

Kosher salt

¾ teaspoon red pepper flakes

If you're familiar with Amatriciana sauce, it's because you've likely had the traditional Italian version of it served with bucatini. Amatriciana is a Roman pasta sauce made of cooked-down tomatoes, guanciale or bacon, and cheese—ingredients that also go beautifully with eggs. For my pasta-less twist, the eggs get cracked right into the sauce and simmered on the stovetop until all of the whites are just set but the yolks are still molten. I think we can all agree that dunking a crispy piece of delicious bread in anything saucy, yolky, or brothy is one of life's greatest pleasures. This recipe guarantees you that pleasure by also nestling big, crispy, craggy croutons right into the tomato sauce as it simmers, so the bottoms soak in all that sauce while the tops stay crunchy.

---

① Preheat the oven to 425°F.

② **Make the croutons:** Tear ¼ loaf of crusty bread into irregular, 2-inch pieces. Toss on a rimmed baking sheet with 2 tablespoons olive oil and ½ teaspoon salt. Bake until deeply golden brown and crisp, 7 to 9 minutes.

③ **Do your mise:**

✦ Chop 1 large onion. **Not sure how to properly chop an onion? I got you.**

✦ Thinly slice 5 garlic cloves.

✦ Dice 8 ounces bacon into roughly ½-inch pieces.

④ **Start the Amatriciana sauce:**

✦ Transfer the bacon to a 12-inch cast-iron skillet and set over medium heat. Cook, stirring occasionally, until lightly golden brown and crisp, 8 to 11 minutes.[1]

✦ Add the onion, garlic, ½ teaspoon red pepper flakes, and 1 teaspoon salt to the skillet and cook over medium heat until the onion is softened and translucent, 6 to 8 minutes longer.

✦ Add 2 tablespoons olive oil and the cherry tomatoes to the skillet. Increase the heat to medium-high and cook, stirring often and smashing some of the tomatoes with the back of a wooden spoon as they begin to burst, encouraging them to release some of their juices. Continue to simmer until about half of the tomatoes have burst and the sauce has thickened slightly, 6 to 8 minutes longer. Remove from the heat and stir in 2 ounces grated Parmesan cheese (½ cup). Taste and season with more salt if necessary.

⑤ **Cook the eggs:**

✦ Nestle the croutons into the tomato sauce so they are half submerged.

✦ Using a large spoon, create 4 divots in the tomato sauce. Working one at a time, crack an egg into each divot. Season the tops of the eggs with salt and the remaining ¼ teaspoon red pepper flakes. Return the skillet to medium heat and cover with a tight-fitting lid (or a baking sheet if you don't have a lid of the right diameter). Cook until the egg whites are just set and no longer translucent, but the yolks are still soft and runny, 8 to 12 minutes.[2]

⑥ **Serve:** Scatter the leaves of 2 oregano sprigs over the top, along with more grated Parmesan. Serve the eggs right out of the skillet.

---

[1] It's best to start bacon in a cold pan set over medium heat, so that it has a chance to gently "render" or dispel all of its fat and turn crisp before the edges burn.

[2] If you like firmer yolks, continue to cook a few minutes longer. You may notice some of the eggs cooking faster than others depending on where they are in the pan, so move the skillet around the burner to encourage even cooking.

Chorizo & Chickpea Carbonara

Serves 4

PRODUCE
½ lemon

DAIRY
4 large egg yolks

1 large egg

2 ounces grated Parmesan cheese (about ½ cup), plus more for serving

PANTRY
Kosher salt

4 ounces cured (Spanish) chorizo (about a 6-inch piece)

1 (14.5-ounce) can chickpeas

3 tablespoons extra-virgin olive oil

Freshly ground black pepper

1 pound dried rigatoni

Carbonara is without question one of the great pasta dishes of all time, and for that, I will forever be grateful to Italy. But there are enough carbonara recipes in this world to last a lifetime, even if you made a different one every single day. So I took a cue from what makes a classic carbonara so delicious—funky salty guanciale (cured pork jowl), lots of umami-laden Parmesan cheese, eggs for richness, and tons of freshly ground black pepper to cut through it all—and came up with this recipe. There is dried Spanish chorizo, a spicy, smoky cured meat that has a lot of the funk and intensity of guanciale but leans a bit smokier in flavor. And I've added crispy chickpeas, which sizzle and fry in the fat that is released from the chorizo as it cooks. The vibe of the dish ends up skewing more Spanish in flavor, but the spirit of the dish and the way it all comes together is quintessentially Italian. Don't let your fear of accidentally scrambling the eggs scare you away—I'll teach ya how to temper the beaten eggs with a splash of pasta water so they don't go into shock when they hit the hot pasta.

---

① Bring a large pot of heavily salted water to a boil.

② **Make the egg mixture:** In a medium bowl, whisk together 4 egg yolks and 1 whole egg. Whisk in 2 ounces grated Parmesan cheese (½ cup).

③ **Start the sauce:**

+ Dice 1 (4-ounce) piece of Spanish chorizo into ¼-inch pieces.

+ Thoroughly drain and rinse 1 (14.5-ounce) can of chickpeas in a fine-mesh strainer.

+ In a large Dutch oven, combine the chorizo and 3 tablespoons olive oil. Cook over medium heat until it just starts to sizzle, about 3 minutes.

+ Add the chickpeas and stir well to coat in the oil. Continue to cook, stirring occasionally and crushing some of the chickpeas with the back of a wooden spoon, until they are crisp in some areas and the chorizo has leeched out some of its red oil, 5 to 6 minutes longer. Coarsely grind lots of black pepper into the pot to bloom the pepper and bring out its aroma. Remove the pot from the heat.

④ **Cook the pasta:**

+ While the chickpeas cook, add the rigatoni to the boiling water and give it a stir. Cook according to the package directions for al dente. Scoop out and reserve 1½ cups of the pasta water, then drain the pasta.

+ Whisk ½ cup of the reserved pasta water into the egg and Parmesan mixture until well combined.

⑤ **Bring it all together:**

+ Transfer the pasta to the Dutch oven along with about half of the remaining pasta water. Turn the heat to medium-low and stream in the egg mixture, stirring vigorously and constantly with a spoon, until the pasta is coated in a thick, creamy, pale yellow sauce. You will see it magically transform from a raw egg mixture to a slightly thickened creamy sauce. Add a splash or two more pasta water if it looks a little too thick and could be saucier.

+ Finely grate the zest of ½ lemon into the pasta. Taste and add more salt and black pepper if you think it needs it.

⑥ **Serve:** Top ith more grated Parmesan and black pepper and serve.

Graziella's Pasta al Pomodoro

Serves 4

PRODUCE
12 garlic cloves
3½ pounds cherry or Sungold tomatoes
1 small bunch basil

DAIRY
2 ounces grated Parmesan cheese (about ½ cup),
plus more for serving

PANTRY
Kosher salt
⅔ cup extra–virgin olive oil, plus more for drizzling
Pinch of sugar, if needed
1 pound dried short pasta, such as orecchiette,
fusilli, rigatoni, cavatappi

This recipe owes all of its simple glory to a darling Italian nonna named Graziella, who housed me, fed me, and taught me to speak Italian during a semester abroad in Florence twelve years ago. She opened my eyes to the principles of cooking simply and gracefully with little more than a few high-quality ingredients. This burst–cherry tomato sauce made a weekly appearance on the dinner table and has remained ingrained in my taste memory ever since. The key to a well-balanced, unctuous tomato sauce is fat, and a lot of it. It cuts through the acidity and sweetness of the tomatoes and transforms them into something well rounded and luxurious.

① Bring a large pot of heavily salted water to a boil.

② **Make the sauce:**

+ Firmly smash 12 garlic cloves, then peel them.[1]

+ In a large Dutch oven, heat ⅔ cup olive oil over medium heat for 2 minutes. Add the garlic cloves and cook, stirring often, until very fragrant but not browned, about 1 minute. Immediately add 1¾ pounds cherry tomatoes to the oil and cook until they begin to burst and release some juices, 7 to 9 minutes.

+ Add an additional 1¾ pounds cherry tomatoes and 1½ teaspoons salt, along with 2 large sprigs of basil.[2]

+ Bring the sauce to a simmer over medium–high heat, then reduce the heat to medium to maintain a simmer and cook until very saucy, thickened, and almost all the tomatoes have burst, 20 to 25 minutes. Remove from the heat. Pluck out and discard the basil sprigs. Taste the sauce and if it's quite acidic, add a small pinch of sugar.[3] Cover to keep warm.

③ **Cook the pasta:** Cook the pasta according to the package directions until al dente. Scoop out and reserve 1 cup of the pasta water, then drain.

④ **Finish the sauce:** Return the tomato sauce to medium heat. Add the pasta along with half of the reserved pasta water. Add 2 ounces grated Parmesan cheese (½ cup) in several handfuls, tossing the pasta with tongs until very well coated; the sauce should cling to the pasta. If it seems like the sauce is a little tight and thick, continue to add some of the reserved pasta water, a splash at a time, until the consistency is right.

⑤ **Serve:** Divide the pasta among 4 bowls. Tear the leaves of the remaining basil over top of each bowl and finish with more grated Parmesan and a drizzle of olive oil.

[1] Be sure they get a good firm smash at the beginning to break them down so they can cook into the sauce; it's totally cool if they break into a few pieces.

[2] Stems and all—you'll pluck them out later on! This will perfume the sauce without leaving wilted brown basil behind.

[3] This is especially likely when cherry tomatoes are not in season and tend to be less sweet, so use your judgment.

Orzo al Limone

Serves 4

PRODUCE
1 medium yellow onion
1 lemon

DAIRY
5 tablespoons unsalted butter
2½ ounces grated Parmesan cheese (about ¾ cup),
plus more for serving

PANTRY
1 cup orzo
Kosher salt and freshly ground black pepper
Extra–virgin olive oil, for drizzling

If you're a mac-and-cheese, buttered pasta, or risotto fan, look no further for your newest favorite dish. Spaghetti al limone—a classic and supremely simple Italian pasta dish composed of lemon juice, butter, and Parmesan cheese—gets a fresh take, featuring orzo instead of spaghetti, which results in a dish that's somewhere between risotto and macaroni and cheese, and I think it's pretty special. The name of the game here is to avoid overcooking the orzo; leave it slightly al dente so that it doesn't turn into a big pot of mush. I've been on a mission to bring back orzo for the last couple of years and it seems to be an uphill battle, so throw me a bone and jump on board, okay?

---

① **Prep your aromatics:**

+ Finely chop 1 yellow onion. **Not sure how to properly chop an onion? I got you.**

+ Using a vegetable peeler, peel 3 (3–inch–long) strips of lemon zest from 1 lemon; set the lemon aside.

② **Start the orzo:**

+ In a large Dutch oven or pot, heat 3 tablespoons butter over medium heat until melted and foamy.

+ Add the onion and cook, stirring often, until softened but not yet browned, 5 to 7 minutes.

+ Add 1 cup orzo, the 3 strips of lemon zest, and 1 teaspoon black pepper and toast, stirring, for 2 minutes.

+ Stir in 3 cups water and 1 teaspoon salt and bring to a simmer over medium heat. Once the water comes to a simmer, reduce the heat to medium–low and cook, stirring occasionally so the orzo doesn't stick to the bottom of the pot, until most of the water has been absorbed (there should still be some liquid at the bottom of the pot), 6 to 8 minutes. Taste the orzo; it should be al dente but not crunchy.

③ **Finish the orzo:**

+ Remove the pot from the heat. Stir in 2 tablespoons butter and 2½ ounces grated Parmesan cheese (¾ cup).

+ Finely grate the remaining zest of the lemon into the pot. Cut the lemon in half and squeeze the juice of both halves into the orzo. Taste and add more salt as needed. Add a few more tablespoons of water, if needed, until it's very creamy and loose.[1]

④ **Serve:** Drizzle the orzo with olive oil and season with black pepper and more grated Parmesan.

---

[1] It tends to thicken as you add the cheese and as it cools, so it's better to err on the looser side here.

Pasta Salad with Morty-d, Mozz & Pistachios

Serves 4 to 6

PRODUCE
2 lemons
1 garlic clove
1 cup basil leaves

DAIRY
1 (1½-ounce) piece Parmesan cheese (about ⅓ cup grated)
12 ounces fresh buffalo mozzarella or burrata cheese

MEAT
8 ounces sliced mortadella, soppressata, or prosciutto

PANTRY
Kosher salt
1½ cups Castelvetrano olives
Freshly ground black pepper
⅔ cup extra-virgin olive oil
1 pound dried rigatoni
⅔ cup roasted, salted pistachios

Two things I need to say about this dish. Number one: Pasta salad gets a really bad rap, and frankly, I'm sick and tired of it. Executed properly and with the right ingredients, pasta salad can be as revelatory, if not more so, than a hot pasta dish. If you ask me, mayonnaise has no place in pasta salad—it starts to congeal and crust the second it hits the table and only gets worse the longer it sits. Vinegar-and-oil-based pasta salads (or lemon juice in this case), on the other hand, only improve with time. As the salad sits, the dressing soaks into the cooked pasta, and it never gloops up or becomes crusty. Number two: I love morty-d. So. Freakin. Much.

① Bring a large pot of heavily salted water to a boil. Go ahead, throw a full ¼ cup salt in there!

② **Make the olive-y dressing:**

+ Firmly smash 1½ cups Castelvetrano olives with the bottom of a glass measuring cup to release their pits. Discard the pits, tear the flesh in half, and transfer them to a large bowl.

+ Finely grate the zest of half of 1 lemon into the bowl. Cut 2 lemons in half and squeeze the juice into the bowl, catching the seeds with your hands.

+ Using a Microplane, finely grate 1 garlic clove and 1½ ounces Parmesan cheese (about ⅓ cup) into the bowl.

+ Stir in ⅔ cup extra-virgin olive oil.

+ Tear 12 ounces buffalo mozzarella and 8 ounces sliced mortadella into bite-size pieces and add them to the dressing, tossing gently to combine. Season with salt and lots of black pepper.

③ **Cook the pasta:** Add 1 pound rigatoni to the boiling water and give it a good stir. Cook according to the package directions until al dente, then drain and rinse in cold water to cool the pasta to room temperature and rinse off any excess starch.[1] Drain well.

④ **Assemble and serve:** Add the pasta to the bowl of dressing. Chop ⅔ cup pistachios and tear 1 cup basil leaves; add to the salad and gently toss everything to combine.[2] Taste and add more salt and black pepper as needed. Serve at room temp or cold.

[1] Normally, you'd use that lingering starch to help thicken your pasta sauce, but because this is a cold side dish, we actually don't want any extra starch.

[2] If not serving immediately, hold off on adding the pistachios (they'll get soggy) and basil (it'll wilt).

Peanutty Pork Noodles with Crunchy Celery

Serves 4

PRODUCE
6 garlic cloves
1 (2-inch) piece fresh ginger
4 celery stalks, plus their leaves

MEAT
1 pound ground pork

PANTRY
Kosher salt
½ cup crunchy peanut butter
¼ cup low-sodium soy sauce
¼ cup unseasoned rice vinegar
3 tablespoons sriracha
3 tablespoons honey
2 tablespoons vegetable oil
1 pound fresh linguine or pappardelle

Peanuts and pork! Two ingredients I particularly love that also happen to love each other. Ground pork is the star (and peanut butter the supporting actor) of these highly addictive noods. If you've ever had peanut butter noodles, the American Chinese riff on the more traditional Chinese dish of cold sesame noodles, then you know the power of combining thick, fatty, creamy nut or seed butters with slippery, slurp-able noodles. Crunchy peanut butter adds both texture and richness to this dish—but you're going to need to add quite a bit of pasta water to thin the sauce to achieve a silky, glossy consistency. The sauce will tighten and thicken as it cools, so err on the looser side. Flavorwise, there's a lot going on here simultaneously—the warm noodles are at once sweet, spicy, fatty, acidic, and umami, which means you're probably gonna have a hard time cutting yourself off. Just thought you'd like a heads-up.

① Bring a large pot of heavily salted water to a boil.

② **Make the sauce:** In a medium bowl, whisk together ½ cup peanut butter, ¼ cup soy sauce, ¼ cup rice vinegar, 3 tablespoons sriracha, and 3 tablespoons honey until well combined. Set this aside; you'll be adding it to your Dutch oven later on.

③ **Prep your aromatics:**
+ Thinly slice 6 garlic cloves.
+ Finely grate 1 (2-inch) piece of ginger. No need to peel it unless it's super gnarly and dirty!
+ Remove the leaves from 4 celery stalks (reserve them for garnish later on). Thinly slice each stalk on the bias into ¼-inch-thick slices.

④ **Sear the pork:**
+ Divide and shape 1 pound ground pork into four 3-inch-round patties. Season the pork all over with 1 teaspoon salt.
+ Heat 2 tablespoons vegetable oil in a large Dutch oven over medium-high heat until just beginning to smoke. Add the pork patties in a single layer and cook, undisturbed, until crispy and brown underneath, 3 to 4 minutes. Use a spatula to flip the patties over and then break them into smaller bite-size pieces.
+ Add the garlic and ginger and cook, stirring often, until very fragrant, 2 minutes longer. Remove from the heat.

⑤ **Meanwhile, cook the noodles:**
+ Add 1 pound fresh linguine to the boiling water and cook according to the package directions until al dente. Scoop out and reserve 1½ cups of the pasta water, then drain the pasta.
+ Add the drained pasta to the Dutch oven along with the peanut sauce and about ½ cup of the reserved pasta water. Turn the heat to medium and cook, stirring and adding more pasta water as needed, until the noodles are well coated, about 1 minute.

⑥ **Serve:** Remove the pot from the heat and stir in the sliced celery. Serve topped with the reserved celery leaves.

Orecchiette with Bacon, Snap Peas & Ricotta

Serves 4

PRODUCE
6 ounces snap peas

DAIRY
2 ounces grated Parmesan cheese (about ½ cup), plus more for serving

4 ounces whole-milk ricotta cheese (about ½ cup)

MEAT
8 ounces thick-cut bacon (6 to 8 strips)

PANTRY
Kosher salt

2 teaspoons freshly ground black pepper, plus more for serving

1 pound dried orecchiette or other short pasta

This dish gives off carbonara × cacio e pepe vibes, with the added bonus of lots of tender, sweet little snap peas and the occasional dollop of creamy ricotta cheese strewn throughout. After crisping up some bacon, you'll use the rendered bacon fat, some starchy pasta water, and a generous flurry of Parm to create a creamy, glossy, emulsified sauce that "naps," or coats, the orecchiette. Look for high-quality fresh whole-milk ricotta cheese, which is far more flavorful than the middle-of-the-road skim-milk stuff you'll find at the grocery store.

---

① Bring a large pot of salted water to a boil.[1]

② **Do some prep:**

+ Using a knife, trim the ends of 6 ounces snap peas and peel and discard their strings. Slice the snap peas crosswise into thirds.

+ Cut the bacon crosswise into ½-inch-wide pieces. Transfer the bacon to a large heavy-bottomed pot and set over medium heat. Cook, stirring often, until golden and crisp, 7 to 9 minutes. Add 2 teaspoons black pepper and stir once or twice to bloom the flavor in the bacon fat. Remove from the heat.

③ **Cook the pasta and snap peas:**

+ Cook the orecchiette until al dente according to the package directions. When there are 2 minutes left on your timer, drop the snap peas into the pasta water along with the orecchiette.

+ Scoop out and reserve 1½ cups of the pasta water, then drain the pasta and snap peas. Add them to the pot of bacon, along with 1 cup of the pasta water (the remaining ½ cup is your reserve in case you need a little more to thin out the sauce at the end).

+ Return the pot to medium heat. While stirring vigorously with a wooden spoon, add 2 ounces grated Parmesan cheese (½ cup), little by little, until the sauce is very creamy and coats all of the pasta. Taste and add salt if you think it needs it.[2]

+ Remove the pot from heat. Add 2 ounces whole-milk ricotta cheese (¼ cup) in 4 small dollops with a small spoon, stirring the pasta just once. This creates little pockets of sweet creaminess as you eat the pasta, interspersed with saltier ones, without the ricotta overwhelming the whole sauce.

④ **Serve:** Divide the pasta among 4 bowls and top with the remaining 2 ounces ricotta cheese (¼ cup) in small dollops. Top with more black pepper and Parmesan.

---

[1] You'll notice that I generally ask you to put an extreme amount of salt in your pasta water. This recipe makes an exception to that rule because there are some naturally salty ingredients (bacon, Parmesan cheese) in the sauce. So definitely season that water, just don't go dumping in fistfuls.

[2] We haven't added any to the sauce until this point because of the salty ingredients, but that doesn't mean you might not need a little extra at the end—you decide!

Paccheri with Pork & Lentil Ragù

Serves 4 to 6

PRODUCE
6 garlic cloves
2 or 3 rosemary sprigs
1 lemon

DAIRY
2 ounces grated Parmesan cheese (about ½ cup), plus more for serving

MEAT
8 ounces ground pork

PANTRY
Kosher salt
3 tablespoons extra-virgin olive oil, plus more for drizzling
6 oil-packed anchovy fillets
3 tablespoons tomato paste
½ cup split red lentils
½ teaspoon red pepper flakes
1 pound dried paccheri or other large tube pasta

It is my pleasure to introduce you to the joy of pasta with pork and lentils. Adding quick-cooking split red lentils to ground pork, garlic, and anchovies—the workhorse ingredients of this ragù—gives this dish the kind of body you'd expect from a long-simmered meat sauce like Bolognese. The lentils give up some of their inherent starchiness to the sauce as they cook, and they break down easily, yielding a full-bodied, deeply flavorful sauce that clings to the noodles.

---

① Bring a large pot of heavily salted water to a boil. It should be salty like the sea!

② **Do some prep:**

+ Firmly smash and peel 6 garlic cloves. Give the garlic a rough chop to break it down into smaller pieces.

+ Strip and finely chop the leaves from 2 or 3 large sprigs of rosemary (you'll have about 1 tablespoon).

③ **Start the ragù:**

+ Heat 3 tablespoons olive oil in a large Dutch oven over medium-high heat. Add 8 ounces ground pork and smash it down in the pot, flattening it to about ½-inch thickness, then break it apart into smaller pieces. Season with ½ teaspoon salt and cook, undisturbed, until browned underneath, 3 to 4 minutes.

+ Reduce the heat to medium. Add 6 anchovies to the oil surrounding the pork. Fry until golden brown, using a wooden spoon to help break them up a bit, about 1 minute. Continue to break the pork into smaller pieces.

+ Add the garlic. Cook, stirring often, until the garlic is softened and just beginning to turn brown at the edges, 1 to 2 minutes.

+ Add 3 tablespoons tomato paste and cook, stirring, until it turns a dark rust color, about 2 minutes longer.

+ Stir in ½ cup split red lentils, 2 cups water, 2 or 3 rosemary sprigs, ½ teaspoon red pepper flakes, and ½ teaspoon salt, scraping up any bits that are stuck to the bottom or the sides of the pot. Once the water comes to a simmer, reduce the heat to medium to maintain a gentle simmer. Cook, stirring occasionally, until the lentils are just cooked through but not mushy, 10 to 15 minutes. If the sauce looks thick and the lentils aren't quite done yet, add an extra splash or two of water. Remove from the heat and cover to keep warm.

④ **Meanwhile, cook the pasta:**

+ Add the paccheri to the boiling water and give it a good stir. Cook the pasta until al dente according to the package directions. Scoop out and reserve 1 cup of the pasta water (a.k.a. liquid gold!), then drain.[1]

+ Return the pot of ragù to medium heat and stir in the pasta. Cook, stirring frequently, while gradually adding 2 ounces grated Parmesan cheese (½ cup) as you go, along with as much of the reserved pasta water as needed. The sauce should be creamy and coat all of the pasta evenly.

+ Stir the juice of 1 lemon into the pasta and add more salt if necessary.

⑤ **Serve:** Divide the pasta among bowls and top with more Parmesan and a drizzle of olive oil.

---

[1] Never throw that stuff out without saving some; it is filled with starchy goodness that will help the sauce thicken and cling to the pasta!

Linguine with Chile Clams & Basil

Serves 4 to 6

PRODUCE
8 garlic cloves
1 pound cherry tomatoes
1½ cups packed basil leaves

DAIRY
4 tablespoons (½ stick) unsalted butter

SEAFOOD
24 littleneck clams

PANTRY
Kosher salt
¼ cup extra–virgin olive oil
2 tablespoons sambal oelek
½ cup dry vermouth or white wine
1 pound dried linguine

Think of this as a mash-up between pasta al pomodoro and white clam sauce, with the added bonus of some serious heat. Sambal oelek, an Indonesian vinegar-based chile sauce, is put to use in an unexpected way here, but it's right at home along with all the garlic and basil. It's a great condiment to add to your roster of spicy things for last-minute zhoozhing on the fly. The key to juicy, plump clams is to avoid overcooking them, which means plucking them out of the pot one by one as they open to stop the cooking and then adding them all back into the pot toward the end to get them nice and saucy.

---

① Bring a large pot of heavily salted water to a boil.

② **Clean the clams:** Submerge the clams in a large bowl of cold water set in the sink, swooshing them around to release any grit. Use a clean sponge to scrub any that seem particularly dirty. Let them sit for at least 10 minutes while you start the broth so they can expel any sand inside them.

③ **Do some prep:**

   ✦ Thinly slice 8 garlic cloves.

   ✦ Cut 1 pound cherry tomatoes in half.

④ **Cook the clams:**

   ✦ In a large Dutch oven, heat ¼ cup olive oil over medium heat. Add the sliced garlic and cook, stirring often, until very fragrant but not browned, 1 to 2 minutes.

   ✦ Add 2 tablespoons sambal oelek and ½ cup dry vermouth. Cook for 2 to 3 minutes to cook off some of the raw alcohol flavor, leaving behind the acidity and slight sweetness of the vermouth.

   ✦ Add the tomatoes and clams and stir once or twice, then cover with a tight–fitting lid. Cook until all the clams open, 8 to 15 minutes. Start checking at around 8 minutes; this timing will vary greatly depending on their size. As they open, transfer the cooked clams to a bowl, letting the remaining clams cook longer (never opening indicates that the clam was dead to begin with—chuck those). Leave behind the tomatoes and liquid; this is your sauce.

⑤ **Cook the pasta:**

   ✦ Once most of the clams are open, get your linguine cooking—drop it into the pot of boiling water and give it a good stir. Cook according to the package directions until al dente.

   ✦ When the pasta is al dente, scoop out and reserve 1½ cups of the pasta water. Using tongs, transfer the pasta to the pot of sauce along with 4 tablespoons butter and about half of the reserved pasta water. Cook over medium heat, tossing often with tongs, until the sauce clings to the linguine, adding more pasta water as necessary. Add the clams back to pot and toss once or twice to reheat.

⑥ **Finish it up:** Remove the pot from the heat and tear 1½ cups basil leaves into the pasta. Taste the sauce and add salt if you think it needs it.[1] Serve right out of the Dutch oven, with tongs and a large spoon for the sauce.

---

[1] We haven't added any yet because clams are notoriously salty by nature, so it's best to be judicious at first.

Big Shells with Escarole, 'Chovies & Mozz

Serves 4

PRODUCE

1 large escarole or radicchio or large bunch of kale

8 garlic cloves

1 tablespoon oregano or thyme leaves

DAIRY

8 ounces fresh whole-milk mozzarella

½ cup heavy cream

2 ounces grated Parmesan cheese (about ½ cup)

PANTRY

Kosher salt

¼ cup plus 2 tablespoons extra-virgin olive oil

¾ cup panko bread crumbs

5 oil-packed anchovy fillets

½ teaspoon red pepper flakes

12 ounces dried large pasta shells

Originally, this dish was destined to be a cheesy baked pasta/casserole kind of sitch. I was hell-bent on including a baked pasta in this book to satisfy all the baked ziti lovers in the house. After testing it out, I had a revelation. Between making a béchamel sauce, boiling the pasta, baking the whole deal, and broiling the top for the crunchy bits (the best part), baked pasta is SO. MUCH. WORK. I'm exhausted just thinking about it. You know what doesn't sound exhausting? All of the joy of creamy, oozy baked pasta made quickly in a Dutch oven and then showered in crispy toasted panko bread crumbs—zero time spent in the oven. It's the best of both worlds, and mark my words, I am never making baked pasta again.

① Bring a large pot of heavily salted water to a boil.

② **Do some prep:**

+ Trim the stem of 1 large escarole head. Cut or tear the leaves into roughly 2-inch pieces. Wash and thoroughly dry the escarole.

+ Thinly slice 8 garlic cloves.

+ Tear 8 ounces fresh mozzarella into ½-inch pieces.

③ **Make the bread crumbs:** Heat 2 tablespoons olive oil in a large Dutch oven over medium-low heat. Add ¾ cup panko and cook, stirring often so it toasts evenly, until golden brown, 6 to 8 minutes. Transfer to a small bowl; season with salt. Wipe out any crumbs left behind.

④ **Make the sauce:**

+ Return the Dutch oven to medium heat. Add ¼ cup olive oil, the garlic, and 5 anchovies and cook, stirring often, until the garlic is softened but not browned, 3 minutes.

+ Add the escarole and ½ teaspoon red pepper flakes, stirring once or twice to coat the escarole in the oil. Cover and cook until the escarole wilts, about 2 minutes. Uncover and continue to cook until any water released has cooked off, about 5 minutes. The bottom of the pot should be relatively dry.

+ Add ½ cup heavy cream, bring the sauce to a bare simmer over medium heat, and simmer until the cream thickens slightly, about 2 minutes.

+ Working with one small handful at a time, add 2 ounces grated Parmesan cheese (½ cup) to the sauce, stirring between additions. Keep stirring until all the cheese has melted and the sauce is smooth. Season with salt. Remove from the heat and cover.

⑤ **Cook the pasta:**

+ Once the water boils, add 12 ounces large shells and stir once or twice. Cook until al dente according to the package directions. Scoop out and reserve 1 cup of the pasta water, then drain.

⑥ **Assemble:**

+ Return the Dutch oven to medium heat and add the cooked shells and ½ cup of the reserved pasta water. Cook, stirring frequently to ensure that all the nooks and crannies get coated, until the sauce thickens again and clings to the pasta, 2 to 3 minutes.

+ Stir in 1 tablespoon oregano. Remove the pot from the heat and add the torn mozzarella cheese, a few handfuls at a time, stirring between additions so that the cheese distributes throughout the pasta in pockets. Taste and adjust the seasoning as needed.

⑦ **Serve:** Scatter about half of the toasted panko generously over the pasta and serve with more panko alongside.

Grains & Legumes

Master Beans

PRODUCE

1 red, yellow, or white onion, or 2 large shallots

1 whole garlic head

1 fresh chile, such as jalapeño, Fresno, or serrano

3 large basil, parsley, or cilantro sprigs or fresh bay leaves

MEAT

2 slices pork product (about 1 ounce), such as bacon, mortadella, ham, or prosciutto (optional)

PANTRY

1 pound dried beans

¾ teaspoon baking soda

1 cup extra-virgin olive oil

Kosher salt

DAIRY

1 Parmesan cheese rind (optional)

Makes 5 cups

I have an incredible amount of love for scratch-cooked beans. People think it's a whole twenty-four-hour to-do, but I'm here to tell that you don't have to flip to the next recipe if you didn't remember to soak your beans overnight. There's a shortcut within the recipe, so no excuses! Of course, there's a time and a place for a canned bean, and don't get me wrong, I use them all the time. But something very special happens when you cover dried beans in a shit ton of olive oil and a Molly-approved amount of salt, mix them with a few bold aromatics, and let them do their thing in the oven while you do literally whatever else you want. The result is a pot of beans that are so flavorful, rich, and creamy, you could simply eat them straight out of the oven. There are many recipes in this book that call for canned beans, but if you've made a pot of these guys, by all means use them whenever a bean is called for.

① **Soak the beans:** Place 1 pound dried beans in a large bowl and cover them with 6 cups cold water. Let them soak at room temperature for at least 6 hours and up to 18.[1]

② Preheat the oven to 300°F.

③ **Build the cooking liquid:**

✦ Drain the beans in a fine-mesh strainer. Add them to a large Dutch oven along with 6 cups cold water and ¾ teaspoon baking soda.[2]

✦ Cut 1 onion into quarters through the root end.

✦ Cut 1 whole garlic head in half crosswise.

✦ Cut 1 fresh chile in half lengthwise. Add the onion, garlic, chile, and 3 large basil sprigs to the beans.

✦ If you have a slice or two of bacon or any other cured pork product on hand and are looking for full-flavored, meaty beans, add that as well. And if you're super lucky and happen to have a Parmesan rind in the fridge— don't miss out on the opportunity to use it here; it imparts a uniquely savory flavor to the beans without reading cheesy.

④ **Cook the beans:**

✦ Add 1 cup olive oil and 5 teaspoons salt to the water. Bring the beans to a bare simmer over medium heat, stirring occasionally.

✦ Transfer to the oven, uncovered, and cook, stirring gently once or twice, until cooked through and tender but not falling apart, 35 to 75 minutes, depending on what type of bean you're using. The tiny ones will cook much faster, so start tasting early if you're using a smallish bean, and always taste more than one to be certain they're done.

⑤ **Eat:** Pluck out and discard any large pieces of onion, garlic, chile, bacon, herbs, and the cheese rind. Taste and add more salt if you think they need it. You can eat these straight out of the pot or use them in any of the recipes in the book that call for beans. They're great hot in their broth, amazing cold when marinated in some oil, vinegar, and herbs, and really just one of life's greatest pleasures to have on hand.

---

[1] The beans need a jump start on absorbing some of the water so that they cook evenly once they're on the stove. If you don't have time to soak them, place the dried beans in a pot and cover them with water. Bring them to a boil, turn off the heat, and let them sit for 10 minutes before draining them. Proceed with the rest of this recipe.

[2] Baking soda helps them stay intact and perfectly shapely—I've tested this, and it's not a hoax.

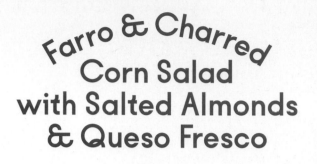

Farro & Charred Corn Salad with Salted Almonds & Queso Fresco

Serves 4

PRODUCE
½ small red onion
4 ears corn
1 cup mint or basil leaves

DAIRY
4 ounces queso fresco or feta cheese

PANTRY
Kosher salt
1¼ cups farro
⅓ cup sherry vinegar or red wine vinegar
1 tablespoon honey
⅓ cup extra-virgin olive oil
½ cup roasted, salted almonds or hazelnuts
Freshly ground black pepper

This grain salad is allllll about texture. You've got chewy al dente farro, juicy kernels of charred corn, crunchy salted almonds, and creamy crumbles of Mexican queso fresco all hanging out together, comingling. You'll cook the farro just as you would pasta, which is the easiest, most foolproof way to cook any grain, so feel free to swap in a different one if you've got it on hand. Barley, wheat berries, freekeh, or spelt would all be fab here. The corn gets charred in a cast-iron skillet, but if you've got access to a real-deal grill, by all means, take this operation outside. This is the kind of dish that only improves with time, so make it in advance and let all the ingredients get to know one another—just don't add the herbs until the end, or they will wilt and blacken as they sit in the sherry vinegar, and you really do hate to see that.

---

① **Cook the farro:** Bring a medium pot of water to a boil. Season well with salt as you would pasta water.[1] Add 1¼ cups farro and boil until cooked through and al dente but not mushy, 20 to 35 minutes. Taste as you go to determine doneness.

② **Meanwhile, pickle the onion:**

✦ In a large bowl, whisk together ⅓ cup sherry vinegar, 1 tablespoon honey, ⅓ cup olive oil, and 1 teaspoon salt.

✦ Peel and thinly slice ½ small red onion through the root end. Add to the dressing and toss to combine.[2]

✦ Once the farro is al dente, drain it in a fine-mesh strainer or colander and rinse with cold water to cool it down. Add the drained farro to the bowl with the pickled onions, tossing to combine.

③ **Char the corn:** Shuck 4 ears of corn. Heat a large dry cast-iron skillet over medium-high heat for several minutes. Add the corn and cook, rotating every few minutes, until charred in spots and bright yellow, 11 to 13 minutes. Transfer the corn to a cutting board to cool. Working one at a time, stand the corn stem-end down in the bowl of farro. Cut the kernels off the cob, starting at the top and working down. Repeat with the remaining corn. **Learn how to do that here.**

④ **Assemble the salad:**

✦ Crumble 4 ounces queso fresco into the farro mixture; tossing to combine.

✦ Roughly chop ½ cup roasted, salted almonds, then toss into the farro mixture to combine.

✦ Tear 1 cup mint leaves into smaller pieces and toss everything together.

✦ Season with lots of black pepper. Taste and adjust the seasoning by adding more salt or vinegar as necessary until it all tastes harmonious.

⑤ **Serve:** Serve at room temperature or cover and transfer to the fridge to chill and then eat cold—both ways are delicious, and this salad is perfect as leftovers.

---

[1] Since you are cooking the farro just like you would pasta, you don't have to worry about nailing the correct amount of water. You'll ultimately drain it.

[2] We are essentially quick-pickling the red onion in the sherry vinegar dressing, so give it a couple of minutes to sit and pickle.

Marinated Lentils with Spiced Walnuts & Lotsa Basil

Serves 4

PRODUCE
3 garlic cloves

1½ cups packed basil leaves

DAIRY
1 (4-ounce) block feta cheese

PANTRY
Kosher salt and freshly ground black pepper

1½ cups black beluga lentils or French green lentils (a.k.a. lentilles du Puy)

1 cup raw walnuts, almonds, or pecans

½ cup extra-virgin olive oil, plus more for drizzling

1 tablespoon cumin seeds

1½ teaspoons ground coriander

⅓ cup golden raisins

⅓ cup red or white wine vinegar

I've got a lotta love for lentils. Any food that tastes great straight on day one and only tastes better as it sits and marinates over a few days is a good food to me. Once you know how to properly cook lentils—like pasta, in a pot of heavily salted water—you've got one of the greatest canvases upon which to express your creativity. Lentils soak up flavors like sponges, so I encourage you to use this recipe as a jumping-off point but not as dogma. Gently heating the oil with lots of aromatics will amplify all their flavors and carry them effortlessly into the lentils once things all gets tossed together. This recipe calls for black or green lentils, both of which tend to hold their shape well when cooked, thus making them perfect for salads.

---

① **Cook the lentils:**

✦ Bring a medium saucepan filled with 2 quarts water and 2 tablespoons salt to a boil.

✦ Add 1½ cups black beluga lentils, give them a good stir, and return the water to a simmer, adjusting the heat as necessary to maintain a simmer while they cook. Simmer until they are cooked through and no longer toothsome but not mushy, 15 to 35 minutes, depending on what type of lentils you have and how old they are. Taste them periodically to evaluate their doneness before draining them.

✦ Drain the lentils in a fine-mesh strainer and let them cool in the strainer while you prepare the walnut dressing. Reserve the saucepan.

② **Make the spiced walnut oil:**

✦ Coarsely chop 1 cup walnuts.

✦ In the reserved saucepan, combine ½ cup olive oil and the chopped walnuts and cook over medium-low heat, swirling the pan often so that they cook evenly, until golden brown, 4 to 6 minutes. Keep an eye on them, as they can turn from toasty to burnt pretty quickly. Remove from the heat.

✦ Add 1 tablespoon cumin seeds and 1½ teaspoons ground coriander and stir to combine. Using a Microplane, immediately grate 3 garlic cloves into the still-hot oil; stir to combine.[1]

✦ Stir in ⅓ cup golden raisins, ⅓ cup red wine vinegar, and 1 teaspoon salt.

③ **Dress the lentils:**

✦ Add the drained lentils back to the medium saucepan with the walnut mixture and gently stir everything to combine.

✦ Thinly slice 1 (4-ounce) block of feta into large ¼-inch-thick planks.

✦ Tear 1½ cups basil leaves in half, or into small pieces if large, and toss them through the lentils. Taste and adjust the seasoning as needed. Divide the lentils among 4 serving bowls. Top each with a few feta planks and black pepper and drizzle with more olive oil.

---

[1] The residual heat from the oil will toast the spices and mellow out the garlic, removing its raw bite.

One-Pot Chicken & Schmaltzy Rice with Lemony Yog

Serves 4 to 6

PRODUCE
1 large white or yellow onion

7 garlic cloves

2 lemons

4 ounces sugar snap peas

1 large bunch dill or cilantro

DAIRY
2 tablespoons unsalted butter

1 cup plain whole-milk yogurt

MEAT
2 pounds bone-in, skin-on chicken thighs (about 6 small)

PANTRY
1½ cups basmati rice

Kosher salt and freshly ground black pepper

¾ cup roasted, salted pistachios

This is comfort food at its best—one pot and supremely satisfying. Chicken thighs get nestled on top of a bed of garlicky rice where they steam together, yielding meat that is impossibly tender. This recipe uses basmati rice—a long-grain white rice that tends to cook up fluffier than jasmine rice, making it perfect for pilaf-y dishes like this one. You'll soak the rice while you prep the chicken and aromatics to give it a jump-start on absorbing some water, which will result in more evenly cooked rice. It's important to get the highest quality basmati rice you can find to ensure even cooking and optimal fluff, especially when sharing real estate with chicken thighs in a one-pot dish like this one.

---

① **Prep the rice:**

✦ Place 1½ cups basmati rice in a medium bowl and cover with room-temperature water. Let the rice soak for 30 minutes.

② **Crisp up the chicken:**

✦ Pat 2 pounds of chicken thighs dry with paper towels to remove any surface moisture; this will encourage crispiness and browning. Season the chicken thighs all over with 2 teaspoons salt and a few good cranks of black pepper.

✦ Arrange the thighs skin-side down in a large, dry Dutch oven. Set the pot over medium heat and cook, undisturbed, until the skin releases easily from the pot and is light golden brown, 8 to 10 minutes.

✦ Once the chicken skin no longer sticks to the pot, move the chicken thighs around a bit in the pot to ensure even browning and continue to cook until the skin is very crisp and deeply golden brown, 6 to 8 minutes longer. Parts of your pot will get hotter than others, so if some of the thighs seem darker golden brown than the rest, swap them for even cooking. When the chicken skin is very crispy, use tongs to transfer the thighs to a plate, skin-side up.

③ **While the chicken cooks, do some prep:**

✦ Finely chop 1 large onion. **Not sure how to properly chop an onion? This should help.**

✦ Finely chop 6 garlic cloves.

④ **Drain the rice:** Drain the soaked rice in a fine-mesh strainer, rinsing with cold water and swirling the rice around with your fingers until the water runs completely clear, 1 to 2 minutes.[1] Set the strainer on top of a kitchen towel to drain any additional water.

⑤ **Add the aromatics and toast the rice:**

✦ Reduce the heat under the Dutch oven (now with only the chicken fat) to medium-low and stir in the chopped onion. Cook, stirring often, until the onion is translucent and soft, about 6 minutes.

✦ Add the chopped garlic to the pot and cook, stirring, until fragrant, about 1 minute. Season with salt and lots of black pepper.

✦ Stir in the rice and cook, stirring constantly, until the grains turn translucent around the edges, 1 minute. We are toasting the rice to coat it in all of that schmaltzy flavor.

---

[1] This helps rinse off some of the excess surface starch clinging to the grains, which can impede fluffiness and yield a gluey outcome.

recipe continues →

+ Add 2 cups water, 2 tablespoons butter, and 1 teaspoon salt and stir to scrape up any bits that are stuck to the bottom of the pot. Bring the water to a boil over medium-high heat. Once the water boils, nestle the chicken thighs back into the pot, skin-side up, along with any accumulated juices. Cover the pot, reduce the heat to low, and cook without removing the lid (we don't want any of that steam to escape!) for exactly 16 minutes. Immediately turn off the heat. Let the rice finish steaming, covered, for 10 minutes.

⑥ **Make the lemony yogurt:**

+ Finely grate the zest of 1 lemon and 1 garlic clove into a small bowl. Stir in 1 cup whole-milk yogurt. Cut the lemon in half. Squeeze in the juice of the lemon halves. Season the yogurt with salt.

⑦ **Chop some stuff:**

+ Cut 4 ounces snap peas crosswise into 1-inch pieces.

+ Coarsely chop ¾ cup roasted, salted pistachios.

+ Finely chop the leaves and tender stems from 1 large bunch of dill, discarding the tough stems. You should have about 1 cup chopped. Yep, that's a ton of dill.

+ Cut a lemon in half.

⑧ **Fluff and finish:**

+ Transfer the chicken to a plate. Fluff the rice with a fork.

+ Add the snap peas, chopped dill, pistachios, and the juice of the halved lemon, fluffing with a fork as you incorporate them all. Taste and adjust the seasoning as needed. Divide the rice and chicken among shallow serving bowls or plates. Spoon some of the lemony yogurt over top and finish with a few cranks of black pepper.

Really Reliable Rice

Makes 3 cups

PANTRY

1 cup long- or short-grain white rice

½ teaspoon kosher salt

People are scared of cooking rice. You know what, eff it—*I'm* scared of cooking rice. Many bad things can happen to what should be just a simple pot of rice: too much water and rice turns to a gluey mush; too little water and the rice is crunchy. Sometimes it sticks to the pan. Sometimes it cooks unevenly. I've made my fair share of less-than-perfect rice, and through it all I've landed on a method that I find to be more or less reliable and consistent. The key to fluffy rice is a combination of both boiling the rice in just the right amount of water, then allowing that water to steam the rice to completion. Really, it's as simple as rinse, simmer, steam, fluff. Do not rush or skimp on any of the steps here; they are crucial to your success.

1. **Rinse the rice:** Place 1 cup white rice in a fine-mesh strainer and set it under cold running water. Using your hands, swoosh the rice around in a circular motion while the water runs through it, until the water runs clear. This could take up to 2 full minutes, no joke. Don't skimp![1]

2. **Steam the rice:**

   + Shake the strainer to allow the excess water to drain off the rice. Place the rice in a medium (3-quart) saucepan that has a tight-fitting lid (this is also crucial, as the lid must trap in the steam to cook the rice properly). Stir in 1¼ cups cold water and ½ teaspoon salt.

   + Set the rice over medium-high heat. Don't walk away just yet; stay nearby. As soon as the water comes to a boil, cover the pot with the lid and reduce the heat to very low. Set a timer for 16 minutes.

   + After 16 minutes, remove the pot from the heat (still covered!) and let the rice steam, covered, for at least 10 minutes. Remove the lid and fluff that fluffy rice with a fork before serving.

---

[1] This is a crucial step in ridding the rice of any starch that clings to its surface, which can hinder fluffiness—and that would be a terrible thing! We're going for extreme fluff.

Big Beans & Spicy Greens Gratin

Serves 4 to 6

PRODUCE

8 garlic cloves

1 large white onion

1 bunch broccoli rabe (about 1 pound)

1 bunch kale, Swiss chard, spinach, or mustard greens (about 1 pound)

DAIRY

8 ounces sharp provolone, cheddar, or Gruyère cheese

2 cups heavy cream

PANTRY

¼ cup plus 3 tablespoons extra-virgin olive oil

1 cup panko bread crumbs

Kosher salt

3 (14.5-ounce) cans butter beans, gigante beans, or other white beans

1 teaspoon red pepper flakes

This is a baked casserole kinda dish that I can truly get behind. It's basically mac and cheese in disguise. Of course, beans are not pasta, but they serve a similar role in this dish, soaking up all of the flavorful, creamy sauce as they bake. And the best part is, all you've got to do is crack open a couple of cans and throw them in, which means it's truly a one-pot meal. A generous blanket of panko bread crumbs on top brings a welcome layer of crunch to this luscious gratin. Not a fan of broccoli rabe? Chopped-up broccolini or broccoli, or double the kale, will be equally delicious. On a slightly unrelated note, one day I asked my husband to describe my food in a few words. His response: "Fun, funky, farty." I've come to realize that (*a*) he is not wrong, (*b*) that is probably what I should have titled my book, and (*c*) this dish is the perfect example of his assessment.

---

① Preheat the oven to 450°F.

② **Toast the panko:** Heat 3 tablespoons olive oil in a large Dutch oven over medium heat. Add 1 cup panko and season with ½ teaspoon salt. Cook, stirring frequently, until the panko is light golden brown, 4 to 5 minutes.[1] Transfer the panko to a bowl to cool. Wipe out the Dutch oven.

③ **Do some prep:**

+ Grate 8 ounces sharp provolone cheese (about 2 cups) and transfer to a medium bowl.

+ Firmly smash and peel 8 garlic cloves. Roughly chop the smashed garlic into smaller pieces.

+ Cut 1 large white onion in half through the root end. Peel and discard the skin. Thinly slice the onion through the root end.

+ Drain and rinse 3 (14.5-ounce) cans of butter beans in a fine-mesh strainer.

④ **Start the gratin:** Heat ¼ cup olive oil in the Dutch oven over medium heat. Add the onions and garlic and cook, stirring occasionally, until the onions are soft and beginning to brown at the edges, 10 to 12 minutes.

⑤ **Meanwhile prep the greens:**

+ Trim off the bottom inch of 1 bunch of broccoli rabe, then chop the bunch crosswise into roughly 2-inch pieces.

+ Strip the leaves of 1 bunch of kale and tear them into 3- to 4-inch pieces.

⑥ **Assemble the gratin:**

+ Add the broccoli rabe to the onions and cook, tossing often with tongs to encourage it to begin to cook down and wilt, about 1 minute. Add the kale, 1 tablespoon salt, and 1 teaspoon red pepper flakes. Cook, stirring, until the kale and broccoli rabe turn bright green and lose some of their volume, 3 to 5 minutes. Remove from the heat.

+ Stir in 2 cups heavy cream and the drained beans. The mixture will look loose but will reduce significantly in the oven as it bakes.

+ Working one handful at a time, stir in all but one large handful of the grated cheese into the pot. It won't fully melt at this point; that will happen in the oven.

⑦ **Bake the gratin:** Scatter the reserved handful of cheese over the top, followed by the toasted panko. Transfer the Dutch oven to the oven and bake until bubbling and thick and a golden brown crust forms around the edges, 20 to 25 minutes. Let sit 5 minutes before serving.

---

[1] It's important to toast the bread crumbs fully, because they won't really take on much more color in the oven, as the moisture in the dish inhibits their browning.

Salading

The Cae Sal

Serves 4

PRODUCE
1 garlic clove

1 lemon

4 romaine hearts

DAIRY
2 large eggs

2 ounces grated Parmesan cheese (about ½ cup), plus more for serving

PANTRY
½ crusty baguette (about 6 ounces)

2 tablespoons extra-virgin olive oil

Kosher salt

Coarsely ground black pepper

4 oil-packed anchovy fillets

1 teaspoon Dijon mustard

½ cup canola or vegetable oil

1 teaspoon Worcestershire sauce

If you only knew the things I'd do for a Cae Sal. Or perhaps you already do. To call it my brand would be to grossly underrepresent what this salad means to me. It is the Greatest Salad of All Time (GSOAT). I've spent a lot of time thinking about, talking about, eating, considering, and developing what I believe is the platonic ideal of a Caesar salad—crisp, cold romaine hearts, a thick peppery, garlicky dressing, lots and lots of Parmesan cheese, homemade croutons, and enough lemon to make it all pop. And while technically you are going to have to make a mayonnaise from scratch in preparing this dressing, it's actually super-duper easy and not as prone to failure as you might think. Trust.

---

① **Make the croutons:** Preheat the oven to 350°F. Tear ½ of a baguette into irregular 1-inch pieces; you should end up with about 3 cups of torn bread. Toss on a rimmed baking sheet with 2 tablespoons olive oil, ½ teaspoon kosher salt, and a few good cranks of black pepper until well coated. Bake until deeply golden brown and crisp, 12 to 14 minutes. Let cool.

② **Make the dressing:**[1]

✦ Separate the yolks and whites of 2 large eggs. Place the yolks in a large bowl (where you'll build your dressing) and reserve the whites for another use. **Here's a quick and easy way to do it!**

✦ Finely grate 1 garlic clove and the zest of about half of a lemon into the large bowl. Squeeze in the juice of half of the lemon.

✦ Finely chop 4 anchovies, then mash them to a paste, using the side of a chef's knife until homogeneous; add to the large bowl.

✦ Add 1 teaspoon Dijon mustard and whisk everything to combine. Place a damp kitchen towel underneath the bowl to stabilize it so it doesn't slip 'n' slide all over the place as you whisk in the oil.

✦ Starting with a very thin stream at first, whisking constantly as you go, incorporate ½ cup of canola oil into the yolk mixture until it is thick, creamy, and pale yellow. **Here's a quick tutorial on how to make mayonnaise by hand!**

✦ Whisk in ¾ teaspoon kosher salt, ¾ teaspoon black pepper, 1 teaspoon Worcestershire sauce, and 1 ounce grated Parmesan cheese (¼ cup). Taste the dressing on a leaf of romaine—it should be salty, cheesy, and lemony. Make any adjustments necessary until it tastes so good that you'd be happy eating a bowl of it alone with a side of crouts.

③ **Prep the lettuce:** Tear the leaves of 4 romaine hearts into 2-inch pieces and transfer them to the bowl of dressing. Squeeze the juice of half of the lemon over the romaine, season with salt, and toss the leaves to coat, avoiding incorporating any of the dressing beneath just yet.[2]

④ **Serve:** Add the croutons and gently toss the lettuce with your hands until well coated. Add 1 ounce grated Parmesan cheese (¼ cup) and toss again. Divide among plates and top with more grated Parmesan and black pepper.

---

[1] You are about to make mayonnaise by hand, BUT it's not as hard as it sounds. The mustard, garlic, and anchovies that get mixed into the egg yolk will help support the emulsion.

[2] It's always a good idea to preseason your greens with some acid and salt so they are zippy and zingy and hold up to the dressing. The lettuce contains water, which is going to dilute the flavor of the dressing, so you'll always need a little extra acid to combat that.

Simple Greens with Any Vinegar-ette

Serves 4

PRODUCE

5 ounces tender lettuces, such as Boston, Bibb, and/or arugula

1 small shallot

1 cup picked tender herbs, such as parsley, cilantro, mint, basil, dill, tarragon, and/or chives

PANTRY

1½ teaspoons Dijon mustard

½ teaspoon honey, maple syrup, or sugar

Kosher salt and freshly ground black pepper

2 tablespoons mixed vinegars, such as red wine, white wine, sherry, rice, and apple cider vinegars

¼ cup extra–virgin olive oil

Flaky sea salt, for serving

Everyone needs a go-to green salad in their back pocket for those times when the majority of your effort is being spent elsewhere in the meal (Butter-basted steak! Roast chicken! Perfect Bolognese!). This salad dressing is extra special because it calls for any, yes, ANY, combo of vinegars you have on hand in your kitchen and a few other common pantry ingredients to create a workhorse dressing that is infinitely riffable. This is a great opportunity to play around with all of those vinegars that have been sitting in your cupboard unused, and breathe new life into them. Combining them makes for a more dynamic and interesting dressing, but you can certainly stick to just one if that's all you have. The most important thing is to be sure your vinegar-to-oil ratio is correct (1 part vinegar to 2 parts oil).

---

① **Do some prep:**

✦ If using whole heads of lettuce, separate the leaves and discard the knobby root ends. Submerge the lettuces in cold water and swoosh them around to release any grit. Drain and spin with a salad spinner until VERY dry.[1]

✦ Finely chop half of a shallot. Transfer to a large serving bowl. **Never chopped a shallot before? I can help you with that.**

② **Make the dressing:**

✦ To the shallot, add 1½ teaspoons Dijon mustard, ½ teaspoon honey, ¼ teaspoon kosher salt, a few good cranks of black pepper, and 2 tablespoons vinegar, whisking to combine. Slowly drizzle in ¼ cup olive oil, whisking constantly until the dressing is emulsified.[2]

✦ Taste and adjust the dressing if needed; it should taste zippy and zingy but also balanced with a touch of sweetness and some bite from the mustard and black pepper. Transfer half of the dressing to a small bowl, leaving the rest behind.[3]

③ **Serve:** Add the lettuces and herbs to the bowl and use your hands to very gently fold to coat them with the dressing. Now you can add that remaining dressing as you see fit; maybe it needs just a smidge, maybe it needs all of it—you decide. Season the salad with flaky sea salt and fold once more to disperse. Serve immediately.

---

[1] Water is the enemy of a crisp, perky salad, and it also repels olive oil, which means if there's any water left behind, your salad dressing won't cling to the leaves, and that would be a total bummer.

[2] "Emulsified" is just a fancy term for thick and creamy with no signs of oil and vinegar separation. A properly emulsified dressing has a totally different mouthfeel than one that is "broken," or not properly emulsified. The latter feels oily on your palate, not smooth and creamy.

[3] This is a safety against overdressed lettuces, because as we all know, you can always add dressing, but you can't take it away. You'll likely use the rest, but this is just best practice for dainty lettuces.

Grapefruit & Burrata Salad with Chile Crisp

Serves 4

PRODUCE
3 garlic cloves
1 medium shallot
2 grapefruit (about 2 pounds total)

DAIRY
8 ounces burrata cheese

PANTRY
⅓ cup extra-virgin olive oil
1 cinnamon stick
Kosher salt
2 teaspoons red pepper flakes
Flaky sea salt, for serving
Crusty bread, for serving (optional)

While, yes, technically this recipe lives within the salad chapter, you will soon learn that this dish is ALL ABOUT THE CHILE CRISP. The best-known version of store-bought chile crisp is made by Lao Gan Ma, which produces myriad chile sauces in China. Its beloved chile crisp is an addictive spicy chile-garlic condiment that's taken the world by storm. If you can get your hands on a jar of it, you won't regret it. Until then, here's a simple version of it you can make at home. The chile crisp gets drizzled over a salad of torn grapefruit and burrata cheese, and if you're smart you'll scoop the whole thing up and schmear it on a piece of crusty bread. This is something of a fruit salad that just so happens to be best enjoyed on toast, and I think we're truly blessed to live in a time when salad no longer means overdressed mesclun mix!

① **Make the chile crisp:**

+ Thinly slice 3 garlic cloves.
+ Thinly slice 1 shallot crosswise into rings.
+ Set a fine-mesh strainer over a small heatproof bowl.
+ In a small saucepan set over medium-low heat, combine ⅓ cup olive oil, 1 cinnamon stick, the garlic and shallot, and ½ teaspoon kosher salt. Cook, stirring, until the oil comes to a simmer, about 2 minutes. Continue to cook, stirring with a fork to separate the shallot rings and swirling the pan occasionally, until the shallots and garlic are golden brown, 13 to 15 minutes. Keep a close eye on them in the last few minutes; they can turn from light golden brown to burnt pretty quickly.
+ Pour the shallot oil into the prepared strainer. Discard the cinnamon stick and let the shallots and garlic cool in the strainer for 2 to 3 minutes, then stir them back into the oil they were cooked in, along with 2 teaspoons red pepper flakes.[1]

② **Prep the citrus:** Trim both ends of 2 grapefruit. Use your knife to follow the contours of each piece of fruit, cutting away the peel and pith and leaving behind only the flesh. **Here's the easiest way to remove all that pith.** Cut about half of the citrus crosswise into ½-inch-thick rounds. Tear the remaining citrus into segments with your fingers, discarding the membrane that holds them all together. You're looking for a mix of irregular shapes, which will vary the texture and look of the dish. It honestly doesn't matter how you get there.

③ **Serve:**

+ Tear an 8-ounce ball of burrata into large pieces, arranging them on a large rimmed platter or plate followed by the grapefruit pieces.
+ Spoon the chile crisp over everything. Season well with flaky sea salt—it'll need quite a bit to make all of that creamy burrata really pop. Serve with crusty bread, if desired.

---

[1] Cooling them outside the oil first ensures that the aromatics stay crisp once they're added back to the oil.

The Minimalist Wedge

Serves 4

PRODUCE
4 garlic cloves
1 bunch chives
2 lemons
1 large iceberg lettuce head (about 1½ pounds)

DAIRY
1 cup plain whole-milk Greek yogurt or sour cream

PANTRY
2 tablespoons extra-virgin olive oil, plus more for drizzling
½ cup panko bread crumbs
Kosher salt
½ cup mayonnaise
Freshly ground black pepper

These days, when there's a wedge salad on a menu, it tends to be a wedge salad of the maximalist persuasion, loaded up like a tray of nachos. This wedge is all about restraint. It is a wedge salad reduced to its most essential, fundamental parts. No bells or whistles. If you ask me, what makes a great wedge truly great is the combination of extremely crisp, cold, refreshing iceberg lettuce (a truly superior lettuce) with an overabundance of tangy, creamy dressing. As far as I'm concerned, the rest of it is fun but unnecessary. You'll double-dress your lettuce, first with fresh lemon juice, kosher salt, and extra-virgin olive oil, and then again with the aforementioned tangy, creamy dressing, to ensure no leaf is left undressed. I will rarely say this, but you should definitely feel free to dress the shit out of this salad. That's what the wedge is all about.

---

① **Make the garlicky panko:**

✦ Lightly smash and peel 4 garlic cloves. Set 1 aside for the dressing.

✦ In a large nonstick skillet, cook 2 tablespoons olive oil and the 3 smashed garlic cloves over medium-low heat, swirling the pan often, until the garlic is fragrant and lightly golden brown, 3 to 5 minutes. Add ½ cup panko and stir to coat evenly in the oil. Cook, stirring often, so the panko toasts evenly, until golden brown all over, 4 to 5 minutes; season with ½ teaspoon salt.

✦ Transfer the panko to a shallow bowl to cool. Pluck out and discard the garlic cloves.

② **Make the ranchy yogurt dressing:**

✦ In a small bowl, stir together 1 cup Greek yogurt, ½ cup mayonnaise, 1 teaspoon salt, and lots of black pepper.

✦ Finely chop 1 bunch of chives. Stir half of the chives into the dressing and set the remaining chives aside for garnish.

✦ Finely grate the remaining 1 garlic clove and the zest of half of a lemon into the dressing. Halve and juice the lemon and stir in the juice. Add a splash or two of cold water to the dressing, stirring to combine, until it reaches a drizzle-able consistency. And of course, always taste and reseason the dressing after adding the water so it doesn't taste flat.[1]

③ **Assemble:**

✦ Remove and discard any floppy, wilty outer layers from a large head of iceberg lettuce. Cut the iceberg into quarters through the root end so you have 4 wedges, leaving the core intact.

✦ Arrange the wedges on a serving platter. Squeeze the juice of the second lemon over the wedges, taking care to get the juice inside some of the layers of lettuce. Season each wedge (again, both inside and out) with salt and drizzle with olive oil.

✦ Generously drizzle the dressing over each wedge, spooning some of it into the layers of leaves and allowing some to drip down onto the plate.[2] You may have some dressing left over; serve that alongside.

✦ Scatter the panko and reserved chives over top and finish with black pepper.

---

[1] It should be zippy and bright, and even slightly too intense on its own, since it's ultimately going to be combined with the salad, which will mellow it out.

[2] There is so much water in iceberg lettuce that you really have to go for it with the dressing in order not to dilute the flavor too much.

The Big Italian

Serves 4

PRODUCE
½ small red onion
1 small garlic clove
1½ pounds ripe, juicy tomatoes (any kind)
2 cups basil leaves

DAIRY
8 ounces fresh mozzarella cheese

MEAT
1 (6-ounce) piece spicy salami or soppressata

PANTRY
6 ounces crusty sesame bread or ciabatta (about ½ loaf)
8 tablespoons extra-virgin olive oil (½ cup), plus more for drizzling
Kosher salt
¼ cup red wine vinegar
1 teaspoon sugar
¾ cup canned quartered artichokes
12 pickled pepperoncini or other pickled peppers

IMO, when it comes to sandwiches, it really doesn't get more iconic than a fully-loaded Italian hoagie. I've taken all the elements of an Italian sub and turned them into a big shareable panzanella-style salad. Don't worry, there's still plenty of bread. This is a study in how to eat a big-ass sandwich and convince yourself you're actually eating a salad. It's remarkable what the brain can do in the name of consumption. Toasting the bread first dries it out, which means that once it gets tossed with a vinegary dressing, it doesn't turn to total mush. Feel free to mix things up and use whatever deli meats and cheeses you have on hand—mortadella, bresaola, prosciutto, provolone, and Parm would all be excellent choices.

① Preheat the oven to 425°F.

② **Toast the bread:** Cut the bread into 1-inch-thick slices. Tear the slices into roughly 1-inch irregular, craggy pieces and toss them on a large rimmed baking sheet with 2 tablespoons olive oil and ¼ teaspoon salt. Bake until golden brown on the outside and crisp, 12 to 15 minutes. Let cool.

③ **Macerate the onions and start the vinaigrette:**

  ✦ Thinly slice ½ small red onion and add it to a large bowl.

  ✦ Finely grate 1 small garlic clove into the bowl. Add ¼ cup red wine vinegar, 1 teaspoon sugar, and 1 teaspoon salt and toss to combine.[1]

④ **Prep and assemble the salad:**

  ✦ Drain the liquid from ¾ cup canned quartered artichokes and, if they are in oil, rinse them in a fine-mesh strainer and pat them dry. (That oil usually isn't particularly tasty.)

  ✦ Cut 1 (6-ounce) piece of salami in half lengthwise. Slice it crosswise into half-moons about the thickness of a nickel.

  ✦ Trim and discard the stems of 12 pepperoncini. Add the artichokes, salami, and pepperoncini to the bowl.

  ✦ If using large tomatoes, cut them in half. Cut around the core, into irregularly shaped 1½-inch pieces (about the size of your croutons). If using cherry tomatoes, cut them in half. Toss the tomatoes into the bowl to coat them in all those vinegary juices.

  ✦ Tear 8 ounces mozzarella into pieces about the same size as the tomatoes and add them right to the bowl along with 2 cups basil and 6 tablespoons olive oil.

⑤ **Serve:** Toss everything several times to encourage the bread to soak up the juices. Taste and add more salt if you think it needs it. Drizzle with more olive oil and serve.[2]

---

[1] Letting the onion and garlic sit in the vinegar will lightly pickle them and mellow out their raw flavor while you do the rest of your prep.

[2] The salad can be made and assembled without the croutons and basil up to 4 hours in advance; add them at the last minute, otherwise the croutons will get overly soggy and the basil will oxidize (turn black) as it sits in the vinegar.

Napa Cabbage Salad with Shredded Chicken, Cotija & Corn Nuts

Serves 4

PRODUCE
1 large garlic clove
2 limes
1 large napa cabbage (about 3½ pounds)
6 small radishes
1 cup packed cilantro leaves and tender stems

DAIRY
½ cup sour cream
½ cup grated cotija cheese, plus more for serving

MEAT
1 whole store-bought rotisserie chicken

PANTRY
¼ cup mayonnaise
Kosher salt
1 (7.5-ounce) can chipotle peppers in adobo sauce
½ cup toasted corn (such as Corn Nuts) or Fritos
Freshly ground black pepper

You likely don't immediately think of cabbage when you think of salad, but this recipe is a testament to just how salad-able the humble cabbage really is. Napa cabbage is softer and more tender than, say, green or purple cabbage, which makes it best suited for this recipe. Using your hands to really squeeze and scrunch the cabbage after it's been seasoned with salt and lime juice will help break it down and tenderize it even further. Think massaged kale, but make it cabbage. This multitextured salad is a great way to quickly turn a store-bought rotisserie chicken into a meal—plus, the leftovers hold up for an easy lunch the next day, in a way that most salads do not. Mexican cotija cheese adds hits of salty crumbles, and you know much I love some salty richness!

① **Make the dressing:**

✦ In a large bowl, whisk together ½ cup sour cream, ¼ cup mayonnaise, ½ cup grated cotija cheese, and ¾ teaspoon salt.

✦ Add ¼ cup adobo sauce from 1 (7.5-ounce) can of chipotles in adobo.

✦ Finely grate 1 large garlic clove and the zest of ½ of the lime into the dressing. Squeeze the juice of both limes into the dressing. Whisk well to combine.

② **Prep and scrunch the cabbage:**

✦ Remove and discard any floppy, wilty, or bruised outer leaves from 1 large napa cabbage. Cut the cabbage in quarters through the root. Thinly slice each quarter crosswise into roughly ½-inch-thick strips.

✦ Add the cabbage to the bowl of dressing, season it with ¾ teaspoon salt, and squeeze and scrunch with your hands to help massage the dressing into the cabbage and break down some of that toughness.

③ **Prep the add-ins:**

✦ Remove and discard the skin of a rotisserie chicken. Pull the chicken meat off the bones, shredding it into bite-size pieces and adding it to the bowl of cabbage as you do.

✦ Thinly slice 6 radishes crosswise into coins and coarsely chop 1 cup packed cilantro leaves and tender stems; add to the salad.

✦ Coarsely chop or crush ½ cup toasted corn with the bottom of a small saucepan or other heavy, flat object; set aside for garnish.

④ **Toss and assemble:** Using tongs, toss the salad to evenly distribute and coat all the ingredients. You can be kind of aggressive with the tossing, since none of these ingredients are particularly delicate. Season the salad with more salt and black pepper as needed.

⑤ **Serve:** Divide the salad among bowls, piling it high 'cause it's more fun to eat that way. Scatter the chopped toasted corn over top, along with more grated cotija cheese.

Sneaky Cottage Cheese Salad

Serves 4

PRODUCE
1 lemon
1 small garlic clove
2 Persian cucumbers, or ½ English (hothouse) cucumber
4 Little Gem lettuce heads or 3 romaine hearts
1 cup dill leaves

DAIRY
½ cup full-fat cottage cheese

PANTRY
½ cup walnuts or almonds
3 tablespoons extra-virgin olive oil
Kosher salt and freshly ground black pepper

This is a sneaky salad. Sneaky because if you just sat down and ate it, you probably would not be able to put your finger on what makes the dressing so sassy. SURPRISE! It's cottage cheese. Cottage cheese has made a major comeback in the last few years, and I for one couldn't be happier about it. Forget everything you thought you knew about the sad, watery, wan diet food of many decades ago, and make this tangy, herbaceous, bright salad of Little Gem lettuce and toasted walnuts that gets bathed in a cottage cheese vinaigrette. A note on Little Gems—they can be tricky to find, but do seek them out whenever you can. They are sweeter, crunchier, and more tender than romaine, not to mention cute as hell. Romaine will do in a pinch.

---

① Preheat the oven to 325°F.

② **Toast the walnuts:** Spread the walnuts out on a rimmed baking sheet and toast in the oven until deeply golden brown throughout, 8 to 10 minutes. Check to be sure they're toasted all the way through by cracking into one. Let the walnuts cool.

③ **Make the dressing:**

✦ Finely grate the zest of about a quarter of a lemon into a large serving bowl. Cut the lemon in half and add the juice from both halves to the bowl.

✦ Finely grate 1 small garlic clove into the lemon juice.

✦ Whisk in ½ cup full-fat cottage cheese, 3 tablespoons olive oil, and lots of black pepper. Season the dressing with salt.

④ **Prep and assemble the salad:**

✦ Cut 2 Persian cucumbers on a bias, rotating the cucumbers as you cut to create 1-inch oblique spears. **Not familiar with the roll cut? Pull up this quick video and I'll show you.**

✦ Chop the toasted walnuts.

✦ Trim off the root end of 4 heads of Little Gems and discard any floppy or bruised outer leaves. Separate the leaves from each head. Tear any large leaves in half, leaving the cute little ones whole (rip big romaine leaves in half or into thirds). Wash and dry them thoroughly; transfer to the bowl with the dressing and toss.

✦ Tear 1 cup dill leaves into smaller pieces and add to the bowl along with the cucumbers and walnuts, tossing everything until all the leaves are well coated. Season the salad with more salt and black pepper as needed. Serve it up.

Ants on a Log
Cel Sal

Serves 4

PRODUCE
10 celery stalks
1 Granny Smith apple
1 small shallot
1 cup packed mint or basil leaves

PANTRY
3 tablespoons unseasoned rice vinegar
1 teaspoon honey
½ teaspoon red pepper flakes
3 tablespoons extra-virgin olive oil
Kosher salt
¾ cup roasted, salted peanuts
8 Medjool dates

There's a reason kids go buck wild for peanut-butter-filled celery stalks topped with raisins, and it's not just because they're fun to look at. It's all about the contrast of sweet and savory, fatty and lean in this crunchy, refreshing celery salad inspired by the beloved "ants on a log" snick-snack of our childhood. I've thrown some adult ingredients in the mix—dates, shallot, fresh herbs—so you won't feel like a four-year-old as you eat it. It's really quite mature. This salad is a study in textures—and proof that salads don't need to contain leafy greens to be called salads. If you're not eating celery salads, I think you're really missing out.

① **Make the dressing:** In a large bowl, whisk together 3 tablespoons rice vinegar, 1 teaspoon honey, and ½ teaspoon red pepper flakes. Slowly stream in 3 tablespoons olive oil, whisking constantly until well combined.[1] Season with salt.

② **Prep the salad, adding the ingredients to the bowl of dressing:**

✦ Pluck off any leaves from 10 celery stalks and set aside. Thinly slice the celery on the bias; add it to the dressing.

✦ Cut out the core of 1 apple by cutting off 4 lobes around it. Arrange the lobes cut-side down on a cutting board and thinly slice them crosswise into half-moons.

✦ Thinly slice 1 small shallot crosswise into rings.

✦ Coarsely chop ¾ cup roasted, salted peanuts or crush them with the bottom of a mug or glass measuring cup. Add the apple slices, shallot rings, and crushed peanuts to the bowl.

✦ Tear the dates into smaller pieces, discarding the pits; add them to the bowl along with 1 cup mint leaves and the reserved celery leaves.

③ **Serve:** Toss everything well to coat in the dressing. Season with salt until it tastes really delicious and serve immediately.

[1] If you add it all at once, you will have a much harder time emulsifying (incorporating) the oil into the vinegar.

Peach & Tomato Salad with Sizzled Halloumi

Serves 4

PRODUCE
2 ripe peaches or nectarines

1 pound ripe heirloom tomatoes

1 lemon

1 cup basil leaves

DAIRY
1 (8-ounce) piece halloumi cheese

PANTRY
5 tablespoons extra-virgin olive oil

2 tablespoons yellow, brown, or black mustard seeds

¾ teaspoon freshly ground black pepper

Kosher salt

Flaky sea salt, for finishing

I'm not sure which part of this salad I am more obsessed with: the slabs of crispy, hot, melty halloumi (a popular Greek cow's-milk cheese) or the crunchy mustard seeds that get toasted in olive oil and somehow end up tasting like buttered popcorn. Peaches and tomatoes get dressed in lemon vinaigrette to macerate for a few minutes, which gives them a chance to release some of their juicy juices and transforms the vinaigrette into something more special than it was at the start. The result is a wild caprese-esque summer salad, and I think you're gonna love it.

---

① **Toast the mustard seeds:** In a small saucepan, combine 3 tablespoons olive oil, 2 tablespoons mustard seeds, and ½ teaspoon black pepper. Cook the seeds over medium heat, swirling the pan, until they begin to pop and become fragrant, 3 to 5 minutes.[1] Remove from the heat and pour the oil into a large bowl, scraping any seeds and spices that stick to the saucepan into the bowl along with it; season the oil with ½ teaspoon kosher salt.

② **Prep the salad, adding the ingredients to the bowl of mustard seeds:**

+ Cut 2 peaches into wedges, discarding the pits.

+ Cut 1 pound tomatoes in half through the root end, then cut them into irregular wedge-shaped pieces about the size of your peaches, discarding the core.

+ Cut 1 lemon in half and squeeze the juice of both halves into the bowl with the peaches and tomatoes. Season with kosher salt and gently toss everything with your hands.

+ Add 1 cup basil leaves and toss to combine. Give the salad a taste and make any necessary seasoning adjustments. (More salt? More lemon?) Let this sit while you carry on.

③ **Sear the halloumi:**

+ Cut 1 (8-ounce) block of halloumi in half on a diagonal to create 2 triangular pieces. Cut the halloumi into ½-inch-thick triangular planks. Break the planks in half and let them dry on a bed of paper towels to wick away some of the surface moisture.[2]

+ Heat 2 tablespoons olive oil in a 12-inch cast-iron skillet over medium-high heat. Add the halloumi in a single layer and sear until deeply brown on both sides and soft and melty inside, 2 to 3 minutes per side.

④ **Serve:** Arrange the halloumi on a serving platter. Add the peaches and tomatoes and pour any remaining vinaigrette over everything. Season with flaky sea salt.

---

[1] Gently heating the spices up in the oil "blooms" the spices, meaning it helps draw out some of their flavor and aroma and infuses the oil.

[2] This will aid in browning. Water is the enemy of caramelization, so the drier, the better.

Winter Greek Salad

Serves 4

PRODUCE
1 large shallot

1 small garlic clove

1 lemon

1 tablespoon fresh oregano leaves, or 1½ teaspoons dried

2 English (hothouse) cucumbers

2 Fuyu persimmons

DAIRY
2 (4-ounce) blocks feta cheese

PANTRY
¼ cup red wine vinegar

½ cup extra-virgin olive oil

Kosher salt and freshly ground black pepper

1 cup Castelvetrano olives

Stuffed grape leaves (a.k.a. dolmas), for serving (optional)

As someone who craves sun like she craves salt, there are depressingly few things to look forward to come wintertime. The two things that make the miserable, cold waiting game tolerable: Christmas and persimmons. You should know that there are two widely available varieties of persimmon, Fuyu and Hachiya. Hachiya are the crown jewel of the persimmon family but ONLY when they are so unbelievably ripe, soft, and heavy that they risk bursting in your palm. Do not eat them otherwise—they contain absurdly high levels of tannins when unripe, and can taste very unpleasant. Truthfully, they are hard to come by, because more often than not, they bruise and rot before they ripen to their fullest potential. Fuyu, on the other hand, are pretty much always down to clown. They are squatter in shape and can be eaten at varying stages of ripeness. They get sweeter as they ripen but even when eaten semi-ripe and still firm, their almost pear-like, snappy texture is a delight. Take my word for it and let them stand in for tomatoes during the wintertime.

---

① **Make the dressing, adding the ingredients to a large bowl:**

+ Thinly slice 1 large shallot lengthwise. Add ¼ cup red wine vinegar, ½ cup olive oil, 1½ teaspoons salt, and lots of black pepper.

+ Finely grate in 1 garlic clove and the zest of half a lemon. Cut the lemon in half and squeeze in the juice of 1 half.

+ Lightly smash 1 cup Castelvetrano olives with the bottom of a mug or glass measuring cup. Discard the pits and add the flesh to the bowl.

+ Tear 1 tablespoon oregano leaves in half as you add them to the bowl. Let the shallot and garlic sit in the dressing to macerate while you prep the salad—the dressing will only improve with time.

② **Prep the veg:**

+ Trim the ends of 2 English (hothouse) cucumbers. Cut the cucumbers into 2-inch(ish) spears by making bias cuts, rotating the cucumber a quarter turn, making another bias cut, rotating again, etc., etc. This is called a roll cut, and it's really hard to explain in words so **just pull up this video and it will all make a lot more sense.** However you get there, you want 2-inch pieces of cukes.

+ Slice 2 Fuyu persimmons crosswise into ⅛-inch-thick rounds, discarding the stem and root ends. Cut the persimmon rounds in half to create half-moons.

+ Cut 2 (4-ounce) blocks of feta crosswise into thin planks.

③ **Combine and serve:**

+ Add the cukes and persimmons to the dressing and toss gently with your hands. Season with salt. Divide the salad among 4 serving bowls, reserving some of the dressing that's accumulated at the bottom for drizzling.

+ Break the feta planks into smaller pieces and scatter them over each bowl. Drizzle the remaining dressing over each salad. Finish with a crank of black pepper and nestle a few stuffed grape leaves in each bowl (if desired).

Cold & Crunchy Green Beans with Garlicky Pistachio Vinaigrette

Serves 4

PRODUCE
1½ pounds green beans, wax beans, or romano beans
1 small garlic clove
2 lemons

DAIRY
1½ ounces grated Parmesan cheese (about ⅓ cup)

PANTRY
Kosher salt
¾ cup roasted, salted pistachios
⅓ cup extra-virgin olive oil
Freshly ground black pepper

Green beans are fibrous and stringy when they're raw, so they almost always benefit from some amount of cooking to help break that down and tenderize them. If you blanch them (a.k.a. boil them) in well-salted water for a few minutes and then immediately plunge them into an ice bath to stop the cooking, they end up tender and snappy but retain their bright green color. Triple win. It also definitely doesn't hurt to then soak said beans in a zippy, bright, garlicky, Parmy vinaigrette and toss them with tons of chopped salted pistachios. Basically, I'm never eating a hot green bean again. I just don't think they're as delicious and refreshing as cold ones, and I'm trying to eat only delicious things in my life.

---

① Bring 4 quarts water and 1½ cups salt to a boil in a large pot.[1]

② **Do some prep:**

✦ Finely chop ¾ cup roasted, salted pistachios until all the pieces are about the size of a lentil.

✦ Trim the ends of 1½ pounds green beans.

③ **Cook the beans:**

✦ Once the water boils, stir in the beans and cook until just tender but not limp, 5 to 6 minutes.[2]

✦ While the beans cook, fill a large bowl with ice and water. Using a spider strainer or tongs, transfer the cooked beans to the ice bath to stop the cooking. Keep them in the ice bath until completely cool.

④ **Make the dressing:**

✦ Finely grate 1 garlic clove and the zest of 1 lemon into a medium bowl. Cut the zested lemon and a second lemon in half and add the juice from both lemons to the bowl, whisking it all to combine.

✦ Slowly stream in ⅓ cup olive oil, whisking as you go. Stir in 1½ ounces grated Parmesan cheese (about ⅓ cup). Season the dressing with salt and lots of black pepper. Stir in the chopped pistachios.

⑤ **Drain and assemble:**

✦ Drain the beans, then transfer them to a clean kitchen towel and pat dry.[3]

✦ Add the green beans to the bowl of dressing, tossing well to coat. Taste and add more salt and black pepper if you think it needs it. Serve them up! These are best served very cold, so keep them covered and refrigerated until serving if you're making them in advance.

---

[1] YES! THAT IS SO MUCH SALT! But the beans are spending only a couple of minutes in the boiling water, and it takes a LOT of salt to penetrate something as fibrous as a green bean. I have tested this outrageous amount of salt, and I promise you, your beans are going to be perfectly seasoned, NOT salty.

[2] Taste one and see if it's done—they shouldn't be fibrous or tough to chew, but you also don't want them to be totally lifeless and mushy. Find that happy, snappy medium.

[3] You want them as dry as possible so as not to introduce any water into the dressing we just made, which will dilute the flavor.

Spicy Creamed Greens with Bacon & Dill

Serves 4 to 6

PRODUCE	MEAT
10 garlic cloves	6 ounces cold thick-cut bacon (about 4 slices)
10 scallions	
2 red Fresno chiles or jalapeños	**FROZEN**
1 cup dill leaves	1½ pounds frozen spinach and/or kale, thawed
DAIRY	**PANTRY**
2 cups heavy cream	1 tablespoon kosher salt, plus more as needed
2 ounces grated Parmesan cheese (about ½ cup)	

In which one of the greatest side dishes America has ever invented gets a minor facelift and becomes my latest and most unhealthy obsession—and hopefully yours, too. Cooking spinach in tons of garlic and even more heavy cream is an undeniably delicious way to go about eating your greens. But throw smoky, salty bacon, spicy fresh chiles, and loads of chopped dill into the mix and the magic really starts to happen. This recipe leans on frozen spinach, mostly because in order to end up with enough creamed greens to feed four to six people, you'd have to wilt down a preposterous amount of fresh spinach. There's nothing wrong with taking the easy way out sometimes.

① **Bang out some prep:**

✦ Thinly slice 10 garlic cloves.

✦ Thinly slice 10 scallions crosswise.

✦ Thinly slice 2 red Fresno chiles crosswise into rounds.[1]

✦ Coarsely chop 1 cup dill leaves.

② **Cook the bacon:**

✦ Cut 6 ounces cold bacon crosswise into ½-inch-wide pieces.[2]

✦ Place the bacon in a large Dutch oven, set it over medium heat, and cook, stirring often, until golden brown and crisp, 10 to 12 minutes.

✦ While the bacon cooks, set 1½ pounds thawed greens in a fine-mesh strainer in your sink and squeeze and press on them firmly to expel as much liquid as possible.

③ **Cook the rest:**

✦ Once the bacon is crisp, add the garlic, scallions, and chiles to the pot and cook, stirring often, until softened but not browned, 3 to 4 minutes.

✦ Add the spinach, 2 cups heavy cream, 1 tablespoon salt, and the chopped dill and stir everything to combine.[3]

✦ Cover the pot, reduce the heat to medium-low, and cook until the greens are completely warmed through and have absorbed most of the heavy cream, 4 to 5 minutes longer. Remove the lid, turn off the heat, and stir in 2 ounces grated Parmesan cheese (½ cup). Taste and add more salt as needed. Transfer the creamed greens to a large serving bowl.

---

[1] It's okay if some of the seeds cling on. If you're spice averse, just use 1 chile, or discard the seeds entirely.

[2] The colder the bacon, the easier it is to cut.

[3] It sounds like a ton of salt, but you just added 2 whole cups of heavy cream to 1½ pounds greens—trust me, it's needed.

Blistered Broccolini with Charred Dates, Lemons & Sesame

Serves 4

PRODUCE
1 pound broccolini
1 lemon
1 garlic clove

PANTRY
½ cup pitted Medjool dates (about 3 ounces)
4 tablespoons extra-virgin olive oil
Kosher salt
1 teaspoon toasted sesame oil

Broccolini is one of those vegetables that can really take an aggressive bit of high heat and benefits from deep, borderline-burnt charring. The thing that makes broccolini so great is that it cooks incredibly fast, so at any given moment you are only about ten minutes away from sitting down to enjoy this dish. Charring the dates caramelizes their natural sugars and brings out an almost toasted-marshmallow-like flavor that contrasts beautifully with the deeply savory side of a charred vegetable such as broccolini.

① **Do some prep:**

+ Trim about 1 inch from the stems of 1 pound broccolini. Halve any very thick stems lengthwise so that they are all about the same thickness.

+ Thinly slice half of the lemon into rounds (discard the thick pithy end). Cut each of those rounds into quarters. We're going to caramelize the lemon pieces. Reserve the remaining lemon half for squeezing later on.

+ Tear ½ cup pitted Medjool dates into smaller bite-size pieces.

② **Get blisterin':**

+ Heat 3 tablespoons of the olive oil in a 12-inch cast-iron skillet over medium-high heat.

+ Add the broccolini and season with salt. Toss it once or twice to evenly coat with oil, then cook, undisturbed, until charred in spots, 3 to 4 minutes. Toss again and continue to cook until bright green, well charred, and tender, 3 to 4 minutes longer. Turn off the heat. Finely grate 1 large garlic clove right into the skillet and toss to coat.[1] Taste a piece of broccolini for seasoning and adjust as needed. Transfer the garlicky broccolini and any little bits left in the pan to a serving plate.

+ Place the skillet over medium heat, add the sliced lemon pieces, torn dates, and the remaining 1 tablespoon olive oil and cook, undisturbed, until the lemons are caramelized in some spots and the dates have darkened in color, 2 minutes longer.

③ **Serve:** Scatter the caramelized lemons and dates over the broccolini and drizzle with 1 teaspoon sesame oil. Finish with a good squeeze of lemon juice.

[1] The heat still present in the skillet will cook the garlic even though it's no longer over a flame.

Charred Cabbage with Salty Peanuts & Nuoc Cham

Serves 4

PRODUCE

1 head purple or green cabbage (3 to 3½ pounds)
3 limes
2 red Fresno chiles or jalapeños
1 garlic clove
¾ cup packed cilantro leaves and tender stems

PANTRY

4 tablespoons extra-virgin olive oil
Kosher salt
3 tablespoons sugar
3 tablespoons fish sauce
½ cup roasted, salted peanuts

Of all the ways to consume a cabbage, I think this may be my favorite. If you're one of those people who feels meh about cabbage, perhaps this could be the recipe that changes that. Cabbage loves a good deep charring to bring out some of its—for lack of a better word—*cabbage-y* flavor. But what cabbage loves even more is to be generously bathed in a bold acidic dressing like Vietnamese *nuoc cham*. If you're not familiar with it, nuoc cham is a pungent, spicy, sour sauce that is a staple in Vietnamese cuisine and has become a go-to flavor bomb of a condiment in my kitchen. Charred cabbage is but one of many ways to use this versatile sauce and is by no means a traditional pairing. For a more traditional application, I encourage you to check out the work of Andrea Nguyen, who has written quite a few landmark cookbooks on Vietnamese cuisine—all of which are definitely worth a deep read.

① Position a rack in the lower third of the oven. Preheat the oven to 450°F.

② **Char the cabbage:**

✦ Remove any floppy, wilty, or sad-looking outer layers from a head of cabbage. Quarter the cabbage through the core.

✦ Place the cabbage quarters in a large bowl and drizzle 3 tablespoons olive oil over them. Toss to coat them in the oil. Season well with salt.

✦ Heat a 12-inch cast-iron skillet over medium–high heat until very hot and nearly smoking, about 4 minutes. Drizzle 1 tablespoon olive oil into the skillet, swirling to coat. Arrange the cabbage wedges in the skillet and cook, undisturbed, until deeply golden brown on the bottom, 8 to 10 minutes. Reserve that bowl!

✦ Using tongs, flip the wedges onto the other cut side and then transfer the skillet to the oven. Roast until the cabbage is tender in the middle when pierced with a knife and deeply golden brown on the bottom, 30 to 40 minutes.

③ **Make the nuoc cham in the reserved bowl:**

✦ Cut 3 limes in half. Squeeze in the juice along with 3 tablespoons sugar, 3 tablespoons fish sauce, and ½ teaspoon salt.

✦ Thinly slice 2 Fresno chiles and add it to the dressing.

✦ Finely grate in 1 garlic clove.

✦ Finely chop ½ cup roasted, salted peanuts and set aside.

④ **Marinate the cabbage:**

✦ Transfer the roasted cabbage wedges to a cutting board and let cool for 5 minutes. Cut each quarter in half crosswise; transfer to a large shallow serving bowl. Season again with salt now that some of the interior parts of the cabbage are exposed.

✦ Pour the dressing over top, turning the cabbage with tongs to coat.

⑤ **Serve:** Top with ¾ cup packed cilantro leaves and tender stems and the chopped peanuts.

Grilled Corn with Sambal-Sesame Butter

Serves 4

PRODUCE
4 ears corn
1 lime

DAIRY
½ cup (1 stick) unsalted butter, at room temperature

PANTRY
¼ cup sambal oelek
1 teaspoon toasted sesame oil
Flaky sea salt
Toasted sesame seeds

In the Northeast, sweet corn is at peak deliciousness at the same time that grilling season is in full swing. But if you happen to live in a place with limited access to a grill, that shouldn't stop you. Shucked corn on the cob can achieve that charred, roasty flavor you associate with grilling simply by giving it some time in a hot, dry cast-iron skillet. The sambal-sesame butter you'll be slathering on the corn would also be epic melted over a seared steak or smeared all over a whole chicken before roasting. A word to the wise: If you can manage to pull your butter out of the fridge an hour or so before tackling this recipe, you'll have a much easier time incorporating the sambal oelek (Indonesian chile sauce) and sesame oil into it at room temperature. If not, cut it into small pieces and let them sit out in the warmest part of your kitchen, or nuke it in 10-second spurts until it's very soft and malleable, but not melted.

① Heat a 12-inch cast-iron skillet over medium-high heat until it's very hot, about 4 minutes.

② **Prep and char the corn:**

+ Shuck 4 ears of corn, discarding the husks and corn silk that stick to the corn. If there are still a few stragglers hanging on, they'll loosen themselves as the corn cooks.

+ Using tongs, arrange the corn in the skillet and cook, rotating slightly every 4 to 5 minutes, until the kernels on all sides are sporadically charred, 15 to 20 minutes total. Set aside.

③ **Meanwhile, make the sambal-sesame butter:**

+ Using a fork, mash together ½ cup (1 stick) room-temperature butter, ¼ cup sambal oelek, and 1 teaspoon sesame oil in a medium bowl until well combined.

+ Finely grate the zest of 1 lime into the butter and stir to incorporate. Cut the lime into 4 wedges for serving.

④ **Serve:** Cut each ear of corn in half crosswise, if you wish. I find they're easier to handle this way, and it helps avoid schmearing butter all over your face as you eat. While still warm, slather each ear generously with sambal-sesame butter and season on all sides with flaky sea salt. Sprinkle with toasted sesame seeds and serve with more sambal-sesame butter and the lime wedges alongside.

Would you rather eat food so salty it burns your mouth or entirely saltless food forevermore?

204

Charred Brussels with Soy Butter & Fried Garlic

Serves 4

PRODUCE
2 pounds Brussels sprouts
4 garlic cloves

DAIRY
5 tablespoons unsalted butter

PANTRY
¼ cup vegetable or canola oil
Kosher salt
2 tablespoons low-sodium soy sauce
2 teaspoons sherry vinegar
¼ teaspoon red pepper flakes
2 tablespoons honey

I'm here to solve a very pressing issue. An issue that involves the proliferation of wan, overcooked, undercharred Brussels sprouts that plague far too many home kitchens. If you've ever had deep-fried Brussels sprouts, you know how delicious those crisp, deeply caramelized edges can be. But frying Brussels sprouts in a tiny apartment kitchen is something I'm simply not willing to do, and I don't think you need to, either. The solution? An empty baking sheet gets thrown into the oven to preheat with the oven, thereby transforming it into something of a large-format skillet. When the Brussels hit the preheated baking sheet, they'll start to sizzle, and crisp immediately—and will take on that beloved deep char after 20 or so minutes in the oven, no hot smelly deep fryer necessary.

① **Preheat your baking sheet:** Place an empty baking sheet in the oven on the bottom rack. Preheat the oven to 450°F.

② **Prep the Brussels and garlic:**

✦ Trim the gnarly brown ends from the Brussels, then cut them in half through the root end. If any of them are particularly small, you can leave those whole—the goal here is that they all cook at the same rate. Place them in a large bowl.

✦ Thinly slice 4 garlic cloves as evenly as possible to ensure that it all crisps at the same rate.

✦ In a small saucepan, cover the garlic with ¼ cup vegetable oil. Set the saucepan over medium heat and cook, swirling the pan often, until all of the garlic is lightly golden brown, 3 to 5 minutes. Remove from the heat and strain the oil through a fine-mesh strainer right into the bowl of Brussels sprouts. Transfer the garlic chips to a small plate to cool. Reserve the saucepan.

✦ Toss the Brussels sprouts in the bowl to coat them evenly with the garlic oil and season lightly with salt.[1]

③ **Cook the Brussels:** Remove the baking sheet from the oven. Add the Brussels and arrange them cut-sides down in a single layer. Return the baking sheet to the bottom rack of the oven and roast until softened and deeply browned on the cut sides, 20 to 25 minutes. Transfer to a serving plate.

④ **Make the soy butter:**

✦ Meanwhile, cut 5 tablespoons butter into ½-inch cubes. They are cut small so that we can gradually add them to the sauce.

✦ In the reserved saucepan, bring 2 tablespoons soy sauce and 1 tablespoon water to a simmer over medium-high heat.

✦ Reduce the heat to medium-low. Begin whisking in the small pieces of butter one at a time, waiting until each has completely melted before adding the next and maintaining a bare simmer the whole time. Once all of the butter has been incorporated, turn off the heat and stir in 2 teaspoons sherry vinegar and ¼ teaspoon red pepper flakes.

⑤ **Serve:** Spoon the soy butter over the Brussels. Drizzle with 2 tablespoons honey and scatter the garlic chips on top.

---

[1] They're going to get doused in soy butter later on, which is already salty, so don't go too crazy with the salt up front.

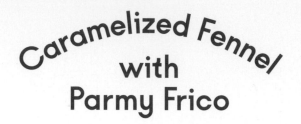

Caramelized Fennel with Parmy Frico

Serves 4

PRODUCE
3 large fennel bulbs with fronds
1 lemon

DAIRY
2 ounces Parmesan cheese, plus more for serving

PANTRY
¼ cup plus 1 tablespoon extra-virgin olive oil
Kosher salt and freshly ground black pepper

This is a love letter to fennel. Why aren't people obsessed with fennel? Fennel is magical because it essentially contains three vegetables in one plant. The bulbs turn more incredibly tender, sweet, and nuanced when roasted until deeply caramelized. The stalks are crunchy, juicy, and anise flavored—perfect for thinly slicing and eating raw. And the fronds, attached to the stalks, are basically free herbs that taste like fennel but look like a wacky, electrocuted version of dill. All parts of fennel are put to use in this recipe, resulting in a dish with many more textures and flavors than there are ingredients. Obviously, the generous coating of Parmesan cheese does no harm here, either. I love you a lot, fennel!

① Position a rack in the lower third of your oven. Preheat the oven to 425°F.

② **Prep the fennel and Parm:**

+ Trim off the long stalks of 3 fennel bulbs, right where they meet the bulb. Reserve about half of them; discard the rest. Trim the root ends of the bulbs if they are looking a little brown and sad. Discard any bruised outer layers of the fennel bulbs. Position each bulb upright on your cutting board, root-end down, and cut into ½-inch-thick planks. Transfer the planks to a large rimmed baking sheet.

+ Drizzle the fennel planks with ¼ cup olive oil, being sure to coat them evenly and all over. Season with salt and black pepper.

+ Using a Microplane, finely grate 1 ounce of Parmesan cheese (about ¼ cup) over the fennel (on top only, no need to flip). Roast until the fennel is deeply caramelized on the underside, 20 to 25 minutes.

+ Remove from the oven and flip each plank. Finely grate 1 ounce more cheese (about ¼ cup) over the caramelized side of the fennel. Return to the oven and roast until tender and browned all over, 10 to 15 minutes longer.

③ **Prep the raw fennel salad:**

+ While the fennel roasts, pluck any fronds attached to the reserved fennel stalks and coarsely chop them. Thinly slice the fennel stalks crosswise into coins. Transfer everything to a medium bowl.

+ Cut 1 lemon in half; squeeze the juice from both halves over the raw fennel. Drizzle with 1 tablespoon olive oil, season with salt and black pepper, and toss well to dress the fennel. Taste and adjust the seasoning if it needs it.

④ **Serve:** Transfer the roasted fennel planks to a serving dish. Scatter the raw fennel salad over top along with more grated Parmesan. Serve warm or at room temp; it's delicious both ways.

Jammy Pepps with Feta & Basil

Serves 4

PRODUCE

3½ pounds mixed color (NOT green!) bell peppers (about 8)

1 red Fresno chile or ½ teaspoon red pepper flakes

8 garlic cloves
½ cup basil leaves

DAIRY

1 (4-ounce) block feta cheese

PANTRY

½ cup extra-virgin olive oil

Kosher salt
1 teaspoon sugar
¼ cup red wine vinegar or sherry vinegar

I have a complicated relationship with bell peppers. When they're raw, I hate them. But give them enough time, some heat, and even more olive oil and they will eventually become jammy, sweet, and intoxicatingly delicious. These long-cooked peppers are particularly tasty when paired with herbs and a salty cheese, like feta, and eaten as you would a caprese salad. But you could also spread them on sandwiches (they will take your hoagie game to the next level), toss them into salads, serve them on an antipasto platter, or spoon them over a piece of chicken or fish with enormous results. They last for quite a while, since they're essentially packed in olive oil, so make a batch or two and keep them on hand for their many uses. Just please don't use green bell peppers in this recipe—even an hour of luxuriating in olive oil can't save those godforsaken creatures.

---

① Preheat the oven to 325°F.

② **Prep the veg:**

+ Remove the cores of 3½ pounds of bell peppers by cutting off 4 lobes on each, leaving behind the cores, stems, and seeds. Cut each lobe into roughly 1½-inch-thick strips. **Never de-lobed a pepp before? Right this way.**

+ Thinly slice 1 Fresno chile crosswise.

+ Firmly smash and peel 8 garlic cloves.

③ **Cook the peppers:**

+ Heat ½ cup olive oil in a large Dutch oven over medium-high heat.[1]

+ Add the bell peppers, Fresno chile, garlic, 1 tablespoon salt, and 1 teaspoon sugar and stir and toss with tongs to combine. Cook until some of the peppers begin to soften a bit and turn golden brown in a few spots, 8 to 10 minutes. Stir in ¼ cup red wine vinegar.

+ Partially cover the pot and transfer it to the oven. Cook, stirring the peppers a couple of times throughout to move things around and encourage even cooking, until the peppers are very soft and jammy, 45 to 60 minutes.

+ Remove the lid and cook until the peppers have caramelized in some spots and the liquid has reduced slightly, 30 to 45 minutes longer. Let cool slightly, then taste and add more vinegar, salt, or sugar as needed until the peppers taste outrageously good.

④ **Serve:**

+ Slice the feta into ¼-inch-thick planks.

+ Spoon the peppers onto a rimmed serving platter along with some of those juices. Break the planks of feta into pieces and scatter them over top. Tear ½ cup basil leaves and scatter over top.

---

[1] It sounds like too much oil, but there are a lot of peppers, and the juices they release are going to mingle with all that olive oil and create a super-luxurious sauce.

Roasted Eggplant with Pickled Raisin & Basil Dressing

Serves 4

PRODUCE

1½ pounds small eggplant, such as Fairy Tale, Italian, or Japanese

1 small shallot

1 cup basil leaves

PANTRY

¼ cup extra-virgin olive oil, plus more for drizzling

Kosher salt

½ cup red wine vinegar

½ cup golden raisins or currants

2 tablespoons sugar

¾ teaspoon red pepper flakes

If you've ever had eggplant caponata, a sweet-and-sour Sicilian dish of long-cooked eggplant, vinegar, and oftentimes raisins, this recipe might resonate with you. Eggplant are sponges for flavor and there is no shortage of sweet/sour/spicy flavor here. Though you could, of course, make this recipe with globe eggplant—the large, teardrop-shaped, dark-purple-skinned kind you most often find in grocery stores—it's worth seeking out some of the smaller, more colorful varieties when in season. There is a whole world of eggplant species out there, and they're pretty easy to come by in the summer months. Smaller ones like Fairy Tale, Japanese, or Graffiti eggplant tend to be less bitter and cook up sweeter and more custardy than the big dogs do, and they're nicer to look at, too.

---

① Position a rack in the lower third of your oven. Preheat the oven to 450°F.

② **Prep and roast the eggplant:**

+ Trim the stems of 1½ pounds small eggplant and halve or quarter them lengthwise, depending on their thickness, so that all of the pieces are about the same width (about 1½ inches thick) and will cook at the same rate.

+ Toss the eggplant pieces on a large rimmed baking sheet with ¼ cup olive oil, coating them as evenly as possible in the oil.[1] Season with salt and arrange cut-side down. Roast until deeply caramelized on the cut side, 15 to 20 minutes. Using tongs, rotate each wedge so that the uncaramelized side makes contact with the baking sheet and continue to roast until the eggplant is very soft and golden brown, 5 to 10 minutes longer, depending on their size.

③ **While the eggplant cooks, make the dressing:**

+ Thinly slice 1 shallot crosswise into rings and separate them with your fingers.

+ In a small saucepan, combine ½ cup red wine vinegar, ¼ cup water, ½ cup golden raisins, 2 tablespoons sugar, ¾ teaspoon red pepper flakes, and ¾ teaspoon salt. Cook over medium-high heat, swirling the pan often, until the liquid has reduced to about a third of what you had originally, 5 to 7 minutes. It should still be loose enough to drizzle—not sticky. If you think you've over-reduced it, add a teaspoon of water to loosen the liquid. Remove it from the heat.

+ Stir the shallots, loosening the rings, into the still-warm raisins.

+ Just before serving and while still warm, gently stir in 1 cup whole basil leaves until just coated in the vinegar.

④ **Plate it up:** Transfer the roasted eggplant to a serving dish. Spoon the warm dressing over top. Drizzle with more olive oil.

---

[1] Spongelike eggplant soak up all the oil so we want to be sure the oil is evenly distributed.

Low & Slow Brocco Rabe

Serves 4 to 6

PRODUCE

2 bunches broccoli rabe (about 2 pounds)

8 garlic cloves

DAIRY

2 ounces grated Parmesan cheese (about ½ cup)

PANTRY

½ cup pickled Peppadew peppers, plus 1 tablespoon brine from the jar

½ cup extra-virgin olive oil, plus more for drizzling

1 (14-ounce) can tomato puree

¾ teaspoon red pepper flakes

Kosher salt

It has taken me a while to accept that some people just don't like broccoli rabe. To me, it is the spicier, sassier sister to broccolini, and I can't get enough of it. If you don't like it, I guess you could skip on to the next recipe, or you could take a chance on me with this one. This recipe employs a low-and-slow method of cooking in which the broccoli rabe braises for three quarters of an hour, until extremely tender. I find it mellows out some of that intensity, breaks down its stemmy toughness, and allows all of the flavors you are cooking in the dish to really meld. Eat this as a side dish alongside a steak, slap it between bread with some provolone and make an epic broccoli rabe and cheese melt, add it to an antipasto and cheese platter, or have it for breakfast with a fried egg.

---

① **Prep the ingredients:**

 ✦ Trim off 1 inch from the stems of 2 bunches of broccoli rabe. Gather the broccoli rabe in a bunch and cut it crosswise into 2-inch pieces.

 ✦ Chop ½ cup pickled Peppadew peppers.

 ✦ Thinly slice 8 garlic cloves.

② **Start cooking:**

 ✦ Heat ½ cup olive oil in a large Dutch oven over medium heat.

 ✦ Add the sliced garlic cloves and cook, stirring often, until very fragrant and just barely beginning to turn light golden brown but no darker at the edges, 3 minutes.[1]

 ✦ Add the broccoli rabe, chopped Peppadews, 1 tablespoon Peppadew brine, 1 (14-ounce) can tomato puree, ¾ teaspoon red pepper flakes, and 1½ teaspoons salt, tossing to combine. Bring to a simmer over medium heat, then reduce the heat to low. Cover the pot and cook, stirring occasionally, until the sauce has thickened and the broccoli rabe is very tender, 35 to 45 minutes.

 ✦ Uncover the pot and increase the heat to medium-high. Continue to cook until the sauce clings to the broccoli rabe and very little liquid remains in the bottom of the pot, 5 minutes. Stir in about 1 ounce grated Parmesan cheese (¼ cup). Taste and add more salt if necessary.

③ **Serve:** Transfer the broccoli rabe to a serving dish and drizzle with more olive oil and top with an additional 1 ounce grated Parm (¼ cup).

---

[1] If they take on too much color, they will turn bitter, and broccoli rabe is already bitter, so we don't need any more of that.

Charred Leeks & Burrata with Walnut Bagna Cauda

Serves 4

PRODUCE
3 large leeks
10 garlic cloves
½ lemon

DAIRY
2 tablespoons unsalted butter

8 ounces burrata or fresh whole-milk ricotta cheese

PANTRY
⅓ cup plus 2 tablespoons extra-virgin olive oil

Kosher salt and freshly ground black pepper

10 oil-packed anchovy fillets

½ cup walnuts

Flaky sea salt

Crusty bread, for serving

I believe that leeks are among the most highly underrated members of the allium family. Onions, shallots, garlic, and scallions get waaaaay more play, and it just isn't okay. Leeks are somewhat of a cross between a scallion, a shallot, and a red onion in taste, and they have a high sugar content, which makes them exemplary for deep caramelization and charring. This is my preferred method for cooking leeks—roasted until almost blackened on their cut sides, and soft and creamy throughout. Of course, getting drenched in garlicky walnut bagna cauda and served with torn burrata does no harm, either. This is the perfect side dish to round out a meal—serve it with lots of crusty bread alongside a roast chicken if you want to experience it my way.

---

① Position an oven rack in the lower third of your oven. Preheat the oven to 400°F.[1]

② **Prep and cook the leeks:**

✦ Trim and discard the dark green tops and hairy root ends of 3 leeks. Peel off and discard the first two layers. Cut the leeks in half lengthwise through the root end. If they seem particularly dirty, rinse them under cold water, keeping the layers intact as best as possible. Pat them dry.

✦ Drizzle a rimmed baking sheet with 2 tablespoons olive oil. Add the leeks and turn with tongs to coat them in the oil. Season all over with kosher salt and black pepper. Arrange the leeks cut-sides down in a single layer on the baking sheet. Roast until softened and deeply caramelized on the cut sides, 14 to 18 minutes.

③ **Make the bagna cauda:**

✦ Firmly smash and peel 10 garlic cloves.

✦ In a small saucepan, combine the garlic cloves, 10 anchovy fillets, and ⅓ cup olive oil. Set the saucepan over very low heat and cook very gently, stirring occasionally and mashing with a fork once the garlic starts to soften, until the garlic and anchovies are totally dispersed, 12 to 14 minutes. The oil will barely simmer as the anchovies fry in the oil.

✦ Meanwhile, finely chop ½ cup walnuts. Add the walnuts along with 2 tablespoons butter to the bagna cauda and continue to cook over low heat until the walnuts are toasted and crisp, 7 to 11 minutes longer.

④ **Plate it up:**

✦ Arrange the leeks on a serving platter, caramelized-sides up.

✦ Tear an 8-ounce ball of burrata into large shards and scatter them on the platter with the leeks, or dollop 8 ounces of ricotta over them.

✦ Spoon the warm walnut bagna cauda dressing over everything; season with flaky sea salt and more black pepper. Squeeze the juice of ½ lemon over top and serve with crusty bread alongside. If you have kitchen shears, they're great for cutting the leeks into smaller, more manageable pieces for serving.

---

[1] The heat source is on the bottom of your oven, so it's a great place to position vegetables in order to get them super charred.

Sweetie P's with Peanut-Chile Salsa

Serves 4

PRODUCE
4 small sweet potatoes (about 2 pounds total)
2 garlic cloves
2 limes

PANTRY
½ cup plus 2 tablespoons extra-virgin olive oil
Kosher salt
½ cup roasted, unsalted peanuts
1 tablespoon ancho chile powder or sweet paprika
1 teaspoon honey
½ teaspoon red pepper flakes

I'm pretty much down to cook anything that can be slathered in some sort of spicy condiment. Chile oils and hot sauces occupy a huge amount of real estate in my fridge, relative to other ingredients. I also happen to be a big fan of toasted nuts. Both of those things are present in this dish. Sweet potatoes are the perfect vehicle for this quick peanut-chile salsa that gets roasty-toasty flavor from ancho chile powder, heat from red pepper flakes, deep nutty notes from peanuts, and a touch of sweetness from honey. I mean, don't tell me you're not excited to eat this.

① Preheat the oven to 425°F.

② **Roast the sweet potatoes:** Scrub 4 small sweet potatoes, then pat them dry. Cut the sweet potatoes in half lengthwise. Place on a rimmed baking sheet. Drizzle with 2 tablespoons olive oil and season with 1½ teaspoons salt, tossing with your hands to evenly coat. Arrange cut-sides down. Transfer to the oven and roast until tender when pierced with a knife and charred on the undersides, 25 to 35 minutes.[1] Transfer the roasted sweet potatoes to a platter.

③ **Meanwhile, make the peanut-chile salsa:**

+ Finely chop ½ cup peanuts so that all pieces are about the size of a lentil. Place in a small pot and cover with ½ cup olive oil. Cook over medium heat, stirring often, until the peanuts are golden brown, 4 to 5 minutes. Remove from the heat.

+ Finely grate 2 garlic cloves right into the oil while it's still relatively hot, stirring to combine. This will cook off some of the raw heat of the garlic and mellow out its flavor. Stir in 1 tablespoon ancho chile powder, 1 teaspoon honey, ½ teaspoon red pepper flakes, and ½ teaspoon salt. Cover to keep warm.

+ Cut 2 limes into 4 wedges each.

④ **Serve:** Spoon the peanut-chile salsa over the sweet potatoes and serve with the lime wedges for squeezing.

[1] Cook time will vary greatly, depending on how thick your sweetie p's are, so just keep an eye on things!

Caesar-ish Potato Salad with Radishes & Dill

Serves 4

PRODUCE

2 pounds baby potatoes, any variety

1 garlic clove

1 lemon

6 radishes

1 cup dill leaves, plus more for finishing

PANTRY

Kosher salt

3 oil–packed anchovy fillets

⅓ cup mayonnaise

1 tablespoon Dijon mustard

Freshly ground black pepper

2 tablespoons extra–virgin olive oil

I'm not sure why the world hasn't already started slathering Caesar dressing on boiled potatoes, but I'm certainly happy to take part in spreading the gospel. A boiled potato is the perfect sponge for the intensely savory flavors of this quick Caesar dressing made with store-bought mayo (no egg yolks or emulsions here!). Like pasta, potatoes can really take it when it comes to salting the water they cook in. If 1 cup of salt seems like a lot, you are not wrong, but this recipe has been tested, tasted, and approved, so rest assured your potatoes won't turn out salty. Their density inhibits them from taking on too much salt, and most of it gets tossed out when you drain them anyway. Take this proudly to your next potluck, but since it's mayo-based, puhlease do yourself a favor and don't let it sit out for hours in the sun!

① **Cook the potatoes:** Place 2 pounds potatoes and 1 cup salt in a large pot and cover with 3 quarts water. Bring to a simmer over medium–high heat. Once the water reaches a simmer, adjust the heat to medium to maintain a simmer and cook until the potatoes are easily pierced with a fork or paring knife. This should take roughly 8 to 10 minutes after the water comes to a simmer, but timing will vary greatly by the size of potato, so focus on the doneness rather than the minutes.

② **While the potatoes cook, make your dressing:**

✦ Firmly smash and peel 1 garlic clove. Add a pinch of salt to the garlic and, using the side of your knife, mash the garlic to a paste.

✦ Finely chop 3 anchovy fillets and then, using the side of your knife, mash them into a homogeneous paste. Combine the anchovy paste with the garlic paste and mash a few more times to combine.

✦ Add the paste to a large bowl along with ⅓ cup mayonnaise, 1 tablespoon Dijon mustard, and 1 teaspoon black pepper. Whisk well to combine.

✦ Slowly stream in 2 tablespoons olive oil, whisking as you go.

✦ Cut a lemon in half and squeeze the juice of both halves into the dressing; whisk to combine. Season the dressing to taste with salt.

③ **Assemble the salad and serve:**

✦ Once the potatoes are cooked, drain them and let cool just until they can be handled. Smash each potato against the cutting board lightly with your palm so they are just crushed and their skins have broken to expose their flesh, but not totally crumbly. Add them to the dressing, tossing to evenly coat.

✦ Thinly slice 6 radishes crosswise into coins. Finely chop 1 cup dill leaves. Add the radishes and dill to the potatoes and toss to coat. Taste and add more salt and black pepper as needed. Top with more dill leaves and serve immediately.

Roasted Squash with Buttered Pine Nuts & Feta

Serves 4

PRODUCE
3 pounds acorn and/or delicata squash
7 garlic cloves
½ lemon

DAIRY
4 tablespoons (½ stick) unsalted butter, at room temperature
1 (4-ounce) block feta cheese

PANTRY
3 tablespoons extra-virgin olive oil
Kosher salt and freshly ground black pepper
⅓ cup raw pine nuts

In the colder months, winter squash are in the peak of their eating season, and therefore possess an unrivaled sweetness and concentration of flavor that you just don't come across during the warmer months. Roasting them at a high temperature coaxes out their natural sugars, which caramelize into a delicious golden crust in the oven. I love the pairing of sweet, tender roasted squash with decidedly savory ingredients (in this case, garlic, pine nuts, and feta), which bring much needed balance to the equation. While technically this is a side dish, I'd be very stoked to eat a big bowl of it as the main event.

---

① Preheat the oven to 450°F.

② **Prep and roast squash:**

+ Trim the stems of 3 pounds acorn and/or delicata squash. Cut them in half through their root ends. Use a spoon to scoop out and discard the seeds and stringy flesh clinging to them. Cut each squash crosswise into 1-inch-thick wedges. Transfer the squash to a large rimmed baking sheet.

+ Lightly smash 7 garlic cloves. Add 5 of them to the baking sheet, leaving them in their skins.[1] Peel the remaining 2 garlic cloves and set aside.

+ Drizzle the squash and garlic with 3 tablespoons olive oil. Season with 2 teaspoons salt and lots of black pepper. Use your hands to toss and turn the squash on the baking sheet so they are evenly coated in the seasonings. Arrange the pieces cut-sides down. Transfer the squash to the oven to roast until deeply charred on one side, 15 to 20 minutes. Using tongs, flip the squash and return it to the oven to finish roasting until the flesh is tender and deeply charred on both sides, 10 to 15 minutes longer.

③ **Make the garlicky pine nuts:**

+ While the squash roasts, melt 4 tablespoons (½ stick) butter in a small saucepan over medium-low heat. Once melted, add ⅓ cup pine nuts and cook, swirling the pan often, until the pine nuts are golden brown and the butter has browned and turned fragrant and nutty, 4 to 5 minutes. Immediately remove the saucepan from the heat.

+ Finely grate the reserved 2 garlic cloves right into the hot pine nut butter and stir to combine. Let cool. Season with salt.

④ **Serve:**

+ Arrange the roasted squash and garlic cloves on a serving platter. Cut 4 ounces feta cheese into ¼-inch-thick planks and scatter them over the squash, breaking them into smaller pieces if desired.

+ Spoon the buttered pine nuts over the squash and feta. Season with more black pepper. Squeeze the juice of ½ lemon over everything.

---

[1] They're going to roast along with the squash, and the skins will protect them from burning in the high heat of the oven.

Raw & Roasted Rainbow Carrots with Sesame & Lime

Serves 4

PRODUCE
1 medium red onion
1½ pounds medium carrots, preferably rainbow
1 lime
1 cup cilantro leaves and tender stems

PANTRY
¼ cup plus 3 tablespoons extra-virgin olive oil
2 teaspoons ground cumin
Kosher salt
2 teaspoons honey or maple syrup
2 tablespoons toasted sesame seeds

I have made some pretty disparaging statements regarding the merits of carrots in my past. But my relationship to food is an ever-evolving one. Thus, after much internal struggle and a few extra rounds of testing, I bring you the first recipe I have ever developed that features, highlights, and even celebrates the humble carrot. They get both roasted at high heat until just tender and sliced raw for added texture and snap. I've dressed them in honey to further accentuate their mild sweetness and tossed them in lime juice, cilantro, and sesame seeds to bring acidity, freshness, and nuttiness to their aid. What results is a real looker of a side dish that is textured and full of fun flavors, and I gotta tell ya, it's the only way I'll be eating any carrots at all.

① Place a large rimmed baking sheet in the lower third of your oven. Preheat the oven to 450°F.

② **Prep and roast the carrots:**

✦ Cut 1 medium red onion in half through the root end. Peel the onion and then cut it into 1-inch wedges through the root end, so they stay intact. Add the onion wedges to a large bowl.

✦ Scrub 1½ pounds medium carrots.[1] Cut half of the carrots on the bias into long spears that are about ¾ inch thick. As you get closer to the tops of the carrots and they are thicker, cut the spears in half lengthwise so they match the other carrots in thickness.[2] Add the carrot spears to the onion wedges along with 3 tablespoons olive oil, 2 teaspoons cumin, and 1 teaspoon salt. Toss well to coat.

✦ Arrange the carrots and onions on the preheated baking sheet in a single layer (reserve the bowl). Roast for 12 to 14 minutes, until the bottoms are browned. Shake the pan to redistribute and turn the carrots and onions and continue roasting until the onions and carrots are charred on both sides and soft to the touch, 8 to 10 minutes more.

③ **Marinate the carrots:**

✦ Finely grate the zest of half of a lime into the reserved bowl. Add 2 teaspoons honey and the juice of the lime and whisk to combine. Whisking constantly, stream in ¼ cup olive oil. Season with salt.

✦ Thinly slice the remaining raw carrots on the bias into oblong coins. Add to the dressing and toss well to coat. Season with salt.[3]

✦ Once the roasted vegetables are finished, let them cool for 5 minutes on the baking sheet, then add them to the bowl with the raw carrots and toss well to combine.

④ **Serve:** Just before serving, add 1 cup cilantro leaves and tender stems and 2 tablespoons toasted sesame seeds and toss to combine. Reseason the salad and transfer to a platter. It's great eaten cold, warm, or at room temperature.

---

[1] If the outsides look kinda gnarly, go ahead and peel them. I usually don't if they're nice clean little thangs.

[2] Consistency in size and shape is key here so that they all cook at the same rate.

[3] They can sit in this marinade for quite some time and will only get more delicious as they soak.

Smooshed & Crispy Potatoes with Salt 'n' Vinegar Sour Cream

Serves 4

PRODUCE
2 pounds baby Yukon Gold potatoes

DAIRY
¾ cup sour cream

PANTRY
Kosher salt
⅓ cup extra-virgin olive oil
Freshly ground black pepper
6 tablespoons distilled white vinegar

Do I really need to convince you to make this recipe? The only thing better than crispy, creamy roasted potatoes is crispy, creamy roasted potatoes piled on top of a puddle of tangy, salt 'n' vinegared sour cream. The key to crispy-on-the-outside, fluffy-on-the-inside potatoes is to boil them in heavily salted water until just tender, then smash and roast them generously coated with olive oil. Don't rush this process—they need that time in the oven to cook off some of their inherent moisture before turning all golden and crisp, and you wouldn't want to prevent that from happening, would you?

① Position a rack in the center of your oven. Preheat the oven to 450°F.

② **Cook the potatoes:** Place 2 pounds baby Yukon Gold in a large pot and fill with 3 quarts water and 1 cup salt.[1] Bring to a boil over medium-high heat. Reduce the heat to maintain a simmer.[2] Simmer the potatoes until tender and easily pierced with a knife, 5 to 10 minutes. The time will vary depending on the size of your potatoes; be careful not to overcook or they'll fall apart when smashed. Drain in a colander and let sit for a few minutes to allow some water to evaporate.

③ **Smash the potatoes:** Transfer the potatoes to a large rimmed baking sheet. Use the bottom of a glass measuring cup or a flat mug to crush each potato until it's about ½ inch thick. Drizzle ⅓ cup olive oil over the potatoes, gently turning them to coat all sides. Taste a potato; if it needs more salt (it probs does), re-season. Top with a few good cranks of black pepper.

④ **Roast the potatoes:** Roast until crispy and golden brown on the underside, 20 to 25 minutes. Remove the potatoes from the oven and drizzle 3 tablespoons distilled white vinegar evenly over. Flip the potatoes with a spatula and continue to cook until very crisp and golden brown around the edges, 10 to 20 minutes longer.[3] Remove from the oven. Taste and season the potatoes with more salt if they need it.

⑤ **Make the salt 'n' vinegar sour cream:** In a small bowl, stir together ¾ cup sour cream, 3 tablespoons distilled white vinegar, and ½ teaspoon salt.

⑥ **Serve:** Spread the sour cream in a shallow bowl or serving platter. Top with the potatoes and a few more cranks of black pepper.

[1] Yes, that is in fact an absurd amount of salt. But most of it is going to get discarded when we drain the potatoes. Promise they won't be too salty!

[2] We start potatoes in cold water so they cook evenly from the inside out as the water heats up.

[3] Depending on how hot your oven is, how crowded the baking sheet is, and what kind of baking sheet you use, this can vary greatly.

Soup

Supremely Creamy Tomato & Cheddar Soup

Serves 4

PRODUCE

1 large Vidalia or yellow onion

1⊙ scallions

¾ cup dill leaves, plus more for serving

DAIRY

3 tablespoons unsalted butter, plus more for serving, if desired

1½ cups heavy cream

3 ounces sharp white cheddar cheese

PANTRY

Kosher salt and freshly ground black pepper

1 tablespoon tomato paste

3 (14.5-ounce) cans crushed tomatoes (preferably fire-roasted)

Crusty bread, for serving (optional)

Flaky sea salt

For the most part, I am really not a big creamy-soup fan. I usually experience palate fatigue after the first few sips and find myself seeking refuge in whatever else is present on the table. But this soup is an exception to that rule. I first tasted a version of this soup at a sweet little French café called Mrs. London's in Saratoga Springs, New York, where I went to college, and the taste of it has been deeply engrained in my memory ever since. If you can't find crushed tomatoes, tomato puree would be a fine substitute, although the soup will end up a bit smoother in texture. Do yourself a favor and seek out some good crusty bread and butter to serve alongside it.

---

① **Prep your aromatics:**

✦ Finely chop 1 large Vidalia onion. **Not sure how? Watch this tutorial.**

✦ Thinly slice 1⊙ scallions crosswise.

✦ Coarsely chop ¾ cup dill leaves.

② **Start the soup:**

✦ Heat 3 tablespoons butter in a large Dutch oven over medium heat until melted. Add the onion, scallions, 1¼ teaspoons kosher salt, and 1½ teaspoons black pepper and cook, stirring often, until the alliums are very soft but not quite brown at the edges, 7 to 8 minutes.

✦ Add 1 tablespoon tomato paste to the onions and cook, stirring often, until the paste begins to stick to the bottom of the pot and turns a shade darker in color, about 3 minutes.

✦ Add 3 (14.5-ounce) cans crushed tomatoes, 1½ cups heavy cream, and 1½ cups water and stir well to combine. Continue to cook until the soup has thickened slightly, letting the flavors meld together, 6 to 8 minutes.

✦ Remove from the heat and stir in 1½ teaspoons kosher salt. Taste and add more salt if needed—canned tomatoes contain varying amounts of salt, so use your best judgment and adjust.

③ **Serve:**

✦ Coarsely grate 3 ounces sharp white cheddar cheese (about 1 cup).

✦ Divide the soup among serving bowls and top each bowl with a generous handful of the grated cheddar cheese, some more black pepper, and more dill leaves.

✦ Set out some good crusty bread and room-temperature butter (if desired) and flaky sea salt for serving.

Would you rather have to eat only burning-hot food for the rest of your life or freeze everything you eat and have to eat it in the form of a Popsicle?

Really Great Chicken Soup (Because You're Worth It)

Serves 4 to 6

PRODUCE
2 large leeks

2 whole garlic heads plus 5 garlic cloves

6 celery stalks

2 medium turnips or parsnips (about 1¼ pounds)

3 large thyme sprigs

MEAT
4 chicken legs (drumstick plus thigh, attached) or 4 thighs and 4 drumsticks (about 2 pounds total)

2 pounds chicken wings

PANTRY
Kosher salt

1 tablespoon whole black peppercorns, plus more for grinding

8 prunes

2 tablespoons extra–virgin olive oil

Is there anything more soul-nourishing than a bowl of perfectly seasoned, deeply chicken-y chicken soup? The key to great chicken soup is packing the broth with lots of chicken bones, which contain collagen and impart both flavor and body in a way that boneless chicken meat alone cannot. You'll use both chicken wings and legs in this soup. The leg meat braises into extreme tenderness as it cooks, before getting shredded into the soup. You may notice that there are no carrots in this soup, and you're right about that. I just don't have any love in my heart for boiled carrots. Turnips and prunes take their place to lend the earthiness and sweetness that carrots like to think they add. You may do as you please.

---

① **Start the broth:**

+ Season 4 chicken legs and 2 pounds of chicken wings all over with 4 teaspoons salt. Place all the chicken in the pot.

+ Cut 2 large leeks in half lengthwise. Separate the dark green parts of the leeks from the white and set the white parts aside; you'll get to those later. Rinse the leek greens to rid them of any grit and dirt.

+ Cut 2 garlic heads in half crosswise.

+ Cut 4 celery stalks crosswise into 2–inch–long pieces. (Set aside any leaves to use later as garnish.)

+ Chop 1 medium turnip (no need to peel!) into 2–inch wedges.

+ Add all of the chopped veg to the pot along with 1 tablespoon whole black peppercorns, 2 prunes, 1 large thyme sprig, and 1 tablespoon salt.

+ Add 12 cups water and bring to a simmer over medium–high heat. Reduce the heat to medium–low(ish) to maintain a simmer and cook, uncovered, about 1 hour. Occasionally skim some of the scoodgy foam from the surface with a large spoon and discard it; this will leave you with clearer broth in the end.

② **Prep the rest of the veg:**

+ Thinly slice 2 celery stalks crosswise.

+ Thinly slice 5 garlic cloves.

+ Cut the leeks crosswise on a bias into 1½–inch pieces.

+ Cut 1 medium turnip into quarters through the root end and then slice each quarter crosswise into ¼–inch–thick pieces.

+ Tear 6 prunes into 2 or 3 pieces.

+ Pick 2 teaspoons leaves from 2 sprigs of thyme.

③ **Shred the chicken:** Once the soup has simmered for 1 hour, use tongs to pluck out the chicken legs and transfer them to a plate to cool. Continue simmering the stock (the longer it simmers, the more flavorful your soup will be). Shred the meat off the bones into bite–size pieces. Discard the skin. Add the bones right back into the broth; they will continue to flavor it.

④ **Assemble the soup:**

+ With the broth still simmering, heat 2 tablespoons olive oil in a large Dutch oven over medium heat. Add the leeks, garlic, and prunes and season them with salt and lots of black pepper. Cook, stirring frequently, until the leeks begin to soften and collapse, 3 to 4 minutes. Scoop out about ¾ cup broth and add it to the leeks. Continue to cook, until the leeks are cooked down and softened but not browned, 10 to 12 minutes.

+ Strain the hot broth right into the Dutch oven. Discard the chicken wings, bones, skin, and vegetables.

+ Add the shredded chicken and the sliced turnips, thyme leaves, and sliced celery and simmer over medium–high heat until the turnips and celery are just cooked through and tender, 4 to 5 minutes. Season the soup with salt— it's likely going to need a lot of it.

⑤ **Serve:** Divide the soup among bowls. Garnish each bowl with black pepper and the reserved celery leaves.

K-bas & Cabbage Soup

Serves 4 to 6

PRODUCE

6 garlic cloves

2 celery stalks

1 large yellow onion

1 pound green cabbage

1 cup dill leaves

DAIRY

Sour cream or plain whole-milk Greek yogurt, for serving

MEAT

12 ounces kielbasa

PANTRY

¼ cup extra-virgin olive oil, plus more for drizzling

Kosher salt and freshly ground black pepper

3 tablespoons tomato paste

2 (14.5-ounce) cans white beans, such as butter, cannellini, or gigante

---

My love for kielbasa runs pretty freaking deep. It's not just a sausage, it's a lifestyle. Kielbasa is perfectly suited to soup because of the complexity of flavor it lends as it simmers. It's porky, salty, smoky, and fatty, and all of those things go a long way when it comes to soup architecture. Of all the pork products you might find in a hearty soup, kielbasa is by far my favorite, so I encourage you to consider it the next time you reach for Italian sausage for minestrone or ham hocks for split pea. This humble but delicious soup is both an homage to my former NYC nabe and a big fat shout-out to my Bassy Posse—you know who you are.

---

① **Do some prep:**

+ Thinly slice 6 garlic cloves.

+ Trim the root ends of 2 celery stalks. Slice the celery crosswise about ¼ inch thick.

+ Chop 1 large yellow onion. **Not sure how? I can help you with that!** Transfer the garlic, celery, and onion to a medium bowl to make space on your cutting board if it's getting jammed up.

+ Quarter a 1-pound cabbage through the root end. Trim out the core of each quarter. Slice the cabbage crosswise into 1-inch-thick strips.

+ Cut 12 ounces kielbasa in half lengthwise. Slice the halves crosswise into ½-inch-thick half-moons.

② **Start the soup:**

+ Heat ¼ cup olive oil in a large Dutch oven over medium-high heat. Add the kielbasa in a single layer and cook, undisturbed, until golden brown and crisp, 4 to 5 minutes. Give everything a good stir to redistribute the kielbasa and cook 2 to 3 minutes longer.

+ Add the garlic, celery, and onion, reduce the heat to medium, and cook, stirring occasionally, until the onion is translucent, 4 to 5 minutes.

+ Stir in the cabbage, 2 teaspoons salt, and lots and lots of black pepper. Continue to cook, stirring often, until the onion is very soft and beginning to stick to the pot and the cabbage is just tender and not crunchy (grab a piece and taste it!), 4 to 5 minutes.

+ Stir in 3 tablespoons tomato paste and cook until the tomato paste starts to stick to the bottom of the skillet and you hear it sizzle a bit louder, about 2 minutes.

③ **Add the beans and broth:**

+ Meanwhile, drain and rinse 2 (14.5-ounce) cans of white beans in a fine-mesh strainer.

+ Stir the beans into the pot, using a wooden spoon to smash about ⅓ cup or so of them against the side.[1]

+ Stir in 4 cups water. Bring the soup to a simmer over medium-high heat. Once it simmers, reduce the heat to maintain a simmer and cook for 15 minutes, until slightly thickened and the flavors have melded.[2]

+ Taste and add more salt and black pepper as needed until it starts to taste really good.

+ Chop 1 cup dill leaves and stir them into the soup.

④ **Serve:** Ladle the soup into bowls. Serve each bowl topped with a dollop of sour cream, more black pepper, and a drizzle of olive oil.

---

[1] This will release their starchy insides, and that starch will help thicken the soup.

[2] The soup should now taste super flavorful, whereas before simmering, it was watery and less developed in flavor. Time is an important ingredient in a good soup.

Overripe Tomato & Bread Soup with Crispy Garlic

Serves 4

PRODUCE
1 large yellow onion

9 garlic cloves

4 pounds very ripe tomatoes

3 large basil sprigs

DAIRY
2 ounces plus 2 tablespoons grated Parmesan cheese (⅓ cup)

PANTRY
5 ounces crusty bread (from about ¼ round country loaf)

⅓ cup plus 3 tablespoons extra-virgin olive oil, plus more for drizzling

Kosher salt and freshly ground black pepper

½ teaspoon red pepper flakes

In the height of tomato season, when your tomatoes are rotting faster than you can keep up with eating them, this overripe tomato soup is here to save you. This is my version of pappa al pomodoro, a Tuscan tomato and stale bread soup that was one of the first recipes I learned to cook back in my college study-abroad days in Florence. I've made it my own by introducing a spicy, crispy garlic oil that's drizzled over the soup before serving, because I never met a spicy condiment I didn't love. Torn crusty bread will function as both a thickening agent in the soup (a very tasty alternative to adding flour, cornstarch, or a roux) and a crunchy Parmesan-smothered crouton for dunking, because what is a soup if not a vehicle for dunkage?

---

① Position a rack in the bottom and upper third of your oven. Preheat the oven to 450°F.

② **Meanwhile, do some prep:**
+ Finely chop 1 large yellow onion. **Need some guidance? Pull up this video.**
+ Thinly slice 9 garlic cloves; set about a third of the sliced garlic aside to use in the garlic oil later.

+ Cut out the cores from 4 pounds ripe tomatoes; roughly chop into 1-inch pieces.
+ Tear 5 ounces bread into 1-inch pieces. You should have about 4 cups torn.

③ **Start the soup:**
+ Heat ⅓ cup olive oil in a large Dutch oven over medium heat.
+ Add the onion and garlic and cook, stirring often, until very soft and fragrant but not browned, 10 to 12 minutes.
+ Stir in the tomatoes, 1 large basil sprig, 1 tablespoon salt, and lots of black pepper.[1]
+ Increase the heat to medium-high and bring the mixture to a simmer, then stir in half of the torn bread. Switch to a whisk and cook, vigorously whisking the soup often to break up the bread into smaller, fairly indiscernible pieces and help distribute and incorporate it into the tomatoes, 3 to 4 minutes. It should still be pretty liquidy and soupy; it's going to cook down further in the oven. Remove from the heat.

④ **Bake the soup and the croutons:**
+ Whisk 2 ounces grated Parmesan cheese (about ½ cup) into the soup. Taste it now and adjust the seasoning if needed.
+ Toss the remaining torn bread on a rimmed baking sheet with a good drizzle of olive oil and 2 tablespoons grated Parmesan. Season with salt and black pepper.
+ Transfer the soup (uncovered) to the bottom rack of the oven and the croutons to the rack above it and bake until the bread is light golden brown and crisp and the soup is thick and bubbling, 16 to 19 minutes.

⑤ **Meanwhile, make the crispy garlic:** In a small saucepan, combine the reserved sliced garlic and 3 tablespoons olive oil over medium heat. Cook, swirling the pan constantly so the garlic cooks evenly, until the garlic is very lightly golden brown all over, 4 to 6 minutes. Remember, it's going to continue to cook in the residual heat of the oil, so don't let it get super dark. Remove the saucepan from the heat and stir in ½ teaspoon red pepper flakes and a pinch of salt.

⑥ **Serve:** Let the soup cool slightly; it will be unbearably hot straight out of the oven. Ladle it into 4 serving bowls. Nestle a few croutons into each bowl and drizzle some of the crispy garlic chips and their oil over the top. Pick the leaves of 2 basil sprigs and scatter them over each bowl.

---

[1] I know, I know, it's a lot of salt, but there's also a lot of water in tomatoes! The soup will be very bland and watery without that much seasoning.

Golden Get-Well Soup

Serves 4 to 6

PRODUCE
1⊙ scallions
1⊙ garlic cloves
1 (4-inch) piece fresh ginger
2 limes
Cilantro leaves and tender stems

MEAT
1½ pounds bone-in, skin-on chicken thighs (about 4 thighs)

PANTRY
2 tablespoons extra-virgin olive oil, plus more for drizzling
1¼ teaspoons ground turmeric
Kosher salt
¾ cup jasmine or basmati rice
Freshly ground black pepper

You couldn't pack more health-inducing goodness into this chicken soup if you tried. It's teeming with all of the restorative properties of ginger and turmeric and thickened with white rice, which swells as it cooks and turns a watery broth into a hearty, comforting porridge. This is exactly what you need when what you need is to get well. Rice acts as a thickening agent when cooked this way, thanks to its naturally occurring starch, so be sure to simmer the soup until the grains of rice are no longer distinct from the broth they cook in—and the whole thing turns rich and cozy. If you've never dipped your spoon into the vast world of grain-thickened porridges, don't stop here. There are many versions, both sweet and savory, that span the globe, from rice-based Asian congee and its many variants throughout the continent to Italian polenta, Jamaican hominy porridge, and hot cereal faves like oatmeal. Though each is distinct, what they collectively share is an ability to comfort and soothe.

---

① **Do some prep:**

+ Thinly slice 1⊙ scallions crosswise, setting aside about ½ cup of the dark green parts for serving.

+ Lightly smash and peel 1⊙ garlic cloves.

+ Thinly slice 1 (4-inch) piece of ginger lengthwise into planks. No need to peel it! Just give it a scrub with some water if it looks dirty.

② **Start the soup:**

+ Heat 2 tablespoons olive oil in a large Dutch oven over medium heat. Add the scallions, garlic, ginger, and 1¼ teaspoons turmeric. Cook, stirring often, until the aromatics are softened and fragrant but not browned, 3 to 4 minutes.

+ Add 1½ pounds bone-in, skin-on chicken thighs, 1 tablespoon salt, 9 cups water, and ¾ cup jasmine rice to the pot.[1] Bring the water to a simmer over medium-high heat. Cook, scraping the bottom of the pot if the rice is sticking and reducing the heat as necessary to maintain a simmer, until the rice breaks down and thickens the soup to a porridge-like consistency, 4⊙ to 5⊙ minutes.

③ **Shred the chicken:**

+ Using tongs, pluck out the chicken and transfer it to a plate to cool.

+ While the chicken cools, use a wooden spoon to fish around for the garlic cloves, which at this point will be very, very soft. Use the back of the spoon to smash the garlic against the inside walls of the pot to crush and incorporate it into the soup. If you feel like it, you can pluck out and discard the sliced ginger at this point as well—it's a little tough to eat, but I usually just eat around it.

+ Once the chicken has cooled, remove and discard the skin. Use two forks to shred the meat from the bones. Discard the bones. Return the shredded meat to the pot and give it a stir.

④ **Season the soup and serve:**

+ Squeeze the juice of 2 limes into the soup.

+ Stir in 1 teaspoon black pepper. Taste the soup and add more salt if you think it needs it.

+ Divide the soup among soup bowls. Garnish it with the reserved sliced scallion greens, some cilantro leaves, a good crank of black pepper, and an additional drizzle of olive oil.

---

[1] In most cases, it's best to first rinse the rice to remove any excess starch that would cause the rice to stick together as it cooks, but since we're aiming for thickened porridge, there's no need to rinse it.

Frispy Chickpeas

Makes 1½ cups

PRODUCE
½ lime

PANTRY
1 (14.5-ounce) can chickpeas
3 tablespoons extra-virgin olive oil
½ teaspoon hot smoked paprika
Kosher salt

Fried and crispy chickpeas (a.k.a. frispy chickpeas) had a real moment about eight years ago. They were popping up on every self-respecting bar menu across the nation in some way, shape, or form. Somehow, they lost their way, and you rarely see them on menus anymore. So, we're bringing them back. 'Cause I love a crispy, crunchy snack like I love a Cae Sal (page 174), which is to say, a lot. Patting the chickpeas dry to rid them of as much surface moisture as possible is key in achieving long-lasting crunch, while slowly shallow-frying them in oil drives out all of their water content to take that crunch factor all the way home.

① **Drain and crisp the chickpeas:**

✦ Using a fine-mesh strainer, drain and rinse 1 (14.5-ounce) can of chickpeas. Line a medium bowl with a double layer of paper towels and pat the chickpeas dry on the towels—this will speed up the crisping process.

✦ Heat 3 tablespoons olive oil in a large nonstick skillet over medium-low heat.

✦ Add the chickpeas to the oil and stir well to coat. Cook, stirring occasionally, until the chickpeas are deep golden brown and crisp, 18 to 22 minutes—taste one for crispiness! They will start out very tender and gradually crisp up all the way through, so be patient.

✦ Line the bowl you used to dry the chickpeas with fresh paper towels.

✦ Using a slotted spoon, transfer the chickpeas to the lined bowl to drain them briefly of any excess oil, then pull out and discard the paper towels.

② **Season and serve:**

✦ Sprinkle ½ teaspoon hot smoked paprika evenly over the chickpeas.

✦ Finely grate the zest of ½ lime over top and season with salt. Toss well to coat.

✦ Eat them as a snack or keep them in an airtight container and toss them into your salads as alt croutons.

Spanakopita Dip

Serves 4

PRODUCE
5 garlic cloves
6 scallions
1 cup dill leaves,
plus more for serving

DAIRY
8 ounces cream cheese
3 tablespoons unsalted
butter
1 ounce grated Parmesan
cheese (about ¼ cup)
4 ounces feta cheese

FROZEN
1 (10-ounce) package
frozen chopped spinach or
kale, thawed

PANTRY
Kosher salt and freshly
ground black pepper
Pita chips, for serving

If you luv spanakopita, the classic Greek spinach/feta/phyllo pie, then you're also gonna luv this dip. True spanakopita (which this is not) is a labor-intensive endeavor, but here you'll find that all of the same flavors come together in just a few minutes on the stovetop. Equipped with the right crunchy vessel for scooping (in this case, pita chips), you've got all the glory and none of the fuss. I do not claim that this dip is any *better* than spanakopita, but do I think it comes pretty damn close in deliciousness.

---

① **Do some prep:**

+ Pull 8 ounces of cream cheese out of the fridge and cut it into 1-inch pieces to bring it to room temperature, which will make it easier to melt.

+ Thinly slice 5 garlic cloves.

+ Thinly slice 6 scallions crosswise. Set aside a small handful of the sliced dark green parts for garnishing later.

+ Finely chop 1 cup dill leaves.

+ Place 1 (10-ounce) package of thawed frozen spinach in a kitchen towel that you don't mind getting a little messy and squeeze out as much liquid as possible.[1]

② **Make the dip:**

+ Melt 3 tablespoons butter in a medium saucepan over medium heat. Add the garlic and scallions and cook until softened and very fragrant but not browned, about 2 minutes.

+ Add the spinach and ¾ teaspoon salt and cook, stirring constantly, 1 minute.

+ Add the cream cheese and 2 tablespoons water. Reduce the heat to medium-low and cook, stirring constantly, until the cream cheese has fully melted, about 3 minutes.

+ Remove from the heat and stir in the chopped dill and 1 ounce grated Parmesan cheese (about ¼ cup). Crumble in 4 ounces feta and stir to combine.

+ Season the dip with salt and lots of black pepper. If it looks a little too thick, add another splash or two of hot tap water until it's a creamy but scoopable consistency—like that of spinach-artichoke dip.

③ **Serve:** Transfer the dip to a serving bowl and garnish with some more dill leaves and the reserved sliced scallions. Serve warm with pita chips alongside.

---

[1] If you forgot to thaw it, you can submerge the package of spinach (unopened) in a bowl of hot tap water to speed things up.

Tomato Toast with Cheddar & Smoky Mayo

Serves 2

PRODUCE
1 small garlic clove

1 lemon

½ pound ripe heirloom tomatoes (about 2 small)

Small handful of chives

DAIRY
3 ounces sharp cheddar cheese

PANTRY
½ cup mayonnaise

2 teaspoons sweet smoked paprika

Kosher salt

2 (1-inch-thick) slices crusty bread

Extra-virgin olive oil

Flaky sea salt

Freshly ground black pepper

WARNING: Attempting this recipe outside the confines of peak tomato season is a crime punishable by law. Seriously. I'm not kidding. Puleeeeeease don't do it. The glory of a truly transcendent tomato toast is perfect high-summer tomatoes, so ripe that their juices and jellies have no choice but to seep out all over your cutting board as you slice them and drip down your face as you eat them. That, and, of course, some garlicky mayo, big shards of sharp cheddar cheese, and lots of crunchy crystals of flaky sea salt.

---

① **Make the smoky mayo:**

+ Finely grate 1 small garlic clove into a small bowl and stir in ½ cup mayo, 2 teaspoons sweet smoked paprika, and ¼ teaspoon kosher salt.

+ Cut 1 lemon in half, squeeze the juice of 1 half into the mayo, and stir to combine. Reserve the remaining half.

② **Prep your ingredients:**

+ Cut ½ pound heirloom tomatoes crosswise into ¼-inch-thick slices.

+ Thinly slice a small handful of chives.

+ Position a rack in the top of your oven. Preheat the broiler. Drizzle 2 (1-inch-thick) slices of crusty bread with olive oil on one side. Broil 3 to 4 minutes, or until golden brown and very crispy on one side.

③ **Assemble and serve:**

+ Slather a few tablespoons of the mayo on the toasted side of each slice of bread.

+ Slice or shave 3 ounces cheddar cheese into big thin shards, scattering them over the mayo.

+ Add the tomatoes, shingling them to cover the surface of the toast as best as possible. Season the tomatoes generously with flaky sea salt. Squeeze the juice of the remaining lemon half over each toast. Drizzle with more olive oil and finish with lots of black pepper. Scatter the chives over top.

Party Nutz

Makes 3 cups

PRODUCE
½ lemon

DAIRY
2 tablespoons unsalted butter

PANTRY
3 cups any combination of raw nuts
1¼ teaspoons red pepper flakes
1 tablespoon onion powder
1½ teaspoons sweet smoked paprika
Kosher salt

If I've learned anything in my years of entertaining, it's that people love a bowl of warm nuts. Spiced nuts are always a good look, but serve them freshly roasted and still warm from the oven, and you've stepped up your entertaining game BIG-time. Toasting nuts brings out all the untapped roasty-toasty flavor within them, but it's important to note that nuts contain a lot of fat, which means they have a tendency to burn easily. You'll cook them at a relatively low temperature (325°F) to ensure they cook evenly and don't burn on the outsides before the insides have cooked. Consider making a double batch of these if you want to have any leftovers.

① Position a rack in the center of the oven. Preheat the oven to 325°F.

② **Season the nuts:** Melt 2 tablespoons unsalted butter in a medium saucepan over medium heat until just foamy. Remove the pot from the heat and stir in 3 cups mixed nuts, 1¼ teaspoons red pepper flakes, 1 tablespoon onion powder, 1½ teaspoons smoked paprika, and 1 teaspoon salt until the nuts are well coated.

③ **Toast the nuts:** On a baking sheet, spread out the nuts in an even layer, transfer to the oven, and roast until golden brown all the way through, 14 to 18 minutes. Check for doneness by cracking into a couple of nuts to be sure they are consistently golden brown throughout.

④ **Finish and serve:** Using a Microplane, immediately (and carefully—they're hot!) grate the zest of ½ lemon over the nuts on the baking sheet and stir well to coat. Taste the nuts and add more salt if needed. Let cool 10 minutes, then serve.[1]

[1] They're great served still warm and also delicious once cooled. If you manage to have any left over, once they're cool, store them in an airtight container at room temperature for up to 2 weeks.

The Right Way to Make Popcorn

Makes 10 cups

DAIRY

4 tablespoons (½ stick) unsalted butter

PANTRY

¼ cup neutral oil, such as canola, vegetable, or grapeseed

½ cup popcorn kernels

Kosher salt

1 teaspoon ground turmeric (optional)

¼ cup nutritional yeast

Freshly ground black pepper

All right, listen up! There's a right way to make popcorn, and there's a wrong way to make popcorn. You know how they drizzle hot melted butter over your popcorn at movie theaters, but it's already in the bag, so only the top third of the popcorn is super buttered, and soggy-ish for that matter, so your hands get slicked in grease? We can fix that. The key to perfect popcorn is introducing all of the fat (whether that be olive oil, vegetable oil, butter, coconut oil, ghee, etc.) at the beginning of the process so that the kernels can fry in said fat. Fried food is crispy food. Fried popcorn is crispy popcorn. If you drizzle oil or butter over the popcorn after it's been popped, it immediately sogs, and its life-span decreases dramatically. This popcorn gets generously coated in nutritional yeast, which is the most important popcorn seasoning out there besides, duh, salt.

---

① **Heat the oil and butter:**

+ Heat ¼ cup neutral oil in a large pot over medium heat until shimmering.

+ Add 4 tablespoons (½ stick) butter, ½ cup popcorn kernels, 1½ teaspoons salt, and 1 teaspoon turmeric[1] (if using) and swirl the pot to evenly coat the kernels in the oil and butter as it melts.[2]

② **Pop:**

+ Once the butter has melted, cover the pot with a tight-fitting lid and cook, shaking the pot occasionally while still covered, until there are 3-second-long pauses between kernels popping, 5 to 6 minutes. Remove the pot from the heat, crack the lid slightly to allow steam to escape, and let sit with the lid cracked for 1 minute to allow any stragglers to finish popping.

③ **Serve:**

+ Transfer the popcorn to a large bowl (it should be quite a bit bigger than the volume of popped popcorn so that you can really get in there and toss in the additional seasoning).

+ Sprinkle ¼ cup nutritional yeast over the popcorn and season with lots and lots of black pepper, tossing and stirring until all of the popcorn is well coated. Let the popcorn cool to room temperature before serving. Taste for seasoning and adjust as needed.

---

[1] The turmeric is totally optional and really only here to stain the popcorn yellow and drive home the buttered movie theater popcorn vibe.

[2] Like with anything else, you've got to season from the start. This will help the salt season the inside of the popcorn as it pops—you'll add more to the outside later on.

Peanuts, Popcorn, Potato Chips

F*ck, Marry, Kill?

Pimiento-ish Cheese

Makes 2 cups

PRODUCE
1 small garlic clove

DAIRY
1 cup labneh, sour cream,
or plain whole-milk Greek yogurt

8 ounces extra-sharp white cheddar cheese

PANTRY
1 tablespoon harissa paste
12 pickled Peppadew peppers
Kosher salt and freshly ground black pepper
Extra-virgin olive oil, for drizzling
Pita chips, crusty bread, breadsticks, cucumber spears,
and/or sliced radishes, for serving

You know who loves pimiento cheese? EVERYONE EVER. It's a slam-dunk kind of dip—creamy, tangy, spicy, fatty, and perfectly suited to all kinds of dippables. There are plenty of recipes for classic Southern pimiento cheese out there. This is not one of them. Labneh (a super-thick and tangy Greek yogurt relative) takes the place of cream cheese in this recipe, while pickled Peppadew peppers and Tunisian harissa bring the heat. Technically, there aren't any pimiento pepps in this version, but the pickled Peppadews are bright and pickle-y, and I promise you won't miss them. I stuck with the classic grated cheddar cheese, because it's just exactly the right ingredient for the job.

---

① Make the dip:

+ In a medium bowl, stir together 1 cup labneh and 1 tablespoon harissa paste.[1]

+ Finely grate 1 garlic clove into the dip.

+ Drain 12 pickled Peppadew peppers; finely chop and add them to the dip.

+ Using the medium holes of a box grater, grate 8 ounces extra-sharp cheddar cheese onto your cutting board. You should have about 2 cups. Add the cheese to the bowl and stir to combine. Season with salt and black pepper and transfer it to a small serving bowl.

② Serve: Drizzle the dip with olive oil before serving and serve with anything you can think of: Ritz crackers! Pita chips! Radishes! Cucumbers! Hard-boiled eggs! Potato chips! Celery!

---

[1] Every brand of harissa varies in spiciness and assertiveness, so this is really just an approximation of how much you should use. Taste the harissa first—if it's super mild and mellow, feel free to add some more until it starts to kick.

Smoked Trout Dip with Potato C's & Salmon Roe

Makes 1½ cups

PRODUCE
½ lemon
½ bunch chives

DAIRY
¼ cup sour cream

SEAFOOD
8 ounces boneless hot–smoked trout fillet
2 tablespoons salmon roe (optional)

PANTRY
¼ cup mayonnaise
Kosher salt and freshly ground black pepper
Crinkle–cut potato chips, for serving

This is kind of like grown-up tuna salad. And because we're grown-ups and we make the rules, we get to eat our trout dip with potato chips, and I think that's pretty special. Smoked trout is full flavored and can handle a decent amount of mayonnaise and sour cream to mellow out its prominent smoky flavor. If you're feeling fancy, and have access to salmon roe, I highly recommend you plop a little on top. People are, for whatever reason, very impressed by fish eggs. So, lean into it and serve this in place of charcuterie at your next dinner party. It takes all of five minutes to pull together.

① **Prep the trout:** Peel off and discard the skin of one 8-ounce fillet of smoked trout. Using your hands, flake apart the trout flesh into approximately ½-inch pieces and place them in a medium bowl, discarding any tiny little pin bones that you may come across.

② **Make the dip:**

✦ Stir in ¼ cup sour cream and ¼ cup mayonnaise until well combined and the trout has broken down—it will look somewhat like tuna salad.

✦ Finely grate the zest of ½ lemon into the bowl and squeeze in the juice; stir to incorporate.

✦ Thinly slice ½ bunch of chives crosswise. Stir in all but about 1 teaspoon chives. Season with salt and black pepper as needed—it likely won't need a ton of salt because smoked trout is naturally salty.

③ **Serve:** Transfer the trout dip to a small serving bowl or dollop it onto a serving plate. Garnish with the remaining chives. Spoon 2 tablespoons salmon roe (if using) on top of the dip. Serve with crinkle–cut potato chips.

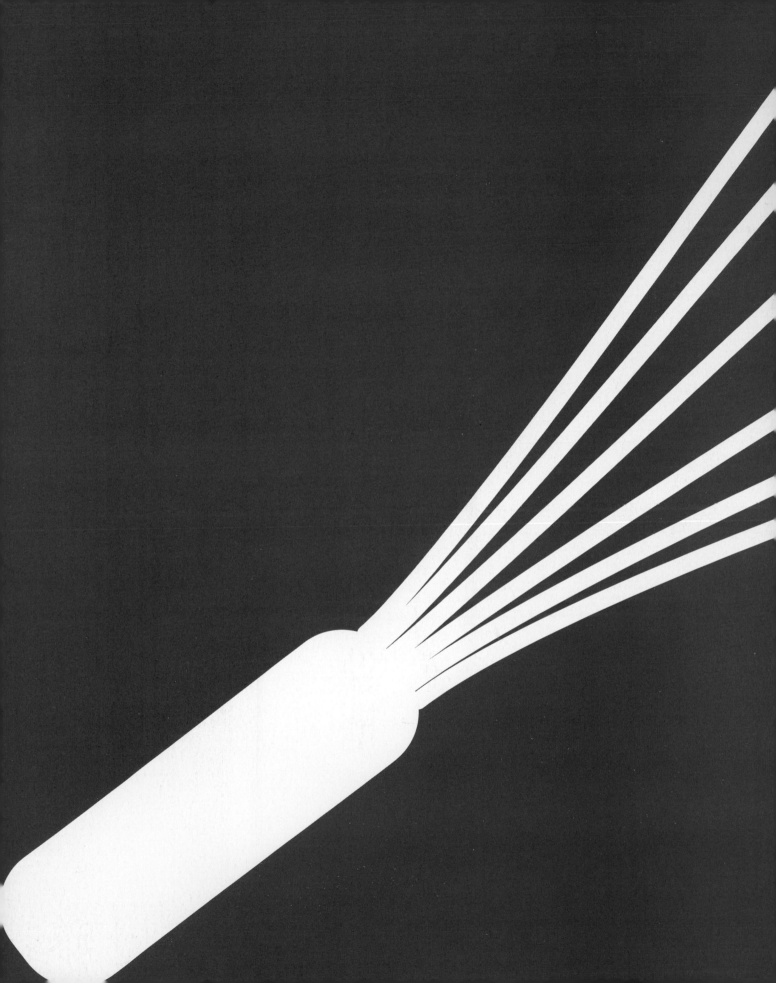

Baking

Blueberry Cornflake Crisp

Serves 6

PRODUCE
6 cups blueberries (about 2½ pints)

1 lemon

DAIRY
½ cup (1 stick/113g) unsalted butter, cold

Vanilla ice cream, for serving

PANTRY
⅔ cup firmly packed (147g) plus ½ cup (110g) light brown sugar

1¼ cups (150g) plus 3 tablespoons (22.5g) all-purpose flour

¾ teaspoon (2g) kosher salt

1 teaspoon ground cardamom

1½ cups cornflakes cereal

Blueberries and corn: one of summer's greatest yet most underrated flavor pairings, IMHO. Cornflakes: one of America's most iconic cereals. Cornflakes crushed into a buttery, cardamom-flecked crisp topping strewn over jammy blueberries: perfection. A fruit crisp is one of the laziest, most hands-off summer desserts out there, meaning it's the best kind of dessert when what you really want to do is prioritize leisure time. Blueberries require zero chopping, slicing, or dicing, unlike some of their stone-fruit counterparts, so your only task is to make the crumb topping, which takes all of 5 or 6 minutes. Less than an hour later, you have a bubbling, juicy, fragrant mess of summer deliciousness just begging for a scoop of ice cream.

---

① Preheat the oven to 375°F.

② **Prep the blueberries:**

+ In a large bowl, stir together 6 cups blueberries, ½ cup (110g) light brown sugar, 3 tablespoons (22.5g) flour, and ½ teaspoon salt.

+ Finely grate the zest of half of a lemon into the blueberries. Cut the lemon in half and squeeze the juice of both halves into the blueberries, catching the seeds with your hands. Toss everything well to combine. Transfer to an 8 × 8-inch baking dish or a cast-iron skillet.

③ **Make the crisp topping:**

+ Wipe out that bowl and use it to put together the topping. Using a wooden spoon, combine 1 teaspoon ground cardamom, 1½ cups cornflakes, 1¼ cups (150g flour, ⅔ cup (147g) light brown sugar, and ½ teaspoon salt, stirring well to combine.

+ Cut ½ cup (1 stick/113g) cold unsalted butter into ½-inch pieces and add them to the bowl with the dry ingredients. Using your hands, pinch and mix the butter together with the dry ingredients until the mixture holds together in clumps when squeezed in your palm. You'll simultaneously be crushing some of the cornflakes, and that's totally okay. Pile the cornflake crumble over the blueberries, clumping some of the crumble as you do so with your hands to create some larger pieces.

④ **Bake and serve:** Bake until the juices are bubbling around the edges and the crumble is golden brown, 50 to 55 minutes. Serve warm with vanilla ice cream.

Black Sesame Shortbread

Makes 16 cookies

DAIRY

10 tablespoons (1¼ sticks/142g) unsalted butter

PANTRY

1½ cups (180g) all-purpose flour

⅔ cup (75g) powdered sugar

1½ teaspoons (4g) kosher salt

¼ cup (35g) black or white sesame seeds

⅓ cup (80g) tahini

Granulated sugar, for sprinkling

Would it be possible to create a melt-in-your-mouth, tenderoni shortbread cookie without relying on an electric mixer and the whole butter-creaming thing? I certainly didn't think so. I was sorely mistaken. This is the anti-cookie. The easiest cookie there is. There are six ingredients. Melted butter and tahini get stirred into a mixture of all-purpose flour, powdered sugar, and salt, and voilà, you've got cookie dough. Melting the butter means you don't need any special stand mixers or electric beaters. Powdered sugar contains cornstarch, which lends a very fine, delicate texture to the shortbread without having to rely on the butter-creaming technique to achieve a tender crumb.

① Position a rack in the center of the oven. Preheat the oven to 325°F. Line a rimmed baking sheet with parchment paper.

② **Melt the butter:** Cut 10 tablespoons (1¼ sticks/142g) unsalted butter into 1-inch pieces. Melt the butter in a small saucepan set over medium heat, swirling occasionally, about 3 minutes. Set aside to cool.

③ **Prep the dry ingredients:**

+ In a medium bowl, whisk together 1½ cups (180g) flour, ⅔ cup (75g) powdered sugar, and 1½ teaspoons (4g) salt.

+ Place ¼ cup (35g) black sesame seeds in a small resealable plastic bag, seal it, and crush them by smashing them lightly with the side of a wine bottle or a rolling pin. (If you have a mortar and pestle or spice grinder, use it.)[1] Add the crushed sesame seeds to the dry ingredients and whisk to combine.

④ **Make the dough:** Whisk ⅓ cup (80g) tahini into the cooled melted butter, then pour the mixture into the dry ingredients, stirring with a spatula until a dough comes together in a rough ball. Using your hands, knead the dough lightly a few times until no floury spots remain.

⑤ **Prep the cookies and bake:**

+ Transfer the ball of dough to the prepared baking sheet and use your hands to pat it into a ½-inch-thick, 8 × 8-inch square. Smooth the surface of the square with the bottom of a measuring cup so that it's nice and flat.

+ Use a fork to lightly prick the dough all over.[2] Transfer the baking sheet to the fridge to chill for at least 30 minutes or up to overnight. If chilling overnight, lightly cover the dough with plastic wrap.

+ Once chilled, cut the shortbread into 16 equal 2-inch squares. Space them out evenly on the baking sheet.

+ Bake the shortbread until lightly golden brown all over, 30 to 40 minutes. While still warm, lightly sprinkle granulated sugar over the surface of the dough—just enough to evenly coat each square. Let the cookies cool on the baking sheet completely before serving.

[1] This will release some of the oils within the seeds and help flavor the dough.

[2] This creates little pockets for the steam to escape so that the cookies bake evenly, yielding a very crisp, melt-in-your-mouth texture.

Brown Butter & Labneh Banana ~~Bread~~ Cake

Makes one 9 × 5-inch loaf

PRODUCE
5 large ripe bananas

DAIRY
10 tablespoons (1¼ sticks/142g) unsalted butter, plus more for the pan

⅓ cup labneh, plus more for slathering

2 large eggs

PANTRY
2 cups plus 2 tablespoons (255g) all-purpose flour

1½ teaspoons (9g) baking soda

1½ teaspoons (4g) kosher salt

1 cup packed (220g) dark brown sugar

1 teaspoon (5g) vanilla extract

1 tablespoon (11g) turbinado sugar, for sprinkling (optional)

Flaky sea salt

I have a bone to pick with all of the banana "breads" of the world. Can we please stop lying to ourselves and acknowledge that banana bread is really just banana cake?? And that explains why when it's good, it's SO good. The only bread-like thing about it is that it's even more delicious when toasted and slathered in butter. End rant. This banana cake is jam-packed with banana flavor, thanks to the four whole bananas inside it and a fifth banana chillin' on top. It is rich and moist, due to the addition of labneh, which, if you've never baked with it before, is a real treat. You could, of course, substitute sour cream or whole-milk Greek yogurt in a pinch, but I encourage you to use labneh, if you can find it. This is a dump-and-stir kinda cake because that's the kinda cake I'm most likely to bake.

---

① Preheat the oven to 350°F. Lightly grease a 9 × 5-inch loaf pan with butter and line it with parchment paper, leaving an overhang on the two longer sides.[1]

② **Brown the butter:** Cut 10 tablespoons (1¼ sticks/142g) butter into about 5 pieces and place them in a small saucepan set over medium heat. Melting the butter in smaller pieces helps it brown more evenly. Cook, swirling the saucepan frequently, until the butter foams up, the foam dies down, and the milk solids (those little white flecks) turn deeply golden brown, 5 to 6 minutes. Let cool.

③ **Mix your dry ingredients:** In a large bowl, whisk together 2 cups plus 2 tablespoons (255g) flour, 1½ teaspoons (9g) baking soda, and 1½ teaspoons (4g) kosher salt.

④ **Combine your wet ingredients:**

✦ Peel 4 ripe bananas, break them into thirds, and place in a large bowl. Using a fork or potato masher, mash the bananas until they are a very thick, mostly homogeneous pulp.

✦ Whisk in ⅓ cup labneh, 2 eggs, 1 cup (220g) dark brown sugar, and 1 teaspoon (5g) vanilla until the mixture is homogeneous, about 1 minute.

✦ Whisk the cooled butter into the wet ingredients, using a spatula to scrape any bits that are stuck to the pan—those contain alllll the flavor; don't waste any of it!

⑤ **Combine and bake:**

✦ Whisk the dry ingredients into the wet ingredients. There may be a few floury patches remaining, but the batter should be mostly mixed.

✦ Scrape the batter into the prepared loaf pan, evening it out with the back of a spoon or a spatula. Peel 1 ripe banana and cut it in half lengthwise. Arrange both halves of the banana cut-sides up, spooning each other, on top of the batter. Sprinkle 1 tablespoon (11g) turbinado sugar (if using) evenly over the batter. This sugar will caramelize on the bananas in the oven, giving them a glossy brûléed effect.

✦ Bake the banana cake until deeply browned and a toothpick inserted into the center of the loaf comes out clean, 1 hour 10 minutes to 1 hour 25 minutes. Let cool in the pan slightly before using the parchment overhang to remove it from the pan.

✦ Serve the banana cake warm or at room temperature with more labneh and flaky sea salt alongside.

---

[1] This overhang will act as a sling later on and aid in removing the bread from the pan. The parchment replaces the need to flour the pan, and it's quite a bit cleaner. No need to butter and flour the parchment.

Salted WaJu Granita

Serves 6

PRODUCE
8 pounds watermelon (1 small or ½ large)
1 lime, for serving

PANTRY
3 tablespoons sugar, plus more if needed
1½ teaspoons kosher salt, plus more if needed

There are few things in this world that I crave more than a cold glass of salted watermelon juice. If you told me I could only drink one beverage for the rest of my life, WaJu would 100p be the bev of choice. So I turned my favorite drink into a food. The thing that makes this granita so special is that you don't need to bust out a blender or food processor to turn the watermelon into juice. You simply grate chunks of watermelon on the fine holes of a box grater, and because of how tender-fleshed the fruit tends to be, it breaks down into juice almost effortlessly. It's a great way to use the second half of that enormous watermelon you cut up for a barbecue but never finished, and is now taking up far more than its fair share of space in your fridge.

① **Prep the watermelon:**

+ Cut 1 small or ½ large watermelon into 4 large pieces (you're breaking the watermelon down into more manageable chunks). Cut off and discard the rind, leaving behind just the bright red flesh.

+ Set a fine-mesh strainer over a large bowl. Using the finest holes of a box grater, grate the watermelon into the strainer.

+ Press firmly on the solids to extract as much juice from the pulp as possible. You should have about 6 cups juice in the bowl, but every watermelon will yield a slightly different amount.

+ Transfer the juice to a 9 × 5–inch loaf pan. Discard the pulp.

+ Whisk in 3 tablespoons sugar and 1½ teaspoons salt (you'll need about 1½ teaspoons sugar and ¼ teaspoon salt for every 1 cup juice that you collected), until dissolved.

② **Freeze the granita:** Transfer the loaf pan to the freezer. Freeze it until hard, 3 to 4 hours, stirring the juice with a fork once or twice as it freezes and scraping the sides, which will freeze first, to encourage the juice to freeze evenly. At this point, you can leave it in the freezer until you're ready to eat it.

③ **Serve:**

+ Once frozen, use a fork to scrape the frozen watermelon juice repeatedly, creating piles of fluffy frozen ice. Transfer the scraped ice into serving bowls as you do so.

+ Cut 1 lime into wedges for serving. Serve each bowl of granita with a lime wedge.

Would you rather eat one chocolate chip cookie every hour on the hour for the rest of your life or never eat a chocolate chip cookie again?

Grapefruit Olive Oil Cake

Makes one 9 × 5-inch loaf

PRODUCE
2 red grapefruit

DAIRY
3 large eggs
½ cup (115g) plain whole-milk Greek yogurt

PANTRY
2 cups (240g) all-purpose flour
½ teaspoon (3g) baking soda
½ teaspoon (2g) baking powder
2 teaspoons (6g) kosher salt, plus a pinch
1½ cups (300g) granulated sugar
1 cup (200g) extra-virgin olive oil, plus more for the pan
¾ cup (85g) powdered sugar
3 tablespoons roasted, salted pistachios

This cake gets its citrusy flavor from several different additions of grapefruit throughout the baking process. If that sounds like too much grapefruit, it's not; the richness and flavor of the olive oil really mellows out the grapefruit's bitterness. Olive oil–based cakes only improve with time once baked (unlike butter-based ones), so this is a great one to make in advance. If you're not sure what size loaf pan you have, measure it from inside edge to inside edge for the most accurate reading. If you measure from the outside of the rim, you'll think your loaf pan has a larger capacity than it really does, and that could cause unwanted overflow.

① **Get yourself ready to bake:**
  - Position a rack in the center of your oven and a second one in the bottom third of your oven. Preheat the oven to 350°F.
  - Lightly grease a 9 × 5-inch loaf pan with about 1 tablespoon of olive oil.
  - Cut a piece of parchment paper as wide as the loaf pan and long enough to hang over the two long edges once it's laid into the pan; line the loaf pan. The flaps that overhang will act as handles for lifting the cake out of the pan later.

② **Combine the dry ingredients:** In a medium bowl, whisk together 2 cups (240g) all-purpose flour, ½ teaspoon (3g) baking soda, ½ teaspoon (2g) baking powder, and 2 teaspoons (6g) salt.

③ **Combine the wet ingredients:**
  - In a large bowl, finely grate the zest of 1½ of the grapefruits—you should have about 2 loosely packed tablespoons of grapefruit zest. Add 1½ cups (300g) granulated sugar and use your fingers to massage the zest into the sugar until it is well combined and the sugar is lightly damp and sandy, about 30 seconds.[1]
  - Whisk in 3 eggs, 1 cup (200g) olive oil, and ½ cup (115g) yogurt until very smooth, homogeneous, and pale yellow.
  - Cut 1 of the grapefruit in half and squeeze out the juice into a large liquid measuring cup, catching the seeds as you do so. Whisk ½ cup of the juice into the wet ingredients. Reserve 2 tablespoons of the remaining juice for the glaze later on.

④ **Combine the wet with the dry:**
  - Whisk the dry ingredients into the wet ingredients until just combined, but no further.[2]
  - Pour the batter into the prepared loaf pan. Place a baking sheet on the lower rack of your oven to catch any potential drippage. Bake on the middle rack until a toothpick inserted into the center of the cake comes out clean, 65 to 85 minutes.

⑤ **Make the glaze:** Finely grate the zest from the remaining ½ grapefruit into a small bowl. Add 2 tablespoons of the reserved grapefruit juice to the bowl (if you don't have enough reserved, you can crack into that second grapefruit) and whisk in ¾ cup (85g) powdered sugar and a pinch of salt until the glaze is thick and smooth. Cover with plastic wrap until the cake has fully cooled.

⑥ **Glaze and serve:**
  - Run a knife around the edges of the cake pan to help release the cake from the sides. Lift the parchment paper up and transfer the cake to a wire rack to finish cooling completely; discard the parchment paper.
  - Once completely cool, drizzle the reserved grapefruit glaze over the cake.
  - Finely chop 3 tablespoons roasted pistachios and scatter them over the cake.

[1] The sugar will act as an abrasive and coax some of the oils and aroma out of the zest as you massage it.

[2] Once the flour comes in contact with the wet ingredients, gluten begins to form in the batter. The more you mix the batter, the stronger that gluten becomes and the tougher your cake will be.

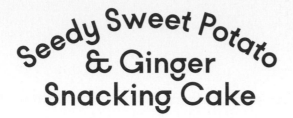

Seedy Sweet Potato & Ginger Snacking Cake

PRODUCE

¾ pound sweet potatoes (about 1 large)

1 (4-inch) piece fresh ginger

DAIRY

2 large eggs

¾ cup (190g) buttermilk

PANTRY

2½ cups (300g) all-purpose flour, plus more for the skillet

2 teaspoons ground cinnamon (6g)

2 teaspoons (6g) kosher salt

1 teaspoon (4g) baking powder

½ teaspoon (3g) baking soda

1½ cups packed (330g) light brown sugar

¾ cup (150g) neutral oil, such as vegetable, canola, or grapeseed, plus more for the skillet

1½ teaspoons (8g) vanilla extract

½ cup mixed seeds, such as pepitas, sunflower seeds, and/or black and white sesame seeds

Makes one 12-inch cake

Conceptually speaking, this sweet potato cake is really no different from a carrot cake. Grated sweet potatoes lend both moisture and sweetness in the same way that carrots would. Technique-wise, this cake couldn't be simpler. Two bowls, a box grater, and a couple of stirs later, and your cake is in the oven. There's freshly grated ginger in the batter, which is much more interesting than ground ginger, if you ask me. You can use any kind of seeds you like for the topping—I happen to love the flavor of toasted sesame seeds with ginger and warm spices, but the world's your oyster in that department.

① **Get ready:**
+ Position a rack in the center of the oven. Preheat the oven to 350°F.
+ Using a paper towel, lightly grease a 12-inch cast-iron skillet with neutral oil.[1] Sprinkle a few tablespoons flour in the skillet and tap it around to evenly coat, being sure to coat the inside edges. Discard any excess flour.

② **Prep your dry and wet ingredients:**
+ In a medium bowl, whisk together 2½ cups (300g) all-purpose flour, 2 teaspoons ground cinnamon, 2 teaspoons (5g) salt, 1 teaspoon (4g) baking powder, and ½ teaspoon (3g) baking soda.
+ In a second large bowl, lightly beat 2 eggs, and then whisk in 1½ cups (330g) light brown sugar, ¾ cup (150g) neutral oil, ¾ cup (190g) buttermilk, and 1½ teaspoons (8g) vanilla until homogeneous and very thick.
+ Peel ¾ pound sweet potatoes and coarsely grate them into the dry ingredients on the large holes of a box grater; you should have about 3 cups grated.

+ Finely grate 1 (4-inch) piece of ginger on the small holes of a box grater into the wet ingredients.

③ **Combine:**
+ Add the dry ingredients to the wet ones. Gently work the ingredients together in large sweeping and folding motions until no floury streaks remain. It's a pretty thick batter, so be sure it's mostly combined.
+ Scrape the batter into the prepared skillet and spread it out using the back of a spoon or spatula into an even layer.
+ Combine ½ cup mixed seeds in a small bowl. Scatter the seeds evenly over the batter.

④ **Bake and serve:**
+ Bake until a toothpick or cake tester inserted into the center of the cake comes out clean, 45 to 55 minutes. Let cool.
+ Run a small knife around the edge of the cake to help release it from the sides of the skillet. Cut the cake into wedges or squares and serve them right out of the skillet.

[1] If you've only got a 10-inch skillet, that will work, too, though the cake may take a little longer to bake since the pan will be fuller.

Salty Date & Cheddar Biscuits

Makes 8

DAIRY

½ cup (1 stick/113g) cold unsalted butter, plus more for serving

6 ounces extra-sharp cheddar cheese

1 cup plus 3 tablespoons sour cream

1 egg

PANTRY

6 ounces Medjool dates (about 1 cup)

2 cups (240g) all-purpose flour, plus more as needed

2 tablespoons (24g) sugar

2 teaspoons (6g) kosher salt

1½ teaspoons (6g) baking powder

½ teaspoon (3g) baking soda

Freshly ground black pepper

Flaky sea salt

I've never met a human who doesn't love a biscuit. And certainly, these sweet/salty/cheesy cheddar-date biscuits will be no exception. The keys to a delicious biscuit are (1) ample fat (butter) to keep them moist, and (2) not overworking the dough, which leads to a tough crumb. Truthfully, it's not all that hard, and the envelope-folding technique you'll learn in this recipe almost guarantees distinct, flaky layers. Keep your ingredients as cold as possible as you make these so that the shards of butter in the dough remain whole and don't melt into it. Cold pockets of butter turn to steam in the oven, which contributes to the biscuits' rise and ultimately their fluffy layers.

---

① Position a rack in center of the oven. Preheat the oven to 425°F. Line a rimmed baking sheet with parchment paper.

② **Cut and chill the butter:**

✦ Cut ½ cup (1 stick) cold butter into ½-inch cubes. Transfer them to a small bowl and chill in the fridge until ready to use.

✦ Remove and discard the pits from 6 ounces Medjool dates. Coarsely chop the dates into ½-inch pieces. (Flour your knife if they're super sticky.)

③ **Prep the dry ingredients:**

✦ In a large bowl, whisk together 2 cups (240g) flour, 2 tablespoons (24g) sugar, 2 teaspoons (5g) kosher salt, 1½ teaspoons (6g) baking powder, ½ teaspoon (3g) baking soda, and a few generous cranks of black pepper.

✦ Set a box grater right over the bowl of dry ingredients and grate 6 ounces sharp cheddar cheese on the large holes of the grater (you'll have about 2 cups grated). Toss the mixture with your hands to combine everything.

✦ Add the chilled butter pieces to the dry ingredients and, using your fingers, pinch and squeeze the butter into the flour until there are no pieces of butter larger than a pea.

✦ Add the chopped dates to the flour mixture and toss to combine, using your fingers to help separate any date pieces that may have clumped together.

④ **Combine, knead, and shape the dough:**

✦ Make a well in the center of the flour. Scrape in 1 cup plus 3 tablespoons sour cream and, using a fork, stir in circular motions until the dough comes together in large clumps.

✦ Using lightly floured hands, knead the dough a few times in the bowl to bring it together into a shaggy mass and incorporate any flour bits at the bottom of the bowl.

✦ Transfer the dough to a lightly floured surface. Knead with the palms of your hands once or twice more to form it into a more uniform mass and incorporate any last floury bits. Don't go too crazy; it just needs to come together, but you should still see some shagginess.

✦ Pat the dough into an 8 × 4-inch rectangle. Fold the short edges of the rectangle toward the center and let them overlap, like a tri-fold business letter. Pat the dough back down into another 8 × 4-inch rectangle. Cut the rectangle in half lengthwise, then slice it crosswise into 4 equal pieces to create 8 squares. Transfer to the parchment-lined baking sheet, spacing them out evenly.

✦ Lightly beat 1 egg in a small bowl. Brush the tops of the biscuits with the egg wash and sprinkle with flaky sea salt.

⑤ **Bake and serve:**

✦ Bake the biscuits, rotating the baking sheet front to back halfway through to encourage even browning, until lightly golden brown on top, 18 to 22 minutes.[1]

✦ Serve warm with more butter and flaky sea salt.

---

[1] The back of the oven is hotter than the front where the door opens, and it's always a good idea to rotate baked goods so they cook at even rates.

Peach & Burnt Honey Cobbler with Cold Cream

Serves 6 to 8

PRODUCE

3½ pounds ripe peaches (about 9 medium)

1 lemon

DAIRY

¾ cup (1½ sticks/170g) cold unsalted butter

1¾ cups (420g) heavy cream, plus more for brushing and serving

PANTRY

3 cups (360g) plus 3 tablespoons (22.5g) all-purpose flour, plus more as needed

½ cup (100g) sugar, plus more for sprinkling

4 teaspoons (16g) baking powder

2 teaspoons (6g) kosher salt

1 teaspoon (3g) ground cinnamon

⅔ cup (222g) honey

Why should you make a cobbler in a world full of crisps, shortcakes, galettes, and pies? Because a cobbler takes cues from all of the best parts of the aforementioned fruit-based desserts and combines them into one. The peaches cook down into a jammy, peak-summer pie-like filling made interesting thanks to the addition of caramelized honey. Meanwhile, the biscuits that top the whole thing are super simps to make, require no special equipment beyond your hands, and end up tasting somewhere in between a tender, fluffy shortcake and the bottom of a double-crust pie as they soak in all of the bubbling juices.

---

① Preheat the oven to 400°F.

② **Make the biscuit dough:**

+ In a large bowl, whisk together 3 cups (360g) flour, ¼ cup (50g) sugar, 2 teaspoons (8g) baking powder, and 1½ teaspoons (4g) salt.

+ Cut ¾ cup (1½ sticks/170g) butter into ½-inch small pieces and toss them into the flour mixture. Use your fingers to pinch and squeeze the butter into the flour mixture, smashing the butter down into smaller pea-size pieces.

+ Make a well in the center of the dry ingredients and, using a wooden spoon and stirring in a circular motion in the well, drizzle in 1¾ cups (420g) heavy cream until a very shaggy dough comes together. At this point, you can switch to using your hands and lightly knead the dough in the bowl to bring the mass together. You may want to lightly flour your hands to avoid stickage. Once the dough has come together into a relatively cohesive mass, lightly flour your work surface and turn the dough out onto the surface.

③ **Shape and cut the dough:**

+ Flour your hands. Pat the dough down into a 1-inch-thick square (about 8 × 8 inches). Cut the square into quarters. Stack the quarters on top of one another in a tower, then firmly press down with the palms of your hands to compress them into a mass again. It should be about 2 inches thick at this point. This technique aids in the creation of lots of flaky layers by literally creating them through stacking. **Pull up this video for a quick biscuit-stacking tutorial; it will all make a lot more sense!**

+ Re-flour your hands and the work surface as necessary and pat the dough into a 1-inch-thick square again. Cut the square into 16 smaller, equal-size squares and transfer them to a rimmed baking sheet. Chill the biscuits, uncovered, for at least 15 minutes and up to 1 hour while you prepare the peaches. If you want to chill them longer, loosely cover them with plastic wrap so they don't develop a skin.

④ **Macerate the peaches:**

+ Cut 3½ pounds peaches into 1-inch wedges (discard the pits). Add them to a large bowl along with ¼ cup (50g) sugar, 3 tablespoons (22.5g) flour, ½ teaspoon salt, and 1 teaspoon (3g) ground cinnamon, tossing well to combine.

+ Squeeze the juice of 1 lemon right into the peaches.

recipe continues →

- ✦ Cook ⅔ cup (222g) honey in a medium saucepan over medium heat until it comes to a simmer and starts to bubble dramatically. Continue to cook, swirling the pan constantly, until the honey is very fragrant and a shade darker in color, 2 to 3 minutes. Immediately pour the warm honey over the peaches, then toss them again to combine.[1]

- ✦ Transfer the peaches and their juices to a 12-inch cast-iron skillet. A 10-inch skillet or 13 × 9-inch baking dish would work well, too.

⑤ **Assemble:**

- ✦ Arrange each of the biscuits on top of the macerated peaches in a helter-skelter but evenly distributed pattern, making sure they don't overlap.

- ✦ Lightly brush the tops of the biscuits with heavy cream and sprinkle with a little sugar.

⑥ **Bake:** Place a baking sheet on the bottom rack to catch any drips. Bake, rotating the handle of the skillet 180 degrees once halfway through, until the biscuits are golden brown and the peach juices are bubbling and very thick, 40 to 45 minutes.[2] Take a peek at the bottom of the biscuits to be sure they are cooked, especially those in the center of the skillet as they'll take the longest. It's okay if they are moister than a typical biscuit: part of the appeal of this dish is the texture of the biscuits soaked in peach juices; you just don't want completely raw dough in the center of the cobbler.

⑦ **Serve:** Let the cobbler cool for at least 20 minutes. Use a large spoon to scoop out portions from the cobbler into bowls and drizzle each with chilled heavy cream.

---

[1] The honey may harden up a bit as it hits the cold peaches, but don't worry too much about it— it will melt and mingle in the oven.

[2] Since the back part of the oven is the hottest part, rotating the pan allows for more even baking.

Miso Apple Tart

Serves 6 to 8

PRODUCE
2 large Pink Lady or Granny Smith apples (about 1½ pounds)

DAIRY
3 tablespoons (42g) unsalted butter, at room temperature

1 large egg

¼ cup (60g) heavy cream

FROZEN
1 sheet store-bought puff pastry, thawed overnight in the refrigerator

Vanilla ice cream, for serving (optional)

PANTRY
⅔ cup packed (148g) dark brown sugar

3 tablespoons almond butter

2 tablespoons white miso paste

All-purpose flour, for dusting

1 teaspoon (5g) vanilla extract

Flaky sea salt

This is the kind of dessert that looks ten times more impressive than it is difficult to make, which is to say, it is the best kind of dessert there is. Puff pastry does all of the heavy lifting that pie dough normally would, and all you've got to do once it's thawed is tear open a package and roll it out. If you like butterscotch and you love salted caramel, then you will be extremely well cared for when you taste the miso-butterscotch sauce that glazes this apple tart. Japanese miso imparts an undeniably savory side to the tart that you can't quite put your finger on but is very welcome nonetheless. The whole thing ends up tasting kind of like a Toaster Strudel, in the best possible way ever.

---

① Position a rack in the center of your oven. Preheat the oven to 400°F. Line a rimmed baking sheet with parchment paper.

② **Make the almond butter frangipane:**

✦ Combine 1 tablespoon (14g) butter and ⅓ cup (74g) brown sugar in a medium bowl. Using a rubber spatula, work the two together, spreading them along the sides of the bowl until the mixture is homogeneous. Add 3 tablespoons almond butter and 1 tablespoon white miso and continue to paddle and mash with your spatula until well combined.

✦ Add 1 egg to the mixture, switch to a whisk, and whisk the egg into the almond mixture.

③ **Prep the apples:** Cut the flesh from 2 large apples in 4 lobes, cutting around the core. Discard the cores. Arrange the apple lobes, cut-sides down, on the cutting board and slice the apples lengthwise into ⅛-inch-thick pieces, keeping them arranged in their lobes so they are easy to fan out.

④ **Roll out and assemble:**

✦ Lightly flour your work surface. Using a wine bottle, cocktail shaker, or rolling pin, roll 1 thawed puff pastry sheet into a 9 × 13-inch rectangle. Transfer the puff pastry to the parchment-lined baking sheet.

✦ Using a small spoon, spread the almond paste in an even layer over the surface of the puff pastry, leaving a ½-inch border.

✦ Arrange the apples on the tart, fanning them out as you place them on the tart in a helter-skelter pattern—leaving the ½-inch border. You may have some slices left over—those are chef snacks!

✦ Transfer to the fridge to chill for 15 minutes.[1]

⑤ **Make the miso glaze:** In a small saucepan, combine ¼ cup (60g) heavy cream, ⅓ cup (74g) dark brown sugar, 2 tablespoons (28g) butter, and 1 tablespoon white miso. Cook over medium-low heat, swirling the pan frequently, until the butter melts. Whisk constantly until the mixture comes to a simmer, the sauce is smooth, and the sugar dissolves, about 1 minute longer. Remove the pot from the heat and whisk in 1 teaspoon (5g) vanilla.

---

[1] It's important that the puff pastry go into the oven as cold as possible. Warm butter melts faster and doesn't release a puff of steam like cold butter does as it cooks, and that steam is what makes the puff pastry "puff."

recipe continues →

⑥ **Glaze the apples:**

✦ Remove the pastry from the refrigerator.

✦ Using a pastry brush, generously brush the apples with the miso glaze. You will have some left over; reserve the remainder.

⑦ **Bake:** Bake until the apples are softened, the almond paste has puffed slightly, and the edges of the pastry are puffed and deeply golden brown, 25 to 35 minutes. Let cool.

⑧ **Serve:**

✦ Just before serving, brush the apples with the remaining miso glaze (if it's cold and thick at this point, you may need to gently rewarm the glaze over medium heat to loosen it up again).

✦ Sprinkle the top with flaky sea salt. Cut the pastry into squares and serve, preferably with vanilla ice cream.

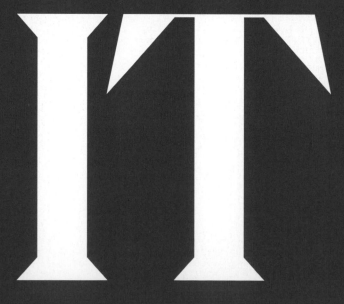

When I take a good hard look at the way I cook at home, it's abundantly clear that I rely heavily on a fully fleshed-out pantry of goods, both homemade and store-bought, to bring variety and vibrancy to my food. Simple recipes can be made a million gazillion times more delicious when you have the right condiments, sauces, and staples to lean on. Many of the recipes in this book feature long-lasting multi-use sauces, marinades, and vinaigrettes, and crispy, crunchy, sprinkly bits that can quickly transform any number of dishes if you make the effort to have them on hand. They're built right into the recipes, but I've also collected them all here, so that should you find your food in need of a quick zhoozh-ing, you'll have an arsenal of yummy condiments to choose from. They're categorized by their predominant flavor profile (Fatty, Salty, Acidic, Umami, Spicy), with an additional section, called Crispy Crunchy, dedicated entirely to texture, so that once you identify what is lacking, you can quickly find a solution. And if you fall in love with any particular condiment and need some inspiration for other ways to consume it, I've made some suggestions in that department, too.

FATTY

Chipotle Lime Dressing
Caesar Dressing
Caesar-ish Dressing
Ranchy Yogurt Dressing
Sneaky Cottage Cheese
Dressing
Kimchi Ranch
Garlicky Yogurt
Classic Aioli
Smoky Mayo
Old Bay Mayo
Tahini Garlic Sauce

SALTY

Soy Butter
Black Olive Mayo

ACIDIC

Greek Salad Dressing
Nuoc Cham Dressing
Any Vinegar-ette
Cilantro Scallion Sauce

Pickled Raisin & Basil Dressing
Pickled Red Onions
Spicy Cukes
Salt 'n' Vinegar Sour Cream
Lemony Yog

UMAMI

Garlicky Pistachio Vinaigrette
Walnut Bagna Cauda

SPICY

Sambal-Sesame Butter
Peanut-Chile Salsa
Red Chimichurri
Chile Crisp

CRISPY, CRUNCHY

Brown-Buttered Nuts
Craggy Croutons
Frizzled Shallots
Crispy Garlic Chips
Garlicky Panko

Chipotle Lime Dressing
MAKES 1½ CUPS

The Vibe: Smoky, Spicy, Creamy

- ½ cup sour cream
- ¼ cup mayonnaise
- ½ cup grated cotija cheese
- ¼ cup liquid from a can of chipotle peppers in adobo sauce
- 1 large garlic clove, finely grated
- Zest of ½ lime
- Juice of 2 limes
- Kosher salt

Combine all of the ingredients in a small bowl and whisk well to combine. Taste and adjust seasoning as needed.

Use it:
- As a dressing for grilled corn
- As a spread on a sandwich
- As a dip with crunchy veg
- Napa Cabbage Salad with Shredded Chicken, Cotija & Corn Nuts (page 185)

Caesar Dressing
MAKES ¾ CUP

The Vibe: Umami, Creamy, Zesty

- 4 oil-packed anchovy fillets, finely chopped and mashed to a paste
- 2 large egg yolks
- 1 teaspoon Dijon mustard
- 1 garlic clove, finely grated
- Zest and juice of ½ lemon
- ½ cup neutral oil
- ¾ teaspoon coarsely ground black pepper
- 1 teaspoon Worcestershire sauce
- 2 ounces grated Parmesan cheese (about ½ cup)
- Kosher salt

In a medium bowl, whisk together the anchovies, egg yolks, mustard, garlic, and lemon zest and juice. Working slowly, add the oil in a very thin stream, whisking constantly as you go, until it is all incorporated and the dressing is thick, creamy, and pale yellow. Whisk in the black pepper, Worcestershire, and Parmesan cheese. Season with salt.

Use it:
- Tossed with warm boiled potatoes
- As a dressing for blanched and chilled green beans
- As a sauce for rotisserie chicken
- The Cae Sal (page 174)

Caesar-ish Dressing
MAKES 1 CUP

The Vibe: Fatty, Creamy, Umami

- 1 garlic clove, smashed, peeled, and mashed to a paste
- Juice of 1 lemon
- 3 oil-packed anchovy fillets, mashed to a paste
- ⅔ cup mayonnaise
- 1 tablespoon Dijon mustard
- 2 tablespoons extra-virgin olive oil
- Kosher salt and freshly ground black pepper

Combine the garlic, lemon juice, anchovies, mayonnaise, and mustard in a small bowl. Whisk in the olive oil and season with salt and black pepper.

Use it:
- As a quick-fix Caesar dressing for romaine, escarole, or kale
- As a dip for kettle chips
- As a sandwich spread
- Caesar-ish Potato Salad with Radishes & Dill (page 220⊙)

Ranchy Yogurt Dressing
MAKES 1¾ CUPS

The Vibe: Tangy, Zesty, Creamy

- 1 cup plain whole-milk Greek yogurt
- ½ cup mayonnaise
- ½ bunch chives, thinly sliced
- 1 garlic clove, finely grated
- Zest and juice of 1 lemon, separated
- Kosher salt and freshly ground black pepper

In a small bowl, stir together the yogurt, mayonnaise, chives, garlic, lemon zest, 1 teaspoon salt, and lots of black pepper. Stir in the lemon juice. Add a splash or two of cold water to the dressing, stirring to combine, until it reaches a drizzle-able but not thin consistency. Re-season the dressing after adding any water.

Use it:
✦ As a ranch-y dip for potato chips
✦ Drizzled over salted cucumbers for a quick cucumber salad
✦ Mixed into leftover roast chicken for chicken salad
✦ The Minimalist Wedge (page 181)

Sneaky Cottage Cheese Dressing
MAKES 1 CUP

The Vibe: Creamy, Zesty

- ½ cup whole-milk cottage cheese
- 1 small garlic clove, finely grated
- 1 lemon
- 3 tablespoons extra-virgin olive oil
- Kosher salt and freshly ground black pepper

Whisk together the cottage cheese, grated garlic, the zest of about a quarter of the lemon, the juice of the entire lemon, and the olive oil. Season to taste with salt and black pepper.

Use it:
✦ As a dressing for crunchy vegetables
✦ Smeared on toast and topped with a poached or boiled egg
✦ As a base for roasted vegetables
✦ Sneaky Cottage Cheese Salad (page 186)

Kimchi Ranch
MAKES 2 CUPS

The Vibe: Ferment-y, Tangy, Thick

- ½ cup labneh or plain whole-milk Greek yogurt
- ½ cup mayonnaise
- 2 teaspoons onion powder
- 1 garlic clove, finely grated
- ½ small bunch chives, thinly sliced
- ¾ cup chopped kimchi
- ½ lemon
- Kosher salt

In a small bowl, whisk together the labneh, mayonnaise, onion powder, garlic, chives, and kimchi. Finely grate the zest of ½ lemon into the dressing. Season with salt to taste.

Use it:
✦ As a dip with potato chips and crudités
✦ Schmeared on toast
✦ On pizza
✦ Hot 'n' Crispy Chicken Cutlets with Kimchi Ranch (page 66)

Garlicky Yogurt
MAKES 1 CUP

The Vibe: Creamy, Tangy, Piquant

- 1 garlic clove, finely grated
- 1 cup plain yogurt
- Kosher salt

In a small bowl, stir together the garlic and yogurt. Season to taste with salt.

Use it:
+ As a spread for sandwiches
+ Swooshed under a plate of roasted veg
+ As a sauce for roasted salmon
+ Spiced, Grilled & Swaddled Chicken Thighs with the Works (page 71)

Classic Aioli
MAKES 1¼ CUPS

The Vibe: Fatty, Creamy, Lemony

- 2 garlic cloves, finely grated
- 2 egg yolks
- 1 cup neutral oil, such as vegetable, canola, or grapeseed
- Juice of 1 lemon
- Kosher salt

Wrap a large, damp kitchen towel around the base of a medium bowl to stabilize it on your work surface. In the bowl, whisk together the garlic and egg yolks. Slowly whisk in the oil, in a very thin stream at first and then more generously once the aioli starts to thicken and lighten in color. **Need a little assistance with that aioli? Pull up this vid to see how it's done.**

Once all of the oil has been added, stir in the lemon juice and season it well with salt.

Use it:
+ ON LITERALLY EVERYTHING
+ Slow-Roasted Piri-Piri(ish) Chicken with Crushed Potatoes & Aioli (page 77)

Smoky Mayo
MAKES 1 CUP

The Vibe: Smoky, Fatty, Assertive

- 1 cup mayonnaise
- 4 teaspoons smoked paprika
- Juice of 1 lemon
- 1 garlic clove, finely grated
- ½ teaspoon kosher salt

In a small bowl, stir together the mayonnaise, paprika, lemon juice, garlic, and salt until well combined.

Use it:
+ Slathered on roast or rotisserie chicken
+ As a base under a pile of crispy potatoes
+ Tomato Toast with Cheddar & Smoky Mayo (page 247)

Old Bay Mayo
MAKES ¾ CUP

The Vibe: Vegetal, Fatty

- ¾ cup mayonnaise
- 2½ teaspoons Old Bay seasoning
- 1 garlic clove, finely grated
- Kosher salt

In a small bowl, stir together the mayonnaise, Old Bay, and garlic. Season with salt.

Use it:

✦ As an alternative dip for Shrimp Cocktail with Dilly Horseradish Cream (page 103)
✦ Slathered on grilled corn on the cob
✦ Alongside crab cakes or fish cakes
✦ Clams on Toast with Bacon & Old Bay Mayo (page 112)

Tahini Garlic Sauce
MAKES 1 CUP

The Vibe: Earthy, Nutty

- ½ cup tahini
- Juice of 1 lemon
- 1 garlic clove, finely grated
- ¾ teaspoon kosher salt

In a small bowl, whisk together the tahini, lemon juice, garlic, salt, and ⅓ cup water. The sauce should be a pourable consistency; if it looks too thick, add another splash of water and whisk to combine.

Use it:

✦ Thinned with more lemon juice as a salad dressing
✦ Drizzled over roasted carrots or sweet potatoes
✦ As a dressing for a grain bowl
✦ Minty Lamb Meatballs with Crispy Cabbage & Tahini Sauce (page 97)

Soy Butter
MAKES ½ CUP

The Vibe: Salty, Sweet, Round

- 2 tablespoons low-sodium soy sauce
- 5 tablespoons unsalted butter, cut into ½-inch pieces
- 2 tablespoons honey
- 2 teaspoons sherry vinegar

In a small saucepan, bring the soy sauce and 1 tablespoon water to a simmer over medium-high heat. Reduce the heat to medium-low. Whisk in the butter, a few pieces at a time, maintaining a bare simmer all the while. Once all of the butter has been incorporated and the sauce looks thick and glossy, remove it from the heat and stir in the honey and vinegar.

Use it:
- As a sauce for crispy-skinned salmon
- Over grilled or seared pork chops
- Drizzled over warm roasted squash
- Charred Brussels with Soy Butter & Fried Garlic (page 207)

Black Olive Mayo
MAKES ¾ CUP

The Vibe: Briny, Salty, Pungent

- 6 tablespoons mayonnaise
- 1 garlic clove, finely grated
- ⅓ cup oil-cured black olives, pitted and chopped

In a small bowl, combine the mayo, garlic, and olives and stir well. No need to season this mayo, since oil-cured black olives are inherently very salty.

Use it:
- On any sandwich that craves a salty note
- As a dressing for potato salad with lots of lemon juice and herbs
- Niçoise Sando with Smashed Egg & Black Olive Mayo (page 129)

Greek Salad Dressing
MAKES 1 CUP

The Vibe: Bright, Kicky, Herbal

- 1 large shallot, thinly sliced lengthwise
- 1 garlic clove, finely grated
- ¼ cup red wine vinegar
- ½ cup extra-virgin olive oil
- ½ lemon
- 1½ teaspoons kosher salt
- Freshly ground black pepper
- 1 tablespoon fresh oregano leaves, or 1½ teaspoons dried

In a medium bowl, whisk together the shallot, garlic, vinegar, olive oil, lemon juice, salt, and lots of black pepper. Tear the oregano leaves in half as you add them to the bowl. Let the shallots sit in the dressing and macerate—the dressing will only improve with time.

Use it:
- ✦ Drizzled over roasted or grilled summer squash
- ✦ As a dressing for cooked grains
- ✦ Winter Greek Salad (page 193)

Nuoc Cham Dressing
MAKES ¾ CUP

The Vibe: Pungent, Sharp, Spicy

- Juice of 3 limes
- 3 tablespoons sugar
- 3 tablespoons fish sauce
- 2 red Fresno chiles, thinly sliced crosswise
- 1 garlic clove, finely grated
- ½ teaspoon kosher salt

In a medium bowl, whisk together the lime juice, sugar, fish sauce, chiles, and garlic. Season with salt.

Use it:
- ✦ As a dressing for smashed cucumbers
- ✦ As a dipping sauce for gingery pork meatballs
- ✦ As a marinade and sauce for grilled zucchini or summer squash
- ✦ Charred Cabbage with Salty Peanuts & Nuoc Cham (page 203)

Any Vinegar-ette
MAKES ¾ CUP

The Vibe: Bright, Acidic

- 1 small shallot, finely chopped
- ¼ cup mix of any vinegars
- 1 tablespoon Dijon mustard
- ½ teaspoon sugar
- ½ teaspoon kosher salt
- Freshly ground black pepper
- ½ cup extra-virgin olive oil

In a medium bowl, whisk together the shallot, vinegars, mustard, sugar, salt, and a few good cranks of black pepper. Slowly drizzle in the olive oil, whisking constantly until the dressing is emulsified, which is just a fancy term for thick and creamy, with no signs of oil and vinegar separation.

Use it:
- ✦ As a dressing for blanched asparagus
- ✦ Stirred into high-quality canned tuna for a bright, mayo-less tuna salad
- ✦ As a marinade for quick-cooking steaks (such as flank or skirt)

Cilantro Scallion Sauce
MAKES ¾ CUP

The Vibe: Spicy, Herbaceous, Fresh

- 4 scallions (white and light green parts only), thinly sliced crosswise
- Leaves from 1 bunch cilantro, finely chopped
- 2 jalapeños, finely chopped
- ¼ cup extra-virgin olive oil
- Juice of 1 lime
- Kosher salt

In a small bowl, stir together the scallions, cilantro, jalapeños, olive oil, and lime juice. Season sauce with salt.

Use it:
- Spooned over sliced steak
- Stirred into labneh or yogurt for a quick dip
- As a sauce for fillets of seared or grilled fish
- Poached Chicken over Brothy Rice with Cilantro Scallion Sauce (page 69)

Pickled Raisin & Basil Dressing
MAKES ½ CUP

The Vibe: Sweet and Sour, Spicy

- ½ cup red wine vinegar
- ½ cup golden raisins
- 2 tablespoons sugar
- ¾ teaspoon red pepper flakes
- ¾ teaspoon kosher salt
- 1 small shallot, thinly sliced crosswise
- 1 cup basil leaves

In a small saucepan, combine the vinegar, raisins, sugar, red pepper flakes, salt, and ¼ cup water. Cook over medium-high heat, swirling the pan often, until the liquid has reduced to about a third of what you had originally, 5 to 7 minutes. It should still be loose enough to drizzle—not sticky. If you think you've over-reduced it, add a teaspoon of water to loosen the liquid. Remove it from the heat. Stir the shallots into the still-warm raisins. Just before serving, while still warm, gently stir in the basil leaves until just coated in the vinegar.

Use it:
- Scattered over a roasted fillet of fish
- Tossed with roasted cauliflower or broccoli
- Spooned over a crusty piece of ricotta-slathered toast
- Roasted Eggplant with Pickled Raisin & Basil Dressing (page 212)

Pickled Red Onions
MAKES 1½ CUPS

The Vibe: Acidic, Sweet, Crunchy

- 1 cup distilled white vinegar
- ½ cup sugar
- 1 tablespoon kosher salt
- 2 medium red onions, cut crosswise into ⅛-inch-thick rings

In a small saucepan, combine the vinegar, sugar, salt, and 1½ cups water and bring to a simmer over medium heat, stirring often to dissolve the sugar and salt. Once the vinegar mixture comes to a simmer, remove from heat and immediately add the onions. Let cool to room temperature. The onions can be made up to several days in advance; they only get better with time.

Use it:
- Tossed in salads
- As a topping for burgers or grilled chicken sandwiches in place of raw red onion
- On a smoked fish, bagels, and shmear board
- Spiced, Grilled & Swaddled Chicken Thighs with the Works (page 71)

Spicy Cukes
MAKES 3 CUPS

The Vibe: Spicy, Crisp, Refreshing

- 1 English (hothouse) cucumber, halved lengthwise, cut crosswise into ⅛-inch-thick half-moons
- 1½ teaspoons kosher salt
- 2 tablespoons unseasoned rice vinegar
- ¾ teaspoon red pepper flakes
- 2 teaspoons sugar

Combine the cucumbers and salt in a medium bowl and toss and scrunch them with your fingers to encourage the salt to get in there. Let the cucumbers sit uncovered in the fridge for at least 15 minutes and up to 2 hours. Tip off and discard any liquid that is left in the bowl. Add the vinegar, red pepper flakes, and sugar and toss well to coat. Keep chilled until ready to serve.

Use it:
+ Stirred into yogurt for a tangy cucumber raita–like dip
+ Alongside a crispy breaded chicken cutlet
+ Scattered over wedges of cold watermelon and seasoned with flaky salt for a sweet-savory fruit salad
+ Miso-Marinated Pork Steaks & a Big Pile of Spicy Cukes (page 93)

Salt 'n' Vinegar Sour Cream
MAKES 1 CUP

The Vibe: Creamy, Acidic, Tangy

- ¾ cup sour cream
- 3 tablespoons distilled white vinegar
- ½ teaspoon kosher salt

In a small bowl, stir together the sour cream, vinegar, and salt.

Use it:
+ Thinned with a little more vinegar and a splash of water as a creamy dressing for hearty greens
+ Stirred into chili or any other spicy braised meat stew
+ As a topping for baked potatoes
+ Smooshed & Crispy Potatoes with Salt 'n' Vinegar Sour Cream (page 226)

Lemony Yog
MAKES 1¼ CUPS

The Vibe: Zesty, Creamy, Tangy

- 1 lemon
- 1 garlic clove, finely grated
- 1 cup plain whole-milk yogurt
- Kosher salt

In a small bowl, stir together the zest of the lemon, the garlic, and yogurt. Cut the lemon in half and squeeze the juice of both halves into the yogurt, stir to combine. Season with salt.

Use it:
+ As a dressing for blanched tender vegetables such as peas or green beans
+ Drizzled into a hearty lentil stew or spicy chili
+ As a dip for cucumbers and radishes
+ One-Pot Chicken & Schmaltzy Rice with Lemony Yog (page 167)

Garlicky Pistachio Vinaigrette
MAKES 1 CUP

The Vibe: Bright, Umami, Crunchy

- 1 garlic clove
- 2 lemons
- ⅓ cup extra-virgin olive oil
- 1½ ounces grated Parmesan cheese (about ⅓ cup)
- ¾ cup roasted, salted pistachios, finely chopped
- Kosher salt and freshly ground black pepper

Finely grate the garlic and the zest of 1 lemon into a small bowl. Add the juice of both lemons, whisking it all to combine. Slowly stream in the olive oil, whisking as you go. Stir in the Parmesan cheese and pistachios. Season the dressing with salt and lots of black pepper.

Use It:
+ As a salad dressing for sturdy greens that the nuts and cheese can cling to
+ Tossed with hot pasta and some pasta water for an alt pesto
+ Spooned over mozzarella or burrata and served with crusty bread as an appetizer
+ Cold & Crunchy Green Beans with Garlicky Pistachio Vinaigrette (page 196)

Walnut Bagna Cauda
MAKES 1 CUP

The Vibe: Intensely Umami, Fatty, Salty

- 10 garlic cloves, smashed and peeled
- 10 oil-packed anchovy fillets
- ⅓ cup extra-virgin olive oil
- ½ cup walnuts, finely chopped
- 2 tablespoons unsalted butter

In a small saucepan, combine the garlic cloves, anchovy fillets, and olive oil. Set the saucepan over very low heat and cook very gently, stirring occasionally and mashing it with a fork once the garlic starts to soften until the garlic and anchovies are totally dispersed, 12 to 14 minutes. The oil will barely simmer as the anchovies fry in the oil. Add the walnuts and butter to the bagna cauda and continue to cook over low heat until the walnuts are toasted and crisp, 8 to 11 minutes longer. Serve warm.

Use it:
+ As a salad dressing for bitter greens (such as radicchio or escarole) with lots of lemon juice added
+ As a dip for crudités
+ Drizzled over roast chicken
+ Charred Leeks & Burrata with Walnut Bagna Cauda (page 216)

Sambal-Sesame Butter
MAKES ¾ CUP

The Vibe: Rich, Spicy

- ½ cup (1 stick) unsalted butter, at room temperature
- ¼ cup sambal oelek
- 1 teaspoon toasted sesame oil
- Zest of 1 lime

In a medium bowl and using a fork, mash the butter, sambal oelek, sesame oil, and lime zest until well combined.

Use it:
+ Slathered on a rested steak
+ Fry an egg in it
+ Tossed with blanched green beans
+ Grilled Corn with Sambal-Sesame Butter & Lime (page 204)

Peanut-Chile Salsa
MAKES 1 CUP

The Vibe: Nutty, Toasty, Crunchy

- ½ cup peanuts, chopped
- ½ cup extra-virgin olive oil
- 2 garlic cloves
- 1 tablespoon ancho chile powder
- 1 teaspoon honey
- ½ teaspoon red pepper flakes
- ½ teaspoon kosher salt

In a small pot, cook the peanuts and olive oil over medium heat, stirring often, until the peanuts are golden brown, 4 to 5 minutes. Remove from the heat. Finely grate the garlic right into the oil while it's still hot, stirring to combine. Stir in the chile powder, honey, red pepper flakes, and salt.

Use it:
+ As a condiment for tacos
+ Spooned over a rice bowl and topped with a crispy fried egg
+ Sweetie P's with Peanut-Chile Salsa (page 219)

Red Chimichurri
MAKES 1¼ CUPS

The Vibe: Smoky, Bright, Spicy

- 1 garlic clove, finely grated
- 3 tablespoons red wine vinegar
- 1 teaspoon sugar
- 1 teaspoon smoked paprika
- 3 tablespoons extra-virgin olive oil
- 1 small shallot, finely chopped
- 1 red Fresno chile, finely chopped
- ½ cup drained roasted red peppers, finely chopped
- Kosher salt

In a small bowl, whisk together the garlic, vinegar, sugar, smoked paprika, and olive oil until combined. Stir in the shallot, chile, and roasted red peppers. Season with salt.

Use it:
+ Stirred into yogurt as a dip
+ Drizzled over roasted broccoli
+ Skirt Steak with Red Chimichurri (page 83)

Chile Crisp
MAKES ½ CUP

The Vibe: Spicy, Crispy, Warming

- ⅓ cup extra-virgin olive oil
- 1 (3-inch) cinnamon stick
- 3 garlic cloves, thinly sliced
- 1 medium shallot, thinly sliced into rings
- ½ teaspoon kosher salt
- 2 teaspoons red pepper flakes

Set a fine-mesh strainer over a small heatproof bowl. In a small saucepan, combine the olive oil, cinnamon stick, garlic, shallots, and salt over medium-low heat. Cook, stirring, until the oil comes to a simmer, about 2 minutes. Continue to cook, stirring with a fork to separate the shallot rings that are nestled together and swirling the pan occasionally until the shallots and garlic are golden brown, 13 to 15 minutes. Strain the oil into the bowl. Let the shallots and garlic cool in the strainer for 2 to 3 minutes, then stir them back into the oil, along with red pepper flakes.

Use it:
+ Drizzled over fried rice
+ Over blistered green beans or asparagus
+ Grapefruit & Burrata Salad with Chile Crisp (page 178)

Brown-Buttered Nuts
MAKES ¾ CUP

The Vibe: Nutty, Fatty

- 5 tablespoons unsalted butter
- ⅔ cup walnuts, finely chopped
- 2 teaspoons Aleppo pepper or other mild chile flakes
- ¼ teaspoon ground turmeric
- ½ teaspoon kosher salt

In a small saucepan, cook the butter over medium-low heat until just melted and foamy. Add the walnuts and cook, stirring occasionally, until very lightly toasted, 2 to 3 minutes. Add the Aleppo pepper and turmeric and continue to cook until the walnuts are toasted and golden brown and the butter is very nutty-smelling and fragrant, 1 minute longer. Remove from the heat and stir in the salt.

Use it:
+ Drizzled over roast fish
+ Stirred into yogurt as a spread for crusty bread
+ As a dressing for cooked lentils or grains (add some lemon juice!)
+ Jammy Eggs with Yogurt and Brown-Buttered Nuts (page 125)

Craggy Croutons
MAKES 3 CUPS

The Vibe: Crunchy, Salty

- ½ crusty baguette (6 ounces), torn into 1-inch irregular pieces
- 2 tablespoons extra-virgin olive oil
- ½ teaspoon kosher salt
- Freshly ground black pepper

Preheat the oven to 350°F. On a rimmed baking sheet, combine the torn baguette with the olive oil, salt, and a few good cranks of black pepper, tossing with your hands until well coated. Transfer to the oven and bake until deeply golden brown and crisp, 12 to 14 minutes. Let cool.

Use it:
+ Stirred into soups to add texture
+ Crushed into smaller bread crumbs with a wine bottle or rolling pin and scattered over pasta
+ As a crouton for any other salad that could use some crunch!
+ The Cae Sal (page 174)

Frizzled Shallots
MAKES 1 CUP

The Vibe: Savory, Sweet, Salty

- 4 large shallots, peeled and thinly sliced crosswise into rings
- 3 tablespoons extra-virgin olive oil
- Kosher salt

In a large nonstick skillet, combine the shallots and olive oil and cook over medium heat, stirring often, until they turn deep golden brown and are charred and crispy around the edges, 10 to 15 minutes, depending how thinly you sliced them. Transfer the frizzled shallots to a small plate and season with salt.

Use it:
+ Tossed into salads as an alt crouton
+ As a topping for sautéed greens
+ Scattered over labneh, with a drizzle of extra-virgin olive oil and a sprinkle of red pepper flakes for a quick-fix dip
+ Extremely Fried Eggs with Frizzled Shallots & Rice (page 130)

Crispy Garlic Chips
MAKES 3 TABLESPOONS

———

The Vibe: Crispy, Pungent, Bitter

- 4 garlic cloves, thinly sliced
- ¼ cup neutral oil, such as canola, vegetable, or grapeseed
- Kosher salt

Set a fine-mesh strainer over a small bowl. In a small saucepan, combine the garlic and oil over medium heat and cook, swirling the pan often, until all of the garlic is lightly golden brown, 3 to 5 minutes. Remove the saucepan from the heat and strain the oil through the fine-mesh strainer into the bowl. Transfer the garlic chips to a small plate to cool. Season lightly with salt. Reserve that garlic oil for roasting vegetables or searing chicken or steak.

Use it:
+ Scattered over charred broccolini
+ As a garnish for a creamy dip
+ Charred Brussels with Soy Butter & Fried Garlic (page 207)

Garlicky Panko
MAKES ⅔ CUP

———

The Vibe: Crunchy, Salty, Fatty

- 3 tablespoons extra-virgin olive oil
- 3 garlic cloves, smashed and peeled
- ⅔ cup panko bread crumbs
- ½ teaspoon kosher salt

In a large nonstick skillet, cook the olive oil and garlic over medium-low heat, swirling the pan often, until the garlic is fragrant and lightly golden brown, about 4 minutes. Add the panko and stir to coat evenly in the oil. Cook, stirring often so the panko toasts evenly, until golden brown all over, 4 to 5 minutes; season with the salt. Transfer to a plate or shallow bowl and let cool. Pluck out and discard the garlic cloves.

Use it:
+ As a topping for a cheesy gratin
+ Scattered over any pasta dish for a salty finish
+ Sprinkled over a piece of tender, slow-roasted fish for textural contrast
+ The Minimalist Wedge (page 181)

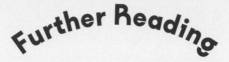

Further Reading

While I am absolutely thrilled that you picked up this book, I will also note that there are many, many other beautiful, informative, and genius cookbooks out there that I encourage you to seek out as further reading. Some of the most blissful moments of my life have occurred while sitting in bookstores, immersed in cookbooks, and surrounded by the culinary wisdom of the many chefs, cooks, and authors that make our ability to cook and eat in the present day so incredibly exciting. Many of the recipes and ingredients used in this book are inspired by the rich cuisines of cultures that are not my own. As I continue to educate myself about their histories through reading, firsthand experience, and travel, I urge you to do the same. Here are just a few of the gems, both old and new, that hold a permanent place in my collection and have both inspired me over the years and educated me as I embarked on writing a cookbook of my own:

Bottom of the Pot, by Naz Deravian

Cooking for Artists, by Mina Stone

The Flavor Bible, by Andrew Dornenburg and Karen Page

Into the Vietnamese Kitchen, by Andrea Nguyen

Japan, by Nancy Singleton Hachisu

Japanese Home Cooking, by Sonoko Sakai

Jubilee, by Toni Tipton Martin

Korean Home Cooking, by Sohui Kim

Marcella's Italian Kitchen, by Marcella Hazan

My Mexico City Kitchen, by Gabriela Camara & Malena Watrous

New World Sourdough, by Bryan Ford

Night + Market, by Kris Yenbamroong

On Food and Cooking, by Harold McGee

Ottolenghi, Plenty, and *Jerusalem,* by Yotam Ottolenghi

Ratio, by Michael Ruhlman

River Café London, by Ruth Rogers

Salt, Fat, Acid, Heat, by Samin Nosrat

Season, by Nik Sharma

Six Seasons, by Joshua McFadden

Vegetable Kingdom, by Bryant Terry

A Very Serious Cookbook, by Jeremiah Stone and Fabian von Hauske

Where Cooking Begins, by Carla Lalli Music

Zaitoun, by Yasmin Khan

The Zuni Café Cookbook, by Judy Rogers

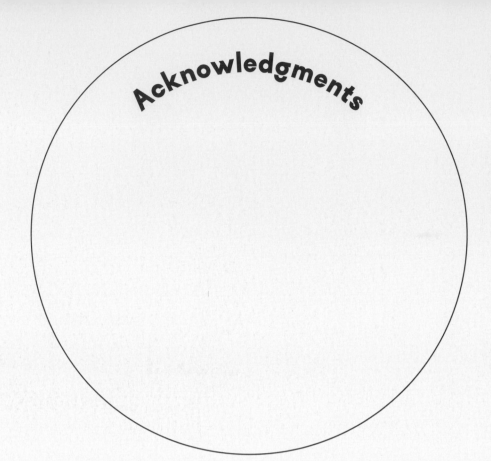

Acknowledgments

To my sweet, sweet husband, Ben: It's ridiculous to even include you in this list of acknowledgments because, frankly, your name should be on the spine next to mine. Thank you for enduring months and months of incessant book talk. Thank you for tasting every recipe in this book and recognizing when my food wasn't "me" when I couldn't. This book is only cool because of you. To my incredible photographers, Taylor Peden and Jen Munk: I never in a million years thought you'd actually want to do this project, and I sort of still can't believe it—your talent is completely unrivaled in the food world and I am so blessed. To my fierce and loyal agent, Nicole Tourtelot: You are such a badass—it's almost unfathomable. Thank you for handling every little thing with such confidence, composure, and grace. To my editor, Jenn Sit: Thank you for asking me to breakfast the first time we met. I was scared shitless, but you lit a fire in me, and this book is the result of that. I am forever grateful for your insights and encouragement. To my fabulous food stylist, Christopher St. Onge: I'm so glad I found you!! I knew we shared an aesthetic when I first saw the way you sliced celery, and it was really all the convincing I needed. I'll never slice my celery any other way. You and your very talented assistants absolutely killed the styling in this book. To my pumpkin-pie-loving prop stylist/Mojo Mama, Eli Jaime: Thank you for bringing the most beautiful props

and, equally, the most ridiculous sense of humor to our set every day. Your talent is rivaled only by your silliness, and I love that for you. To my fab French design team, Violaine & Jérémy: Sans vous deux, mes plus grands rêves de design n'auraient jamais pu être réalisés. Et comme vous seuls savez si bien le faire, vous avez réussi à les rendre encore plus grands et encore plus beaux. Merci du plus profond de mon cœur, pour ce travail accompli dont je suis extrêmement fière. To Yeah-Ya: Thank you for swooping in and so effortlessly saving the day in a time of crisis. I promise to cook for you and feed you any time you want, no questions asked. To Ali Slagle, the most efficient, organized recipe tester I know: Thank you for all of your hard work and focus, and for always keeping the big picture in mind as you cooked through Every. Single. Recipe. In this book. To Andrea Nguyen, thank you for all of the insightful wisdom and experience you so generously brought to this book. To my parents, Jill and Doug: WOW. This goes without saying, but your unwavering support of me, of my career, and of the journey that is my first published cookbook is one of the greatest gifts I'll ever be lucky enough to receive. Thank you from the bottom of my heart. To my brother, Adam: As long as you are my older brother, everything I do I'll do to impress you, and this book is no exception. We are the bad babies. Don't you ever forget it. To the world's sweetest weenie,

Tuna: You are the longest and most delicious little hot dog I've ever known, and waking up next to you every day is an absolute joy. To my Babela: I am so proud of the competent cook you've become over the last few years. Thank you for cooking through so many of my recipes, for your thorough notes and at times ridiculous questions. There's a lot of *crema* in this book—I did that for you. To Sam Russell a.k.a. Tiff a.k.a. Shmuel: Thank you for reading and cooking your way through this book and coming to my aid when I needed it the most. You are an absolute gem. To Yoland and Jared: Thank you for being my cheerleaders and my most reliable recipe testers. Your enthusiasm for this book did not go unnoticed. To mi Nora, my culinary soul sister: Thank you for all the sound advice, brainstorming, and ideating you always provide. There's no one in this world I enjoy cooking and eating with more than you. For the last time, I'm so sorry I left you hanging on our first date. To the Biggest Dog, Declan: Thank you for being so unbelievably insightful and wise and helping to shape all of my thoughts and ideas since day one of this endeavor. We are the happy ones, don't ever forget it. To Milky and Little Ms. Schmultz: Thank you for answering every annoying question I've ever asked you about how to manage my social. I know you think I am "offline," but having you two by my side makes me feel a little closer to the possibility of getting back on. To my

former boss turned Cheese Queen and Friend4Lyfe, Carla: I've said it before but I'll say it again, thank you for seeing in me whatever it was you did and opening the door to the world of BA for me. It has been an absolute honor and privilege to work under you, with you, and alongside you. There are exactly zero moms as cool as you, and I can't wait to see what the future holds for us both.

To my Test Kitchen Fam, Andy, Chris, Sohla, Brad, Claire, and Gaby: Working alongside the six of you for the last four years has been the greatest honor of my professional career. You are easily the most talented, thoughtful, creative, and F–U–N cooks I've ever known. Thank you for making work feel like play every day of my life. To @grossypelosi: Thank you for loving my chicken wings children like they are your own, and for all of the beautifully curated objects you surround yourself with that are featured in this book. To Era Ceramics, Caraway, Caroline Hurley, Design Within Reach, East Fork Pottery, and Great Jones: Thank you for generously donating so many beautiful, perfect, vibey products—all of which brought so much life to this book. And lastly, but certainly not least, to everyone on the team at Potter: Thank you for believing I deserve to write a cookbook and for putting so much energy, spirit, and enthusiasm into the making of this book. It has been nothing short of a dream come true.

PEEP THESE TECHNIQUES!

CHOP AN ONION

DE-LOBE A BELL PEPPER

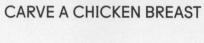

CARVE A CHICKEN BREAST

CARVE A CHICKEN

CORN OFF THE COB

MAKE AIOLI

FIND THE GRAIN

CHOP A SHALLOT

STRAIN EGG WHITES

DEVEIN
SHRIMP

REMOVE
CITRUS PITH

STACK BISCUITS FOR
FLAKY LAYERS

SLICE FENNEL

SCOOP AND LEVEL FLOUR

THE THREE-FINGER PINCH

SEPARATE EGGS

BUTTER BASTE

THE ROLL CUT

CITRUS SEGMENTS

MEET TUNA

Index

What Shall We Do Without Us?

The Voice and Vision of Kenneth Patchen

with an afterword by James Laughlin

A YOLLA BOLLY PRESS BOOK PUBLISHED BY

Sierra Club Books

San Francisco

FIRST EDITION

Certain of the works reproduced in this book were originally published
in *Hallelujah Anyway,* copyright 1960, 1961, 1962, 1963, 1964, 1965, 1966 by Kenneth
Patchen, and *But Even So,* copyright 1968 by Kenneth Patchen, published
by permission of New Directions Publishing Corporation. All works not
appearing in the foregoing, copyright 1984 by The Regents of the University of California. "Remembering Kenneth Patchen" copyright 1984
by James Laughlin. All rights reserved. No part of this book may be
reproduced in any form or by any electronic or mechanical means,
including information storage and retrieval systems, without permission
in writing from Sierra Club Books. Printed by Dai Nippon Printing
Company, Ltd., Tokyo, Japan.

A YOLLA BOLLY PRESS BOOK

What Shall We Do Without Us? was produced in association with the publisher at The Yolla Bolly Press, Covelo, California under the supervision
of James and Carolyn Robertson.

The original picture poems, manuscripts, letters and first editions are a
part of The Kenneth Patchen Archive and are located in Special Collections, University Library, University of California, Santa Cruz. The
University gratefully acknowledges the Friends of th UCSC Library for
their long-standing support of the Archive.

"Kenneth Patchen: Principal Works" was compiled by Jonathan Clark,
who also made the original color transparencies from which this book
was reproduced. The bibliography is published here by permission of
Mr. Clark. Photograph of Kenneth Patchen by Chester Kessler, published
by permission of Robert E. Johnson.

The Sierra Club, founded in 1892 by John Muir, has devoted itself to the study and
protection of the earth's scenic and ecological resources—mountains, wetlands,
woodlands, wild shores and rivers, deserts and plains. The publishing program of
the Sierra Club offers books to the public as a nonprofit educational service in the
hope that they may enlarge the public's understanding of the Club's basic
concerns. The point of view expressed in each book, however, does not necessarily
represent that of the Club. The Sierra Club has some fifty chapters coast to coast,
in Canada, Hawaii, and Alaska. For information about how you may participate
in its programs to preserve wilderness and the quality of life, please address
inquiries to Sierra Club, 530 Bush Street, San Francisco, CA 94108.

LIBRARY OF CONGRESS CATALOGING IN PUBLICATION DATA
Patchen, Kenneth, 1911–1972.
What shall we do without us?
"A Yolla Bolly Press book."
Bibliography
I. Laughlin, James, 1914–   II. Title.
PS3531.A764W45   1984   811'.54   84-4891
ISBN 0-87156-843-8
ISBN 0-87156-818-7 pbk.

Acknowledgments

The producers of this book and its publisher extend their appreciation to Miriam Patchen, who, from the start, has given the project her enthusiastic support. They also wish to thank Jonathan Clark for permission to reprint, in this volume, his selected bibliography of Patchen works.

Special thanks are extended to Rita Bottoms, Special Collections Librarian at the University of California, Santa Cruz, who is responsible for the care of, among other resources, The Kenneth Patchen Archive. Her vision and cooperation were essential to the making of this book. Appreciation is also extended to Allan Dyson, University Librarian, and to Carol Champion and Paul Stubbs of the Special Collections staff.

Everyman is me,
I am his brother.
No man is my enemy.
I am Everyman
and he is in and of me.
This is my faith,
my strength,
my deepest hope,
and my only belief.

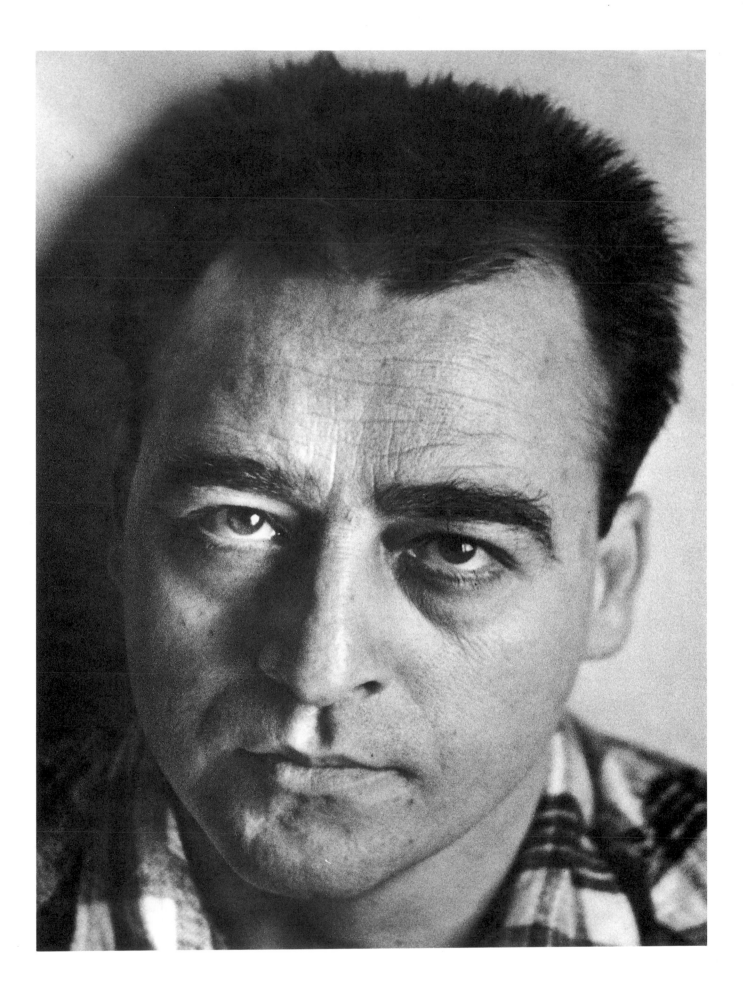

THE LION PART

& that which is water lily, sea gull,
Heather, crimson-dotted butterfly,
Lizard, ant, and heart-shaped leaf,
White panther, lynx, marsh frog,
Grass, dogs, and little paradise beetles—
Oh, it's a lot of business we have,
Being part and substance of everything
That lives! O yes this tall trade of ours,
This business of being represented here
On earth in all these funny-wonderful
Shapes and guises such as... well, ostriches,
Walruses, elephants and three-toed galuttos...
No, this business of being alive
Is not really 9,824 feet long,
Or Alexander the Great (was it?) wide,
And Jesus Buddha Johnny Jepps high...

And to think ... it all started out like any other

World

Peace or we all perish

or

Intended, one might almost have been led to believe, to last for a good long time

Kenneth Patchen

for miriam · on our twenty-eighth wedding anniversary · 28 June 69

What can you do up here
that you can't go on doing
just as vilely on earth?
Patchen

The World
Is Nothing
That Can
Be Known

in the shadow
we shall see
the color of
God's eyes
again

Patchen

beyond Love

there is no belief

IN THE LONG RUN

This is
a race
where everybody
ends up

in a tie, sorta

Kenneth Patchen

The birds
are
very
careful
of
this
world

Ha! a lot of good
that'll do them!

(Behind those desks
some mighty
dangerous
guys
are sitting, Baby.)

Patchen

The World's Not
Enough Really

For The
Kind of Rent
We Have To Pay
To Live In Us

Patchen

IT'S A LWAYS TOO SOON OR TOO LATE

Fact is,

the train don't come on time for nobody

except those who should walk all the way to hell on their own backs

THE BEST HOPE

Is that one
of these days
the ground
will get disgusted
enough just to walk
away~ leaving
people with nothing
more to stand on
than what they

have so bloody well
stood for up to now

Patchen

Do you think that somebody will find us in time?

Yeah, I'm afraid so. That's the one thing they're bloody good at.

Sure, Leroy,
There Is
A
Kindness
Of
Willing
& A Cruelty
Of Won'ting
Still—no dog ever
Doubt his dogness
The maple tree
Never mistake
Himself—for
Any other cuss
But a man—
Who is us?

Patchen

the CONTINUOUS CHRIST

dying rising O seasons
of Earth Sky Sea Air
in one Touching Hearing
the Seeing of the Sun
and these mistaken
& pathetic imaginings

"man"

"bird"
"fish"
beast
"flower"
"stone" "lake" "tree"
Forever-leaving
arriving always

O this
Animal
where

all "reason"
denies it standing

into that unmoving
Nothing Everything ness

back & forth
and yet again
O
Eternity's Single Clockman
"Life" "Death"
hallucinatory mask

All things are
all things
True?
And if
not,
how not...
Then, my
little two-legged flea,
name me one
single thing
that is <u>not</u>
all
things!
Eh?

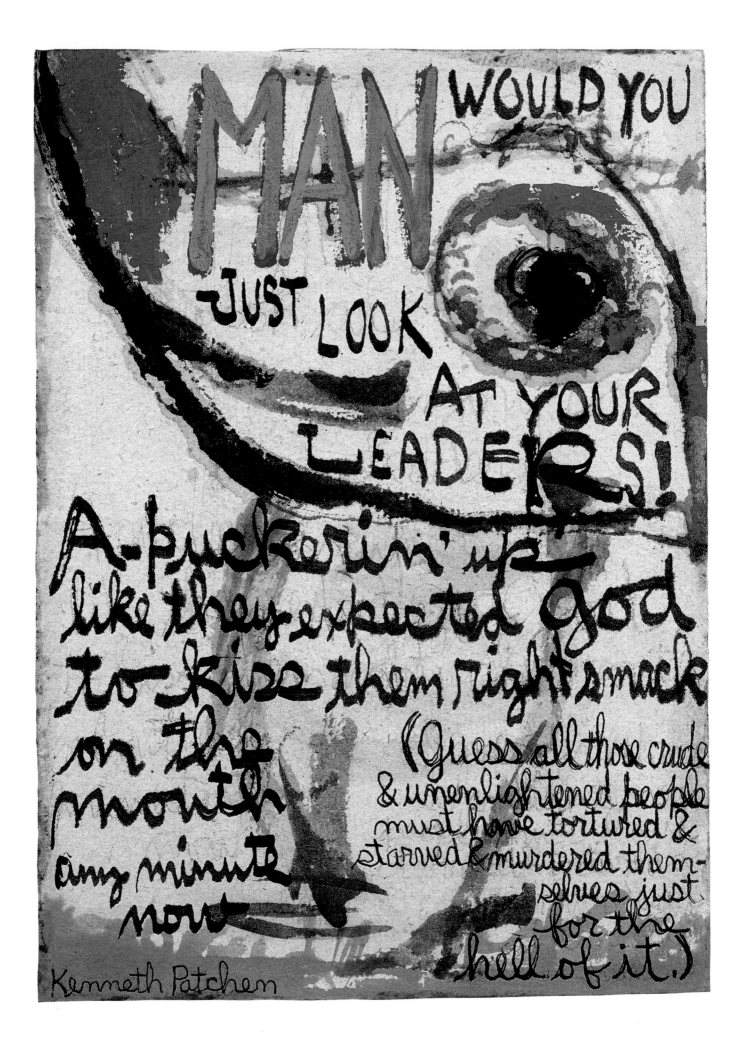

Which of us is not flesh?

Last

and first, in that common cause. Beyond

this— I would like to be able to say... to say more

Snow is the only one of us that leaves no tracks

Kenneth Patchen

The concerns of the heart

Feeling, I must remind you, is the poet's sign—
O let the print of her hurrying sandal
be unrecorded in the meadow's thousand deaths
yet upon his heart it has signed the angel's name. For him the distance of the world is never less than when he is forced to think how all he loves must soon be taken away

Kenneth Patchen

The One

Who comes
To Quest-
ion Him-
self

Has cared for mankind

Patchen

O TAKE HEART, MY BROTHERS

Even now...with every Leader
& every Resource & every Strategy
of every Nation on Earth

arrayed
against
Her—
Even now
O even
Now! my
Brothers

Life is in no danger
of losing the argument!
—For after all....
(As will be shown)
She has only to change the subject.

Kenneth Patchen

Remembering Kenneth Patchen

The poet's publisher, James Laughlin, recalls their association

Sometimes it is strange what the memory retains. Where are the pieces that the film editor cut and dropped on the cutting room floor? I think I knew Kenneth Patchen for about thirty-three years. That would be from old letters; I never kept a diary. And the scenes of Miriam and Kenneth which survive are not in narrative sequence. They jump around in time, a flickering black and white film. There isn't much sound, though I can hear Kenneth's deep, deliberately slow voice and Miriam's liquid laughter. Surely it must have been Miriam's laughter which kept Kenneth going through those years of agony when his back was constant pain and the pain was battering his spirit.

The first scene shows Patchen and his young wife Miriam at the Oikemuses' farm near Concord, Massachusetts. That would be in 1938. I had been corresponding with Kenneth for over a year, because I was impressed by his first book of poems, *Before the Brave,* which Random House published in 1936. The writer of the jacket copy, who was not off the mark, spoke of Patchen's "social and revolutionary principles," and said that "he scorns the devices of his poetic elders and seeks by experimentation new and more dynamic verse forms." Not exactly Bennett Cerf's kind of book, but it certainly was mine. So I was happy when Random House let him go and he signed on with New Directions. His first book with us was *First Will and Testament* in 1939.

But back to the farm. I noted how very tidy the Oikemuses kept their place. If the edges of the picture are out of focus, the center is not. Miriam was, and is, more than pretty. There is the light from within, the radiance of the illumined heart. And Kenneth, before illness demolished him, was a handsome man. Those eyes were gentle, but there was such an intensity in his glance. He always looked at people, not around them. He looked into me and sometimes I hated to think what he might be seeing there. Miriam had told me that her parents, who came from Finland, were socialists. One reason I came to Concord was to look into that; I was planning to ask the Patchens to come run the New Directions office in Norfolk. It was on the family place, which was presided over by that miraculous survivor from an earlier age, my Aunt Leila. She was a lady of infinite good works, but her social and political views were somewhat retarded. Once I had met the Patchens, and the Oikemuses, I knew there would be no problem. They were not *Reds*. They were fine people, good people; they were pacifists.

I always suspected that some of Patchen's social awareness and his powers of protest may have come from the Oikemuses. He never, so far as I know, professed himself a socialist, and I'm sure that he never signed on with the communists, though there were a lot of them around in his younger days whom he could have known; I think he distrusted parties of the left as much as he did those of the right. But the concern for social justice was one of the strongest drives in his life, and one of the paramount themes of his poetry, and he submitted some of his early work to journals of the left.

We heard about "under God" from the Founding Fathers, and our politicians still love to mouth the phrase. Patchen was very much "under God." He wanted to get us all under God's wing.

> I am going to tell you the story of my mother's
> Meeting with God.
> . . .
>
> She walked up to where the top of the world is
> And He came right up to her and said
> So at last you've come home.
> . . .
>
> My mother started to cry and God
> Put His arms around her.
> . . .
>
> She said it was like a fog coming over her face
> And light was everywhere and a soft voice saying
> You can stop crying now.
>
> "Do the Dead Know What Time It Is?"

Often Patchen's idea of God is melded with the theme of pacifism. He would have been a conscientious objector were it not for his back. He spoke out constantly against war, and it was this, perhaps more than anything else in his writing, which made him such a hero to the young. The theme of pacifism is sometimes stated through Patchen's identification with animals:

> Because the snow is deep
> Without spot that white falling through white air
>
> Because she limps a little—bleeds
> Where they shot her
>
> Because hunters have guns
> And dogs have hangmen's legs
>
> Because I'd like to take her in my arms
> And tend her wound
>
> Because she can't afford to die
> Killing the young in her belly
>
> I don't know what to say of a soldier's dying
> Because there are no proportions in death.
>
> "The Fox"

Which God was Patchen's God? Probably not the Christian God, though many cadences and references in his poetry show that he had read the King James Version closely. Perhaps his God was a Being whom he created to give him the answer that he needed in his battle to save the world. I suppose that only innocents, or fools, imagine that they can save the world. And poets, those innocents, often try. Pound, for all his errors, partly meant that the *Cantos* should help reform the economic system. He dreamed of a *paradiso terrestre*. One of the dominant themes in Williams's *Paterson* is that of the new, "redeeming language," and it is clear that he hoped its consequences, if he could realize it, might be social as well as poetic. From his idol, William Blake, Patchen derived his own concept of a prophetic poetry. He did not write poems for amusement; he had a message. And, happily, he was not a *vox clamantis in deserto*. Over a period of perhaps fifteen years, he, along with Henry Miller, was one of the most popular American writers among young people in America.

Religion and politics. In Patchen's work they go together. His ethic is brotherhood. "Do unto others . . ." and if we all pull together we can save ourselves and our beautiful earth. His God is the spiritual force which can bring the *paradiso terrestre*. Of brotherhood he wrote:

> The bloodhounds look like sad old judges
> In a strange court. They point their noses
> At the Negro jerking in their noose;
> His feet spread crow-like above these
> Honorable men who laugh as he chokes.
>
> I don't know this black man.
> I don't know these white men.
>
> But I know that one of my hands
> Is black, and one white. I know that
> One part of me is being strangled,
> While another part horribly laughs.
>
> Until it changes,
> I shall be forever killing; and be killed.
>
> "Nice Day for a Lynching"

Thanks to the chronology in Larry R. Smith's excellent critical book on Patchen in the Twayne United States Authors Series, it is possible to run our film backwards. Patchen was born in Niles, Ohio, in 1911, where his father was a steelworker for Youngstown Sheet & Tube. The family moved to Warren in 1915, where there was another Youngstown mill, and there Kenneth grew up. His mother was a Catholic and wanted him to become a priest. In the poems, he speaks of his father with respectful affection:

> When I was five years old my father got hurt
> Very badly in the mill; they carried him in
> Through the kitchen of our house—two men
> at his head, two at his feet—and carted him upstairs.
>
> "Anna Karenina and the Love-Sick River"

But in a remarkable, and I think autobiographical, story, "Bury Them in God," which appeared in the New Directions 1939 anthology (and was reprinted in the 1972 book *In Quest of Candlelighters*) we see that there was a problem of sensitivity between father and son. The narrator's beloved younger sister has just died, and he writes:

> My father walks into the kitchen with the alertness of one expecting great events. . . . "When did she die?"
>
> I cannot answer. I want to pound him with my fists. You dirty, cheap, sweaty-nosed monster. . . . Noreen is dead! Does it make no difference to you? "When did she die?" as calmly as "Is supper ready?" I can see him at the head of the table, making thick noises with his lips as he wolfs the best pieces of meat . . .

"Bury Them in God," which seems to have escaped the notice of most writers about Patchen, may deserve some attention. To me, it is clearly autobiographical. I once showed it to a psychiatrist friend; he was fascinated. "This is a missing persons report," he said. I think I can identify two areas on which a psychiatrist might speculate, one within the Patchen family and one outside it, that is, how a young writer saw his role in the world. It would take a geneticist of some imagination to determine how the stork brought a prophetic, language-obsessed poet to the Patchen household. Kenneth must have been more than a mystery to his parents; he must often have been an annoyance. Imagine the friction and, for him, the frustration.

In the story, Swanson, the narrator's cynical friend says, "You got . . . the prettiest damned sister who kicks the bucket and maybe you wanted to sleep with her . . . so what?" Swanson is surely coloring the nature of the relationship to make his point, but would it not have been natural for Patchen to transfer to his sister the affection he could not feel for his parents because he thought they did not understand him? Later, would Miriam with her understanding and complete devotion, become the perfect replacement for his beloved sister? How much resentment, how much anger, conscious or unconscious, might Patchen have had against his father and mother?

And then, if there was such anger, how much of it might later have been trans-
ferred to the leftist establishment, a potential sheltering and guiding parent, when it
did not accept his early revolutionary poetry? Swanson is described as the leftist
poet, "who came in clean and hard on the wave of proletarian writing and was left
high and dry when it receded." In Swanson's failure with the leftists is Patchen talking
about his own first book, *Before the Brave?* How much did its lukewarm acceptance by
the leftist journals hurt him? In the story, he goes on to say of Swanson: "He writes
anger now. He has bogged down in hating people who are not worthy of notice."
I find this statement, "He writes anger," very important for understanding Patchen's
work. And I link familial and political anger. We must face it. Patchen often does
write anger. Take such a poem as "The Hangman's Great Hands."

> And all that is this day . . .
> The boy with cap slung over what had been a face . . .
> Somehow the cop will sleep tonight, will make love
>   to his wife . . .
> *Anger won't help. I was born angry.*
> *Angry that my father was being burnt alive in the mills;*
> *Angry that none of us knew anything but filth and poverty.*
> *Angry because I was that very one somebody was supposed*
> *To be fighting for*
> Turn him over; take a good look at his face . . .
> Somebody is going to see that face for a long time.

Underneath the gentleness of spirit and the faith in love, there was deep anger.
I remember that boiling anger from late-night conversations in 1945 when the
Patchens were living near Abingdon Square in Greenwich Village. They were renting
a little two-room house built in a backyard. It was a rather dingy place, but Miriam,
as she always somehow managed to do, made it cheerful and attractive. All evening
Kenneth drank coffee; I used to think he would burst from it. At first the talk was
quiet. (So often I wondered, over the years, how the glorious, rich language of the
poems could come out of such a plain-talking, almost hesitant speaker. Henry Miller
has recorded Patchen's "awesome silence. It seems to spring from his flesh, as though
he had silenced the flesh. It is uncanny. Here is a man with the gift of tongues and
he speaks not. Here is a man who drips words but he refuses to open his mouth."
Miller is exaggerating, but not altogether.) After a few hours and more coffee Patchen's
emotion would build, and the anger would begin to sound out. The rhetoric would
become pyrotechnical. Most of it focused on the bad state of the world, the successful
poets he didn't like, and the stupidity of the editors of *Partisan Review* who would not
publish him.

Patchen had worked in the steelmills to earn money to go to college at Wisconsin.
He was a good athlete. I've been told that he had a football scholarship, but had to
give it up because of a heart condition. (There may also have been a football injury

that started the lifelong problems with his back.) But he was also a man of letters, and thought of himself as such, from the age of seventeen, when he had two sonnets accepted by the *New York Times*. A lady I once met, who had dated Patchen when they were growing up together in Ohio, spoke of him as "the aesthetic type" and rather a dandy. He knew all about the French poets, she told me. Which French poets? She couldn't remember. Swanson, in the story, mentions Villon. Could he have read Rimbaud? That would fit. Patchen is often compared to the surrealists; Charles Glicksberg called his work "surrealism run amok." I think the accusation is mistaken; the comparison is far too easy. What surrealist art looks like these picture poems? None that I know of. I think that two very different mechanisms of imagination are operative in Patchen. Some of Patchen's fantasy poems are *dreamlike*, but they are definitely not oneiric dictations according to the surrealist rules. Instead, they combine a fusion of word and image with an often whimsical fantasy.

I go back to that story "Bury Them in God" because so many of the techniques and strategies which Patchen would later develop in such prose books as *Memoirs of a Shy Pornographer* and *The Journal of Albion Moonlight* appear in it for the first time. (The visual tricks, the concrete poetry of *Sleepers Awake* came later.) Collage structure of the parts in contrasting styles replaces sequential narrative. There is verbal exaggeration for comic effect, and slang is mixed in with literary style for the same purpose. Shift of persona occurs as Swanson takes over as the narrator. We find a kind of prose poetry in the impressionism of some passages. Here is the use of italics for parody-tags of biblical prose (*And he said, How can I, except some man shall guide me? . . . and forthwith the angel departed from him*) which are inserted without break into a tough-style paragraph in which the narrator imagines that he is beating his mother with a "board with a long nail sticking out of it." There is the syncopated, intimate dialogue between the lovers. All of the stylistic ingredients are there which will later be elaborated and refined—or almost all of them.

Let's make this scene short. I don't like the way I see myself in it now. No whip, but Simon Legree. It is later in 1938, and the Patchens have come to Norfolk to do all the dirty work of running New Directions while I flit around the country. The office is on the family place on the flank of Canaan Mountain, where my aunt has converted a small stable into a work place—a neo-Georgian, white brick stable. The horse boxes have gone and are replaced with shelves and work tables for Kenneth and a desk for Miriam. The cottage where they live is connected to the office by a breeze-way. The cottage is at the edge of the forest—birches, beeches, pine and hemlock—and across Mountain Road is the sheep meadow. There are rhododendrons and azaleas in the yard. And half a mile down the forest road is Tobey Pond. Very lovely? Well, not entirely. The cottage is a mile from the village, and the Patchens have no car. My aunt's grumpy chauffeur, Frank, and the farmer, taciturn Joe, are dragooned into driving the book packages down to the post office and bringing back the Patchens' groceries. This, they feel, is beyond the call of their duties, and they grouse about it. If the Patchens need something unexpectedly, they have to walk for it. And Norfolk (population about 1700) is not exactly lively. It has a very fine little library which Kenneth uses; otherwise a drugstore, a hardware store, and the post office. The nearest real town with a movie theater is seven miles away and there are no buses. Oh yes, a nice quiet place for a poet to write—after eight or ten hours of packing books and posting ledgers. Miriam and Kenneth have all the grubby work, including proofreading, while I have the fun of reading manuscripts and corresponding with authors. And woe betide them if there are any slip-ups. I am obsessed with making the business go, and I come down on them with a sarcasm which is almost hostility.

How they put up with it as long as they did I don't know; except that Kenneth desperately wanted me to publish his books. As I did, actually for some thirty years, though never all of them that he wanted me to do. But I did love his picture poems, and New Directions published three collections of them; *Hallelujah Anyway* (1966), *But Even So* (1968), *Wonderings* (1971), and four of his illustrated books of poetry and prose: *Because It Is* (1960), *Hurrah for Anything* [in *Doubleheader*] (1966), *Aflame and Afun of Walking Faces* (1970), and *In Quest of Candlelighters* (1972). The earliest two of this last group of books, which arc illustrated with pen, charcoal, and wash drawings, show the genesis of the later picture poems, in which there is no longer "illustration," but the fusion of words and pictures into an integrated "poem."

Henry Miller was one of Patchen's most ardent boosters. Miller promoted Patchen and sought help for him as often as he could. His essay "Patchen: Man of Anger and Light" had wide distribution because it was included in his book *Stand Still Like the Hummingbird*. At the time (1946) I was pleased, but now as I reread it I am less happy about it as a permanent part of the record. Much of it is misleading for Miller did what he so often did: he wrote himself into his subject. Patchen would not have disagreed with what Miller wrote in the pages about the position of the artist, but the ideas, and their expression, are Miller's as we find them in his other writings, and not Patchen's. What troubles me more is some outright distortion in the descriptions of Patchen. To support his metaphor of the "snorting dragon," who is a "gentle prince" inside, Miller calls Kenneth a monster and a "fizzing human bomb." He goes on to say, "He is inexorable; he has no manners, no tact, no grace." Well, that is simply not the Patchen I knew. Kenneth was no *schmeichler*, but he had courteous manners and he never exploded in my presence. Miller is much more to the point when he focuses on Patchen's books:

> Patchen uses the language of revolt. . . . It is in his prose works that Patchen uses this language most effectively. With *The Journal of Albion Moonlight,* Patchen opened up a vein unique in English literature. These prose works, of which the latest to appear is *Sleepers Awake,* defy classification. Like the Wonder Books of old, every page contains some new marvel. Behind the surface chaos and madness one quickly detects the logic and the will of a daring creator. One thinks of Blake, of Lautréamont, of Picasso—and of Jakob Boehme. Strange predecessors! But one thinks also of Savonarola, of Grünewald, of John of Patmos, of Hieronymous Bosch—and of times, events and scenes recognizable only in the waiting room of sleep.

Bosch was a favorite of Miller's. He called one of his best books *Big Sur and the Oranges of Hieronymous Bosch.* Had Patchen seen reproductions of paintings such as "The Garden of Earthly Delights" when he began to draw the strange little animals of the picture poems? Probably he had. But they are not of the same zoology. To me, the Bosch creatures are malign and somehow kinky. Those of Patchen are loving and happy.

It is 1947, and I have come down from the Litchfield Hills to see the Patchens near Old Lyme, Connecticut. It is a sylvan scene. The little red cottage they are renting is in the woods a bit outside the village. There is a sedate black cat named Pushkin. Kenneth's back is hurting him so he can't join us when we go for a walk among the trees. But where are Kenneth's *green* deer? For him deer are green. They are green in some of the poems and in *Memoirs of a Shy Pornographer,* the book which has my hand covering "porn" on the jacket. And years later, when he was hoping for a uniform edition of his books, which I was never able to materialize for him, he wanted it to be called the Green Deer Series. It's not hard to imagine what green deer symbolized for him: the natural continuum, the bond between man and the animals which the Indians understood, the preservation of our environment, even the imagination itself. And the deer are related to the fanciful animals and birds which appear in the picture poems.

I came away from Old Lyme feeling that I had found Kenneth happy. Despite his back and the usual financial worries, he seemed more relaxed, more accepting. I took with me an intensified sense of the quality of the affection that bound Kenneth and Miriam to each other and enabled them to sustain each other and to keep his life going. He read me some of the love poems he was writing to her. It is hard to make a choice from the many lovely love poems that Kenneth wrote to Miriam. She was his Sita, Sita the wife of Rama in the *Ramayana*, who is still venerated in India as the perfect wife.

> O my darling troubles heaven
> With her loveliness
>
> She is made of such cloth
> That the angels cry to see her
>
> Little gods dwell where she moves
> And their hands open golden boxes
> For me to lie in
>
> She is built of lilies and candy doves
> And the youngest star wakens in her hair
>
> She calls me with the music of silver bells
> And at night we step into other worlds
> Like birds flying through the red and yellow air
> Of childhood
>
> O she touches me with the tips of wonder
> And the angels cuddle like sleepy kittens
>
> "O My Darling Troubles Heaven with Her Loveliness"

To be sure, there are lapses in such a poem. It would be hard for a big man to sleep in a golden box of a size little gods could carry around. The sunset may be red and yellow but the air isn't. Wonder does not have tips. It's easy to see why the establishment critics, when they deigned even to notice Patchen, made fun of him as sentimental. Certainly it is a sentimental poem. But for me it works, despite the slapdash imagery. The intensity of the feeling carries it. The feeling is communicated. Every poet who is in love doesn't have to be Cavalcanti describing love in the Aristotelian terms of the *Donna mi pregha*. There are kinds and kinds of poetry and they can all work if the passion is there. It was Patchen's "sentimentality," and related excesses, which made him a too easy target for the new critics and the professors of English who gave him the bastinado all his life. But there were a few of them who could see both sides of the coin. James Dickey was one, a very good poet and critic, who wrote in *Sewanee Review* in 1958 (collected in *Babel to Byzantium*, Farrar, Straus, & Giroux, 1968):

> Patchen is still, despite having produced a genuinely impassible mountain of tiresome, obvious, self-important, sprawling, sentimental, witless, preachy, tasteless, useless poems and books, the best poet American literary expressionism can show. Occasionally, in fragments and odds and ends nobody wants to seek out any more, he is a writer of superb daring and invention, the author of a few passages which are, so far as I can tell, comparable to the most intuitively beautiful writing ever done . . .

If there is such a thing as pure or crude imagination, Patchen has it, or has had it. With it he has made twenty-five years of notes, in the form of scrappy, unsatisfactory, fragmentarily brilliant poems, for a single, unwritten cosmic Work, which bears, at least in some of its parts, analogies to the prophetic books of Blake . . .

He has made and peopled a place that would never have had existence without him: the realm of the "Dark Kingdom," where "all who have opposed in secret are . . . provided with green crowns," and where the vague, powerful figures of fantasmagoric limbo, the dream people, and, above all, the mythic animals that only he sees, are sometimes as inconsolably troubling as the hallucinations of the madman or the alcoholic, and are occasionally, as if by accident, rendered in language that accords them the only kind of value possible to this kind of writing: makes them obsessive, unpardonable, and magnificent.

When Patchen was writing, the environmental movement had not yet become the public concern that it is today. We had experienced the shock of Hiroshima, and in the East, Governor Rockefeller was telling us to build shelters under our houses, but few of us realized, or were willing to believe that a nuclear war would be total devastation, wiping out all life on the planet. But Patchen understood it very well. Yet there was then no accepted tradition of environmental poetry as we have it now, at its finest, in the work of such a poet as Gary Snyder. Jeffers had celebrated the Big Sur and Everson the country north of San Francisco. Frost had given us rural New England, and Rexroth was writing his great philosophical mountain poems of the Sierra Nevada. These were the poets most available to Patchen, but his passion demanded a stronger, more accusatory voice. In one of the picture poems he tells the politicians:

> I proclaim this international
> shut your big fat flapping mouth week

And in another he tells the industrialists and their bankers:

> The birds are very careful of this world
> Ha! a lot of good that'll do them!
> (Behind those desks
> some mighty dangerous guys are sitting, Baby.)

And he warns us all:

> The words that speak up from the mangled bodies of
> human beings
> This is the fallout that covers everything on earth now
>
> The best hope is that one of these days
> the ground will get disgusted enough just to walk away
> leaving people with nothing more to stand *on*
> than what they have so bloody well stood *for* up to now

In the extended form of his written poems Patchen could develop his themes more richly, though sometimes a poem becomes too rich, with image piled pell-mell on image until clarity is lost and the reader feels overwhelmed by so much sensory stimulation. Here are two short poems which do not get out of control and in which we can identify with Patchen's intimate connection with nature and the animal world:

> The quail flutters like a forlorn castle falling
> *I do not mean her harm*
>
> She thinks I wish to hurt her young;
> The little things are somewhere hidden.
> They move their tiny mouths but do not cry.
>
> I cannot ever hurt thee, little bird
> I cannot ever hurt thee
>
> I have but a bullet left
> And there are so many things to kill.
>
> "The Quality of Mercy"

> They stand contentedly, chewing
> *What does it mean to live now?*
>
> They are solid and the muscles move
> Easily in the oil of their blood
> *What does it mean to live now?*
>
> They put their faces together like children
> And their great gentle eyes look at me
> *What does it mean to live now?*
>
> I run my hand along their necks, lovingly.
>
> "Plow Horses"

The Journal of Albion Moonlight is surely Patchen's most important prose book. In the summer of 1940 (he was then living on Bleecker Street in the Village) he wrote me that he had begun work on it and, intrigued by the title, I asked him what kind of book it would be. I quote at some length from his reply because it is an historic statement, both about the book and about himself, which has never been published:

I attempt to write the spiritual account of this summer. I do so on several levels . . . realizing that I must give corporal presence to the journal's narrator, I decided to surround him with semi-fictional characters, who would act in the capacity of lending definition and interest to the things which Albion Moonlight chose to record. Should these characters conform to the accustomed time-and-space machinery of the novel? No, I had no intention of writing either a murder mystery or a love story, and even less to write a novel of ideas— it was my task to keep inviolate my intention of writing a journal of this summer—a summer when all the codes and ethics which men lived by for centuries were subjected to the acid tests of general war and universal dis-illusionment. I had *to recreate that chaos* . . . uncharted horror and suffering and complete loss of heart by most human beings.

I have used the narrative method in this manner: it has been my weapon against the false and sterile reality of the story books—I have satirized the creaking framework of the whodidit and what'stohappennext fairy tale; I have, I think kept the reader on his toes—I have made him a participant—I have removed the obvious landmarks and encouraged him to accept the book for what it is: an attempt to evaluate the world in the precise terms by which the world will force its will on him.

I introduce a little novel into the journal. This is done in order that I may attack the problem in an oblique way, to be able to write about the characters as though they were already the public property of the novelist, and not only the companions of Moonlight—to give them histories outside the confines of the journal, to indicate that they had a flesh and blood existence before the summer of 1940.

I am at a place in the writing now where Adolf Hitler comes to Moonlight after a bombing raid. I intend a long dialogue between them—in which Hitler asks Moonlight for advice, for a way out.

The meaning of my book? It means a thousand and a thousand things. What is the meaning of this summer?

I must confess that when Patchen sent me the completed manuscript of *Moonlight* I was baffled. I wasn't yet ready for it. (Both Pound and Thornton Wilder had warned me about the time-lag that is inevitable, for ordinary readers at least, when a work of real originality appears.) I sent the manuscript to Edmund Wilson for his appraisal. His report is vintage Wilson and should someday be published in full to show what Patchen was up against with the literary establishment, and why he was so bitter about its power. I'll give a few lines from it: "It is a mixture of Rimbaud, the Dadaists, Kafka and a number of other things—with a considerable talent of Patchen's own for improvising a rigmarole of images, ideas and dialogues. I haven't found it exactly boring to read: there is a lot of verbal felicity, and there are many unexpected and amusing things . . . he has talent and he ought to be encouraged; but he is still pretty juvenile." Wilson ended his report with a nice New England touch: "I skipped large sections of the latter part of the book, so you need only pay me $40." So the first edition of *Moonlight* was published by Kenneth and Miriam themselves. But later I saw the light and it was added to the New Directions paperback list and there became, for us at least, a bestseller.

It is interesting, I think, to compare what our greatest literary critic, Edmund Wilson, found in *The Journal of Albion Moonlight* with what two of Patchen's peers, the poets William Carlos Williams and Kenneth Rexroth, saw in the book. Williams's review is titled "A Counsel of Madness," and Rexroth's, "Kenneth Patchen: Naturalist of the Public Nightmare." (Both pieces are included in Richard Morgan's invaluable *Kenneth Patchen: A Collection of Essays*.)

Williams's prose style for criticism is blessedly unique, for its syntax which challenges us to think in new ways, for its subjectivity—a man writing about poetry who has written some of the best—and for its curiously prowling mode. He circles around his subject like a dog sniffing trees; when he finds the right one, he lets fly.

For what we're after is a cure. That at its best is what the book's about. A man terribly bitten and seeking a cure, a cure for the bedeviled spirit of his day. Nor are we interested in a Punch and Judy morality with a lily-white soul wrapped in a sheet—or a fog, it doesn't matter which. We are ready and willing to accept a low down human spirit which if it didn't have a hip-joint we'd never be in a position to speak of it at all. We know and can feel for that raving reality, bedeviled by erotic dreams, which often enough is ourselves. This book is from the gutter.

The story is that oldest of all themes, the journey, evangelical in purpose, that is to say, with a purpose to save the world from impending doom. A message must be got through to Roivas, read the name backward.

He must get through a message to the people such as they are who have lost hope in the world. . . .

Patchen slams his vivid impressions on the page and lets them go at that. He is investigating the deformities of truth which he perceives in and about him. Not idly. He is seeking, the book is seeking, if I am correct, a new order among the debris of a mind conditioned by old and persistent wreckage. . . .

Where does the journey take place did I say? In America? Why not? One place is like another. In the mind? How? What is the mind? You can't separate it from the body or the land any more than you can separate America from the world. We are all one, we are all guilty.

Whether or not this book is a good one (let's not talk prematurely of genius) I believe it to be a right one, a well directed one and a hopeful one. It is the sort of book that must be attempted from time to time, a book to violate all the taboos, a racial necessity as it is a paradisical one, a purge in the best sense—suggesting a return to health and to the craft itself after the little word-and-thought pansies have got through their nibbling.

. . . the work of a young man. . . . He voices the world of the young—as he finds it, screaming against what we, older, have given him. This precisely is the book's prime validity.

Williams and Rexroth were friends, but their approaches to criticism were totally different. Williams was instinctive and intuitive; Rexroth was the erudite comparatist, at home in all literatures, including the Oriental. But he was also a superb literary streetfighter. In his essay, Rexroth begins by situating Patchen in relation to the pre–World War I liberals:

> The silentiaries of American literature . . . have ceased to be able to tell good from evil. One of the few exceptions is Kenneth Patchen. His voice is the voice of a conscience which is forgotten. He speaks from the moral viewpoint of the new century, the century of assured hope, before the dawn of the world-in-concentration camp. But he speaks of the world as it is. Imagine if suddenly the men of 1900—H. G. Wells, Bernard Shaw, Peter Kropotkin, Romain Rolland, Martin Nexo, Maxim Gorky, Jack London—had been caught up, unprepared and uncompromised, fifty years into the terrible future. Patchen speaks as they would have spoken in terms of unqualified horror and rejection. He speaks as Emile Zola spoke once—"A moment in the conscience of mankind."

> It is difficult to say if the artist and the prophet ever really merge. . . . Artist and prophet seem perpetually at war in Blake and D. H. Lawrence. But there comes a point when the minimum integrity necessary to the bare functioning of the artist is destroyed by social evil unless he arise and denounce it. . . .

> Against a conspiracy of silence of the whole of literary America, Patchen has become the laureate of the doomed youth of the Third World War. He is the most widely read younger poet in the country. Those who ignore him, try to pass over him, hush up his scandalous writing, are read hardly at all, unwillingly by their English students and querulously by one another. Years ago Patchen marked out his role. "I speak for a generation born in one war and doomed to die in another." . . . He is never published in the highbrow quarterlies. In a market where publishers spend millions to promote the masturbation fantasies of feeble-minded mammals, his books have made their way into the hands of youth, the hands that are being drafted to pull the triggers, the youth that is being driven to do the dying—for the feeble-minded mammals and their pimping publishers.

Much has been written about Patchen's graphic work, with the writers often seeing in it what they came to it wanting to see, so perhaps it is best to begin with what Patchen himself said about it. In an interview with the poet Gene Detro Patchen tells us:

> I don't consider myself to be a painter. I think of myself as someone who has used the medium of painting in an attempt to extend—give an extra dimension to the medium of words. . . .

> There is always . . . between words and the meaning of words, an area which is not to be penetrated . . . the region of magic, the place of the priestly interpreter of nature, the man who identifies himself with all things and with all beings, and who suffers and exalts with all of these.

> It is not the nature of the artist to know what his true influences are . . . I think that the mystery of life will ring in the work, and when it rings most strongly, truly and honestly, it will ring with a sense of mystery. [And with a sense] of wonder, childlike wonder . . . a sense of identification with everything that lived. . . .

> I feel that every time he [Paul Klee] approached a new canvas it was with a feeling that "well, here I am, I know nothing about painting, let's learn something, let's feel something"—and this is what distinguishes the artist of the first rank, the innovator, the man who *destroys* [my italics. JL], from the man who walks in the footsteps of another.

Almost without exception, the writers on Patchen's picture poems see a connection with Klee, as do I. I would urge readers to look at Jürg Spiller's *Paul Klee: The Thinking Eye*, New York, Wittenborn, 1961.

What interests me most in the picture poems are the "creatures," and whether or not they descend from the ordinary animals of the earlier words-only poems. Barring the green deer, those earlier ones were recognizable animals such as we see around us. But now, in the picture poems, there have been drastic metamorphoses. I don't recall hearing Kenneth talk about Ovid, but like Ovid he has changed many mortals into strange creatures, even into trees or plants. They inhabit an unreal, a surreal world; yet it is also our world because they are talking to us in our language. These lopsided, deformed little birdies and beasties are often brightly colored as a child would color them with his crayons, and diminutive as a child's toys. It was a necessity to Patchen to preserve the innocence, the "wonder," as he put it, of childhood. One of his names for this realm was "The Dark Kingdom." That wonder was part of his defense against a bad world. Kenneth called the first collection of his poems in England *Outlaw of the Lowest Planet*. Yes, the creatures are outlaws, but not bandits. They do not attack us. They are benevolent, they wish us well. They warn and advise us. They offer us what comfort they can.

Patchen's handwriting—he used the same script for the picture poems as he did in his letters—provokes curiosity. What would a graphologist say about it? Did Kenneth flunk the Palmer Method which doubtless was taught in the grade schools of Warren, Ohio? James Schevill, the San Francisco poet who is now Professor of English at Brown, says of it:

> Patchen's distinctive handwriting adds to the effect of his work. A round, rolling scrawl, it is a kind of American anticalligraphy, calling attention to its demerits as classical penmanship, voicing its humorous desire to wander around in words and encounter laughing mysteries. It is the handwriting of a man who has endured a lifetime of pain, who has transformed that pain into a singular joy. . . . After closer inspection what may seem to be crude penmanship becomes a large, wide-eyed scroll of wonder. Beware again of calling it naive. The shape of a painful will, doggedly enduring, searching, is everywhere evident.

The power of Patchen's imagination is evident in his poem titles. No one, not even Tennessee Williams, has thought up more tempting, more suggestive titles. Here are a few chosen at random from the *Collected Poems*:

"A Letter to a Policeman in Kansas City"

"A Letter on the Use of Machine Guns at Weddings"

"Avarice and Ambition Only Were the First Builders of Towns
    and Founders of Empire"

"Boxers Hit Harder When Women Are Around"

"The Character of Love Seen as a Search for the Lost"

"Do the Dead Know What Time It Is?"

"I Got the Fat Poet into a Corner and Told Him He Was Writing
    'S—T' and Couldn't Get Away with It."

"Can the Harp Shoot Through Its Propellers?"

"The Reason for Skylarks"

These wonderful titles are little poems in themselves and they sound the great range of Patchen's poetic œuvre. But when we come to the picture poems, we find a slightly different kind of title-as-poem. The picture poems are like extended titles. They do not juxtapose disparate images as the other poems do. In the picture poems, once a metaphor or a conceit is established, it is usually maintained throughout. No doubt this was because of the limited space available for word-language on the fairly small sheets which Patchen, painting on a board in bed, had to work. Sometimes there are only a score of words, seldom many more. This obligatory compression led Patchen to tiny fables, to apothegms—some serious, some comic—to epigrammatic, often sardonic jokes, to free-verse limericks. Could one call some of them Patchenesque, fantasy haikus?

Caring is the only daring / oh you know it

What shall we do without us?

I got me the blue dawg blues / If the Devil don't wag this world, / How come
all you lousy cats / Lickin' away at his shoes!

I have a funny feeling / that some very peculiar-looking creatures out there
are watching us

That one about the creatures out there who are watching us succinctly states, as we
shall see, the central motifs, both visual and substantial, of the picture poems.

The world is nothing that can be known / in the shadow we shall see the color
of God's eyes again / beyond love there is no belief

To think it all started out like any other world / intended, one might almost
have been led to believe, to last a good long time

All at once is what eternity is

Everyman is me, / I am his brother. No man is my enemy. I am Everyman and
he is in and of me. / This is my faith, my strength, my deepest hope, and my
only belief.

Peace now for all men / or amen to all things

The next scene is in San Francisco. It must be about 1952, on one of my trips to the
City of Poets from Utah, where I have been trying, rather ineffectually, to run the
ski lodge at Alta—as a supplement to the meager earnings of New Directions. The
Patchens are renting a tiny apartment on the second floor of one of those non-
descript little wooden houses which must have been built by the thousands after the
great earthquake and fire of 1906. I think it was on Telegraph Hill, not far from
Ferlinghetti's City Lights Bookstore (and from New Joe's in North Beach where the
maritata soup was the staple of my diet).

Allen Ginsberg met Patchen in San Francisco at about this time and described
him as looking "like a mild longshoreman." But today he looks tired and weak. He
is feeling miserable. His back is hurting steadily, and he is bitter about his poverty.
Miriam is not there because she has had to take a fulltime job selling perfume in a
department store to support them. He misses having her with him and he hates it that
she should have to work. He is down on a world that does not provide for poets.
If I were not so involved with the ski resort, could more of his books be sold? I blame
his sales on the mentality of the clerks in most bookstores. (At one time he did try
to cater to mass taste and wrote the novel *See You in the Morning*; it made a fair bit of

money but not enough to make such hack work tolerable.) "But the stores do buy Eliot," he says, "there are stacks of Eliot in Paul Elder's." "Eliot has fooled them," I tell him. "Eliot has convinced them he is British; ever since the Civil War the Boston Brahmins have thought that if a book were British it must be literature."

I change the subject to Pound's Social Credit, and how Ezra believes that when his economic theories are adopted the National Dividend will provide a living for artists and writers. Kenneth is dubious. "The politicians are the worst. They hate artists and they are afraid of writers who expose their lies. And there are no Medicis or Maecenases anymore." I know what's coming, though he spares me and doesn't say it. My aunt had once told Kenneth how her cousin Duncan Phillips gave the painter Arthur Dove a stipend. But there wasn't anything like that I could do for Patchen. I hadn't yet received an inheritance and was financing New Directions from my allowance, then begging from my family when a printer refused to do any more work till I paid up. Patchen's hope was that his idea for a poetry & jazz program might catch on and make money. With his back, he could hardly contemplate a tour, but there were recordings and the radio. I was never in San Francisco at the right time to hear a performance, but I'm told they were very good indeed, and I have the Cadence and Folkways records, which even I, who have never cared much for jazz, find exciting.

I went downtown to visit Miriam at work at The City of Paris. I could see why they had put her in perfumes on the first floor right near the main entrance. She was so handsome and had such zest for the sale. I spotted her the moment I came in the store and stood aside to watch. She was working on an overdressed lady whose expression of anxiety clearly indicated that she needed help with her personal life. Which exotic essence would put things right for her? Miriam dabbed little drops of different scents on the lady's wrist, and they both smelled and discussed. A decision was finally made, and the lady paid and went off beaming.

When I came to the counter Miriam pretended not to know me. "And what can I do for you, young man?" she asked, with an engaging smile. She produced a purple crystal bottle in the shape of a swan and gave me the treatment. The stuff smelled so awful—it must have been pure civet—that we burst out laughing and hugged each other. She had told me on the phone that her lunch relief would appear at noon, as she did, and we repaired to the cafeteria for a BLT and malt.

Yes, she was very worried about Kenneth. His back seemed to be getting worse, there might have to be another operation, and he was in deep depression. Nevertheless he was writing well and was doing quite a bit of drawing. She didn't really mind the work except that she hated leaving him alone all day. Nothing could get Miriam down. And nothing ever did, even when things got worse later.

At first intermittent, when in 1937 Miriam reported a "violent attack of back disability," becoming more frequent and finally completely disabling, pain was the dominant factor in Patchen's physical life. I never really understood exactly what was the matter with Kenneth's back. Over the years there were different diagnoses, several operations and finally one which was almost certainly botched. I know of no clinical summary by a medical writer, but James Schevill gives an account of the agonies of the sixties in his memoir "Kenneth Patchen: The Search for Wonder and Joy," which is one of the most sensitive pieces written about Patchen. Jim Schevill was a good Samaritan indeed; he often drove Kenneth from Palo Alto to Berkeley for his medical consultations and assisted him, I suspect, with his expenses.

At one time or another many distinguished writers helped raise money for Patchen's medical bills. In 1950 there were benefit readings and concerts through a fund set up by Eliot (yes, T. S. Eliot, who didn't like Patchen's poetry at all; I remember his frown when I first showed him a Patchen book in his office at Faber & Faber), Thornton Wilder, Auden and MacLeish, with the backing of Cummings, Marianne Moore, Williams, Edith Sitwell and many others. Later there would be benefits sponsored, as I recall, by Ferlinghetti, Schevill, and the rest of the San Francisco poets.

How did Patchen come to terms with his suffering? How did it affect his ability to work and his creativity? Henry Miller put these questions to him. Patchen's written reply is revealing:

> The pain is almost a natural part of me now—only the fits of depression, common to the disease, really sap my energies and distort my native spirit. I could speak quite morbidly in this connection. The sickness of the world probably didn't cause mine, but it certainly conditions my handling of it. Actually, the worst part is that I feel I would be something else if I weren't rigid inside with the constant pressure of illness; I would be purer, less inclined to write, say, for the sake of being able to show my sick part that it can never become all powerful; I could experience more in other artists if I didn't have to be concerned so closely with happenings inside myself; I would have less need to be pure in the presence of the things I love, and therefore, probably, would have a more personal view of myself.

I have heard mean-spirited people say that Patchen's illness was psychosomatic, that it was the sickness of the world, or at least his obsession with it, which caused his pain. One of them quoted Schiller's dictum that it is the spirit which controls the body. I don't buy that. It was Patchen's indomitable spirit which kept his body from killing him long before it did. (But I cannot analyze what he meant by needing "to be pure in the presence of the things" he loved.)

This last scene is the saddest. One would think that those three Greek ladies would have provided a good end for a good poet, but it doesn't always happen that way. Archie MacLeish was vigorous and writing to the end, but Rexroth lay so paralyzed that for months he could only raise one hand, Pound was in deep depression for years, and Williams, wrecked by his strokes, was in a fury of frustration because he could only type the poems of *Pictures from Brueghel* with one finger at a snail's pace and he had so much more in his head he wanted to write.

It must be in the mid-sixties and I am calling on the Patchens in their little house on Sierra Court in Palo Alto. It's a nice neighborhood, a quiet street, trees, and a yard behind the house where Miriam is training the black squirrels to come to her to be fed. It's the best house they ever lived in. How they were able to buy it I can't guess, unless Miriam had an inheritance. Patchen did not receive his $10,000 grant from the National Foundation of Arts and Humanities until 1967. Again, Miriam has made the rooms attractive, warm, and cheerful. There are several of Kenneth's strongly colored paintings on the walls, and his treasure, the tiny torn scrap of a Blake etching given to him by the English poet Ruthven Todd. Small as it is, the fragment can be identified. It is the opening two lines of Blake's "America: A Prophecy":

> [The Guardian Prince of Albion] burns in his nightly tent:
> [Sullen fires across the Atlantic gl]ow to America's shore,

It seems clear what the "sullen fires" meant to Patchen: a prophetic warning of the nuclear holocaust he feared. The lines from the poem, presumably in Blake's own hand, are etched in at the bottom of the plate, while above them floats the figure of a little angel. There we have, I'm sure, the chief source of inspiration for the mixing of words and drawing in Patchen's picture poems. Of course, Blake usually separated the lines of language from the drawings on the plate, while Patchen mingled the words with the visual shapes, making them a part of the design. But from the frequent references to Blake in his letters to me, I believe that Patchen thought of himself as a successor, wishing only to find a structure which would not seem like plagiarism or parody.

I asked my friend Aleksis Rannit at Yale what he thought about a Blake/Patchen connection. (Aleksis is a great Estonian poet-in-exile, but art history is his hobby.) His reply was to the point: "In the style of *drawing* itself, Patchen is not influenced by Blake (his affinities are with Ben Shahn, Calder, Miro, Rouault, Chagall, Matisse, Goya, Klee, etc.) but *compositionally* he is. If you look at such drawings-poems as: 'Check! Questions are the best things, answer, Bub' (1962), 'All right, you, may a-light' (1962), 'The King of Toys' (1964), and 'A Crown of Clouds' (1968), you see that his idea, like Blake's, is to create a piece of *tapestry*. This is true only when Patchen is using his own handwriting for the poems (not the typeset text) and especially when the space given to the text of the poem is larger than that for the drawing. This way Patchen enlarges the imaginative scope of his work in the direction of *abstraction* and *decoration*, which, as in the case of Blake, become the condition rather than the aim of his labor. The principal difference between Patchen and Blake is that Blake, as artist and poet, remained an innocent man of the pre-Fall spirit, while Patchen, a civilized artist, has eaten lots of fruit from the Tree of Knowledge."

Back to Sierra Court. Miriam is expecting me. She has a signal for the telephone. If it is a friend, you ring three times, then hang up, then ring again at once, and she answers. (I'm not sure why this system is necessary because they see few people.) When I come in, Miriam tells me that Kenneth has had a bad night and has taken a painkiller, but should be able to see me soon. In about an hour he calls from the bedroom and she goes in to help him and give him coffee. Soon she invites me to follow. The bedroom is also his studio since he can't move about. It is a sunny room, with an orderly litter of painting things: pots of different kinds and colors of paint, brushes in jars, stacks of completed drawings on the dresser. I haven't seen Kenneth for over a year, and I'm afraid I show my shock at his appearance. He is sitting up in bed against a pile of pillows and he looks terrible. But let Norman Thomas tell it from his portrait of Patchen in *Outsider* magazine:

> At midmorning his face is grey and the lines at the side of the mouth are
> deep, his eyes sunken and dark with miserable night memories. When he
> moves it is with so much care and with such apprehension. For all his nights
> are long; all his sleep is troubled.

Miriam brings me a chair and I try to talk with Kenneth. But it isn't easy for me because it is so hard for him. I think he is still drugged from the painkiller. His voice is very low. It seems to come from somewhere deep down inside him—a submerged, undersea voice—and he speaks more slowly than ever.

As if grasping for the only thing which he knows will revive his spirits, Kenneth asks Miriam to help him get started painting. She raises his knees under the blanket and rests his painting board against them. The pillows must be arranged so that he is more upright to work on the board. A half-completed picture poem is tacked to the board. I can't now remember which one it was, but think he was working with acrylic paint and a felt pen that day. Patchen experimented with many media and techniques: earth pigment colors, Sumi ink, casein, watercolor, collages with the interesting paper John Thomas brought him, perhaps even oils, I'm not sure. Once he wrote me:

> Lately I've been messing around with "lift" drawings, an old, old technique
> which Klee was fond of. "Messing around" exactly describes what one does
> in the beginning.

I pull my chair close to the bed to watch. The movements of his hand, like his speech, are slow and deliberate. As best I make it out, with acrylic you can't do it over, as you can with oils. It has to be right the first time. He seems to know in his head what he wants to do next. He had started this one the day before, at the top, and now he is moving down the sheet, alternating the pen for the lettering with the brush for the figures and the background. I do remember that the background was a rich orange.

"Kenneth," I ask him, "I've always wanted to know: when you compose these things, which comes first in your mind, the poem or the picture?"

He stops work and gives me a long look, then, I hope it was so, an almost affectionate smile. "Laughlin," he says, "you're asking me: which comes first, the chicken or the egg?" (In all the years I knew him he always called me "Laughlin," never "J.")

Miriam brings in coffee. Kenneth says, "You know Laughlin won't drink coffee." We laugh. It's true, I hate coffee. What I really would like at this point is a good stiff drink. But I don't think there's anything like that in the house. I settle for tea. I'm afraid I'm tiring him so I make an excuse to go. But Kenneth insists on giving me a present. He asks Miriam to bring him the stack of paintings. He goes through them carefully and picks out a beauty, not a picture poem but one of the earlier large paintings without words. It hangs now in my office in New York. I want a lot of people to see it. As I leave the bedroom, he calls me back. "Laughlin," he tells me, "when you find out which comes first, the chicken or the egg, you write and tell me." I never saw Kenneth again. He died in that bedroom on January 8, 1972.

Drawings on this and the preceding pages
are from *Hurrah for Anything* and are reprinted by
permission of New Directions Corp.

Kenneth Patchen: Principal Works

Before the Brave. New York: Random House, 1936. Poems.

First Will and Testament. Norfolk, Connecticut: New Directions, 1939. Poems.

The Journal of Albion Moonlight. New York: The Author, 1941. Prose. (Available as New Directions Paperbook 99)

The Dark Kingdom. New York: Harriss & Givens, 1942. Poems.

The Teeth of the Lion. Norfolk, Connecticut: New Directions, 1942. Poems.

Cloth of the Tempest. New York: Harper Brothers, 1943. Poems and drawings.

Memoirs of a Shy Pornographer. New York: New Directions, 1945. Prose. (Available as New Directions Paperbook 205)

As Astonished Eye Looks Out of the Air. Waldport, Oregon: Untide Press, 1946. Poems.

The Selected Poems of Kenneth Patchen. New York: New Directions, 1946. Poems. (Available as New Directions Paperbook 160)

Sleepers Awake. New York: Padell, 1946. Prose. (Available as New Directions Paperbook 286)

Panels for the Walls of Heaven. San Francisco: Bern Porter, 1946. Prose poems and drawings.

Pictures of Life and of Death. New York: Padell, 1946. Poems.

They Keep Riding Down All the Time. New York: Padell, 1946. Prose.

See You in the Morning. New York: Padell, 1947. Prose.

Red Wine and Yellow Hair. New York: New Directions, 1949. Poems.

Orchards, Thrones and Caravans. San Francisco: The Print Workshop, 1952. Poems.

Fables and Other Little Tales. Highlands, North Carolina: Jonathan Williams, 1953. Prose.

The Famous Boating Party. New York: New Directions, 1954. Prose poems.

Poems of Humor and Protest. San Francisco: City Lights, 1954. Poems. (Available as City Lights Pocket Poets Series No. 3)

Hurrah for Anything. Highlands, North Carolina: Jonathan Williams, 1957. Poems and drawings.

When We Were Here Together. New York: New Directions, 1957. Poems.

Poemscapes. Highlands, North Carolina: Jonathan Williams, 1958. Prose poems.

The Love Poems of Kenneth Patchen. San Francisco: City Lights, 1960. Poems. (Available as City Lights Pocket Poets Series No. 13)

Because It Is. New York: New Directions, 1960. Poems and drawings. (Available as New Directions Paperbook 83)

Doubleheader. New York: New Directions, 1966. Contains *Hurrah For Anything, Poemscapes* and *A Letter to God*. (Available as New Directions Paperbook 211)

Hallelujah Anyway. New York: New Directions, 1966. Picture poems. (Available as New Directions Paperbook 219)

Collected Poems of Kenneth Patchen. New York: New Directions, 1968. Poems. (Available as New Directions Paperbook 284)

But Even So. New York: New Directions, 1968. Picture poems. (Available as New Directions Paperbook 265)

Aflame and Afun of Walking Faces. New York: New Directions, 1970. Selections from *Fables*, with new drawings. (Available as New Directions Paperbook 292)

Wonderings. New York: New Directions, 1971. Picture poems and drawing poems. (Available as New Directions Paperbook 320)

In Quest of Candlelighters. New York: New Directions, 1972. Contains *Panels for the Walls of Heaven, They Keep Riding Down All the Time,* and two prose works. (Available as New Directions Paperbook 334)

Patchen's Lost Plays. Santa Barbara, California: Capra Press, 1977. Plays.

ABOUT KENNETH PATCHEN

Smith, Larry R. *Kenneth Patchen*. Boston: Twayne Publishers, 1978. (Twayne's United States Authors Series Number 292.) Critical biographical study with bibliography.

Morgan, Richard G. *Kenneth Patchen: A Bibliography*. Mamaroneck, New York: Paul P. Appel, 1978.

Morgan, Richard G., editor. *Kenneth Patchen: A Collection of Essays*. New York: AMS Press Inc., 1977. Principal essays and reviews by various authors on Kenneth Patchen, 1941–1976.

Veres, Peter. *The Argument of Innocence: A Selection from the Arts of Kenneth Patchen*. Oakland, California: The Scrimshaw Press, 1976. Color reproductions of picture poems, painted books and sculpture; biographical essay.

Detro, Gene. *Patchen: The Last Interview*. Santa Barbara, California: Capra Press, 1976. (Capra Chapbook Series Number 40)